MAN CANNOT SPEAK FOR HER

Susan B. Anthony. Kansas Collection, University of Kansas Libraries.

MAN CANNOT SPEAK FOR HER

_____ *VOLUME I* _____

A CRITICAL STUDY OF EARLY FEMINIST RHETORIC

Karlyn Kohrs Campbell

PRAEGER

New York
Westport, Connecticut
London

Library of Congress Cataloging-in-Publication Data

Campbell, Karlyn Kohrs.
    Man cannot speak for her / Karlyn Kohrs Campbell.
        p. cm.
    Bibliography : p.
    Includes index.
        Contents: v. 1. A critical study of early feminist rhetoric—v. 2. Key texts of the early
    feminists. ISBN 0–275–93266–4 (set)
        ISBN 0–275–93269–9 (pbk. : v. 1 : alk. paper).—ISBN 0–275–93267–2 (pbk. :
    v. 2 : alk. paper)
        1. Feminism—United States—History—Sources. 2. Speeches, addresses, etc.,
    American—Women authors—History and criticism. 3. Political oratory—United States—
    History. 4. Women's rights—United States—History. 5. Rhetoric—Political aspects—
    United States—History. 6. Rhetoric—Social aspects—United States—History. 7. Women
    orators—United States—History. I. Title.
    HQ1154.C28 1989b
    305.4'2'0973—dc 19   88–37438

British Library Cataloguing in Publication Data is available.

A hardcover edition of *Man Cannot Speak For Her: Volume I*
A Critical Study of Early Feminist Rhetoric is available from
Greenwood Press (Contributions in Women's Studies, 101;
ISBN: 0–313–25649–7).

Library of Congress Catalog Card Number : 88–37438
ISBN: 0–275–93266–4 (set)
ISBN: 0–275–93269–9 (v. 1)
ISBN: 0–275–93267–2 (v. 2)

First published in 1989

Praeger Publishers,
One Madison Avenue, New York, NY   10010
A division of Greenwood Press, Inc.

Printed in the United States of America

∞

The paper used in this book complies with the Permanent Paper Standard issued by the
National Information Standards Organization (Z39.48–1984).

10 9 8 7 6 5 4 3 2 1

Contents

	Acknowledgments	vii
1.	Introduction	1
2.	The Struggle for the Right to Speak	17
3.	Responding to Opposition Based on Theology: Proposing a Single Moral Standard	37
4.	Woman's Rights Conventions: Ideological Crucibles	49
5.	A Movement in Transition: The Debate of 1860	71
6.	Adapting to Males: Addressing State Legislators	87
7.	Seeking a Judicial Route to Suffrage: Anthony in Behalf of Herself	105
8.	Social Feminism: Frances Willard, "Feminine Feminist"	121
9.	The Humanistic Underpinnings of Feminism: "The Solitude of Self"	133
10.	The Heavy Burdens of Afro-American Women: Sex, Race, and Class	145
11.	The Coming of Woman Suffrage: The Orator, the Organizer, and the Agitator	157
12.	After Woman Suffrage	181
	References	193
	Index	207

Acknowledgments

Many of the virtues of this project are due to others. Wil Linkugel first stirred my interest in the rhetoric of early feminists. Students at the University of Kansas tested and refined my ideas. Most particularly, I thank Charles Conrad for his work on the 1860 convention debate, Adrienne Christiansen for her study of Clarina Howard Nichols, Claire Jerry for her analysis of the suffrage press and of Clara Bewick Colby and the *Woman's Tribune*, Mari Tonn for her criticism of the rhetoric of Mary Harris "Mother" Jones, Bonnie Dow for her research on Frances Willard, and Tom Burkholder for sharing his discoveries about populist women.

I owe a special debt to the Women's Studies Program at the University of Kansas, in particular to Janet Sharistanian and Shirley Harkess, who brought the program into existence and made it a fine venue for feminist scholarship.

Deborah Dandridge was both guide and friend as I learned about the history of Afro-American women and, more specifically, about their clubs in Kansas. As a result of her work, the women of the Kansas Association of Colored Women's and Girls' Clubs shared their experiences and enlarged my understanding of feminism, past and present.

The University of Kansas and the University of Minnesota provided faculty development and travel grants that made much of the research and writing involved in this project possible.

In volume I, chapter 7 is a revision of an essay originally published in *The Jensen Lectures: Contemporary Communication Studies* ed. John I. Sisco (Tampa: University of South Florida, 1973), pp. 117–32. Chapters 9 and 10 are revisions of articles that appeared in the *Quarterly Journal of Speech* 66 (1980):304–12, and 72 (1986):434–45, respectively. The University of South Florida and the Speech Communication Association have graciously granted me permission to reprint this material.

Finally, there is Paul, my partner in everything, and my best editor.

These and many others, particularly my former students, made contributions; the errors of fact, taste, logic, and proportion are my own.

Karlyn Kohrs Campbell
Minneapolis, Minnesota

1

Introduction

Men have an ancient and honorable rhetorical history. Their speeches and writings, from antiquity to the present, are studied and analyzed by historians and rhetoricians. Public persuasion has been a conscious part of the Western male's heritage from ancient Greece to the present. This is not an insignificant matter. For centuries, the ability to persuade others has been part of Western man's standard of excellence in many areas, even of citizenship itself. Moreover, speaking and writing eloquently has long been the goal of the humanistic tradition in education.

Women have no parallel rhetorical history. Indeed, for much of their history women have been prohibited from speaking, a prohibition reinforced by such powerful cultural authorities as Homer, Aristotle, and Scripture. In the *Odyssey*, for example, Telemachus scolds his mother Penelope and tells her, "Public speech [*mythos*] shall be men's concern" (Homer 1980, 9).[1] In the *Politics*, Aristotle approvingly quotes the words, "Silence is a woman's glory" (1923, 1.13.12602a.30), and the epistles of Paul enjoin women to keep silent. As a result, when women began to speak outside the home on moral issues and on matters of public policy, they faced obstacles unknown to men. Further, once they began to speak, their words often were not preserved, with the result that many rhetorical acts by women are gone forever; many others can be found only in manuscript collections or rare, out-of-print publications. Even when reprinted, they frequently are treated as historical artifacts from which excerpts can be drawn rather than as artistic works that must be seen whole in order to be understood and appreciated. As a rhetorical critic I want to restore one segment of the history of women, namely the rhetoric of the early woman's rights movement that emerged in the United States in the 1830s, that became a movement focused primarily on woman suffrage after the Civil War, and whose force dissipated in the mid-1920s. I refer to this as the early movement in contrast to contemporary feminism.

This project is a rhetorical study, which means that all of the documents analyzed in the chapters that follow and anthologized in volume II are works through which woman's rights advocates sought to persuade others of the rightness of their cause. In the broadest sense, rhetoric is the study of the means by which symbols can be used to appeal to others, to persuade. The potential for persuasion exists in the shared symbolic and socioeconomic experience of persuaders (rhetors) and audiences; specific rhetorical acts attempt to exploit that shared experience and channel it in certain directions.

Rhetoric is one of the oldest disciplines in the Western tradition. From its beginnings in ancient Greece, it has been a practical art, one that assesses a persuader's efforts in light of the resources available on a specific occasion in relation to a particular audience and in order to achieve a certain kind of end. As a result, rhetorical analysis has focused on invention, the rhetor's skill in selecting and adapting those resources available in language, in cultural values, and in shared experience in order to influence others.

The aim of the rhetorical critic is enlightenment — an understanding of the ways symbols can be used by analyzing the ways they were used in a particular time and place and the ways such usage appealed or might have appealed to other human beings — then or now. Rhetorical critics attempt to function as surrogates for audiences, both of the past and of the present. Based on their general knowledge of rhetorical literature and criticism, and based on familiarity with the rhetoric of a movement and its historical milieu, critics attempt to show how a rhetorical act has the potential to teach, to delight, to move, to flatter, to alienate, or to hearten.

The potential to engage another is the aesthetic or symbolic power of a piece of persuasive discourse. Such assessments are related to a work's actual effects. However, many rhetorical works fail to achieve their ends for reasons that have little to do with their style or content. In a social movement advocating controversial changes, failure to achieve specific goals will be common, no matter how able and creative the advocates, whether male or female. For example, a woman might urge legal changes to give a wife a right to her own earnings, but in a single speech to men opposed to the very idea of a woman speaking, she cannot succeed in practical terms, even though her speech is powerful and noteworthy. If she were extremely skillful, she might increase awareness of the plight of married women and arouse sympathy for them among some members of the audience. As a result, critics must judge whether the choices made by rhetors were skillful responses to the problems they confronted, not whether the changes they urged were enacted. Nevertheless, where evidence of impact exists, it will be noted, although such evidence is not a reliable measure of rhetorical skill, because it, too, can be the product of extrinsic factors.

Selecting appropriate terminology to refer to women in the early movement has proved something of a problem, because the meanings of some key terms have changed. I call the activists of the earlier movement feminists only in the sense that they worked to advance the cause of women. To themselves, they were woman's rights advocates (working for the rights of woman) or suffragists (working for woman suffrage), and for the most part, I shall retain these labels. In the United States, only their opponents called them "suffragettes," whereas in Great Britain, the radical wing of the movement, the Women's Social and Political Union, led by Emmeline and Christabel Pankhurst, adopted this epithet as their own. The term "feminism" existed in the mid-nineteenth century, but it meant only "having the qualities of a female." In the 1890s the term came into use, primarily by anti-suffragists, to refer negatively to woman's rights activists, that is, those committed to the legal, economic, and social equality of women. After the turn of the century, the term became more acceptable, and mainstream suffragists used the term but redefined it (Shaw 1918, in Linkugel 1960, 2:667-83; Cott 1987, 3-50); early in this century more radical feminists in the National Woman's Party claimed it as their own. As this study will demonstrate, women in the early movement differed over goals; my use of "feminism" here is inclusive and catholic, referring to all those who worked for the legal, economic, and political advancement of women, beginning in the 1830s.

References to individual women also required decisions. Except for chapter 2, in which I refer to Sarah and Angelina Grimké by their first names in order to distinguish between them, I have consistently referred to women by the names they used themselves, for example Ida B. Wells, Lucy Stone, and Carrie Chapman Catt, or I have used their birth and married names to refer to them after initial identification, for example Cady Stanton and Coffin Mott. I do so to retain their identities as well as to indicate kinship, as in Martha Coffin Wright and Lucretia Coffin Mott. This may seem a bit cumbersome, but I can find no alternative that seems consistent with my principles and theirs. When names changed subsequent to or during movement activism, such changes are indicated in brackets, as in Antoinette Brown [Black-well].

MOVEMENT HISTORY

Woman's rights agitation was in large measure a byproduct of women's efforts in other reform movements. Women seeking to end slavery, to attack the evils of alcohol abuse, and to improve the plight of prostitutes found themselves excluded from male reform organizations and attacked for involving themselves in concerns outside the home. A distinctive woman's rights movement began when women reformers recognized that they had to work for their own rights before they could be effective in other reform efforts.

Many early woman's rights advocates began as abolitionists, but because they were excluded from participation in male anti-slavery societies, they formed female anti-slavery societies and ultimately, as chapter 2 describes, they began to press for their own rights in order to be more effective in the abolitionist struggle (Hersh 1978). Both Lucretia Coffin Mott and Elizabeth Cady Stanton dated the beginnings of the woman's rights movement from 1840, the year when five female delegates from U.S. anti-slavery societies, one of whom was Coffin Mott, were refused seating at the World Anti-Slavery Convention in London. The outrage they felt at the debate that culminated in the denial of women's participation in the convention fueled their decision to call a woman's rights convention, a decision that eventuated in the Seneca Falls, New York, convention of 1848. Because the struggle to abolish slavery was so closely related to the earliest efforts for woman's rights, and because female abolitionists' speeches show them struggling to find ways to cope with proscriptions against speaking, the next chapter analyzes this connection, and texts by abolitionist women are included in volume II.

Woman's rights activism took an organized form at the 1848 Seneca Falls convention at which Elizabeth Cady Stanton made her first speech, and the movement's manifesto, the "Declaration of Sentiments," was introduced and ratified. Local, regional, and national woman's rights conventions were held until the outbreak of the Civil War in 1861. During the war, women activists bent all their efforts toward supporting the Union cause, primarily through work on the Sanitary Commission, and toward abolishing slavery, primarily through the Woman's National Loyal League. Because of their important contributions, women expected to be rewarded with suffrage.

Instead, they were told that their dreams were to be deferred. Woman suffrage was so controversial that it was feared it would take suffrage for Afro-American males down to defeat. As a result, in 1868, the Fourteenth Amendment for the first time introduced the word "male" into the U.S. Constitution. Bitterness and frustration caused the movement to split into rival organizations in 1869. However, a final effort was made to obtain suffrage through the courts. Based on the argument that the Fourteenth Amendment had defined citizenship, and that citizenship implied suffrage, in 1872 Susan B. Anthony and other women registered and voted, or attempted to do so. In 1875, however, the Supreme Court rejected that argument, making a separate federal amendment necessary.

During this period a major impetus toward woman suffrage came from an unexpected source — the temperance movement. This reform effort, like abolitionism, was a major source of woman's rights advocates. The struggle against the evils of alcohol abuse caught fire in 1874, and the Woman's Christian Temperance Union (WCTU) was founded. Per capita consumption of alcohol by Americans in the 1820s is estimated to have been three times that of 1980, and by 1909, Americans spent almost as much on alcohol as they did on all food products and nonalcoholic beverages combined. In the 1820s, hard liquor was inexpensive, cheaper than beer, wine, milk, coffee, or tea; only water was cheaper, and it was often polluted. Consumption of alcoholic beverages had been an integral part of U.S. life since colonial times, and alcoholic beverages were thought to be nutritious and healthful. Such traditions and beliefs, combined with low cost, increased consumption (Rorabaugh 1980; Lender and Martin 1983). In 1870, there were some 100,000 saloons in the country, approximately one for every fifty inhabitants (Giele 1961, 41).

Women were vulnerable to the effects of alcohol abuse. Although some women became drunkards, primarily due to the high alcohol content of patent medicines, alcoholism among males was the major problem. Women married to drunkards were at the mercy of their husbands. As late as 1900, in thirty-seven states a woman had no rights to her children, and all her possessions and earnings belonged to her husband (Bordin 1981, 7).

Temperance was an acceptable outlet for the reformist energies of women during the last decades of the nineteenth century. Unlike earlier woman's rights and woman suffrage advocacy, which implied at least a redefinition of woman's sphere, temperance work could be done by a "true woman." Because brothels were often attached to saloons, alcohol was perceived as an inducement to immorality as well as a social and economic threat to the home. Women who struggled against its use were affirming their piety, purity, and domesticity. Because the sale and consumption of alcohol was associated with immorality, and because temperance work implied no change in woman's traditional role, churches that opposed other reforms supported temperance activities. WCTU branches often grew out of existing churchwomen's organizations. As a result, temperance efforts exacted fewer social costs from women than did work for other woman's rights. Although the WCTU accepted traditional concepts of womanhood, it came to argue that woman's distinctive influence should be extended outside the home via the vote. Consequently, woman suffrage became acceptable to more conservative women (and men), who had rejected it before, when presented as a means for woman to protect her domestic sphere from abuses related to alcohol.

In 1890, the rival suffrage organizations merged into the National American Woman Suffrage Association (NAWSA). Although 1890 was the year Wyoming became the first state to give women the right to vote, in the period around the turn of the century women activists made little progress. Anti-suffrage activity was at its height, and movement leadership was in transition as the initiators died and a younger generation took over. With the rise of the Progressive movement, particularly in the West, the climate for woman's rights improved. Women such as the Rev. Dr. Anna Howard Shaw traveled throughout the nation speaking in support of woman suffrage. In 1915, the skilled administrator Carrie Chapman Catt assumed leadership of NAWSA, developing a "Winning Plan" to maximize pressure on Congress to pass a suffrage amendment. Finally, Alice Paul and her cohorts in the National Woman's Party (NWP) paraded, picketed, and demonstrated in order to draw attention to the issue and to keep it at the top of the congressional agenda. These efforts, energized by the pressures of World War I, led to passage of an amendment and its ratification on August 26, 1920. For the first time, all U.S. women were eligible to vote in the 1920 elections.

Sadly, that achievement meant less than women activists had hoped. Few women voted, and in a short time it became clear that women did not form a distinct voting bloc or constituency. The limited meaning of woman suffrage was manifest in 1925 when an amendment prohibiting child labor failed to gain ratification, and that event symbolizes the end of the early movement.

Many causes contributed to the demise of the movement. In the

"Red scare" of the 1920s, women activists were attacked for their support of progressive causes, including the Parent-Teacher Association (PTA) and the Young Women's Christian Association (YWCA). Activists also hastened their own end by bitterly dividing over the equal rights amendment, introduced in 1923 at the behest of the National Woman's Party. On the one hand, the NWP took an inflexible and absolute natural rights position, rejecting any special legal consideration for women. In opposition, the League of Women Voters, descendant of NAWSA, and women trade unionists, among others, fought to retain protective legislation, which would have been imperiled by such an amendment. Conflict over similar issues and over the ERA persists among U.S. women, underlining the links between the earlier movement and contemporary feminist concerns.

THIS STUDY

In these volumes, I have analyzed and anthologized discourse that appeared at critical moments in this movement and that represents particular issues or groups within the movement. But, although some of these works have great historical significance, all of them were selected for their rhetorical significance, in order to reveal the variety and creativity of woman's rights advocacy. In this sense, the works anthologized and analyzed are persuasive masterworks of the early movement. As such, they contributed to the development and survival of that movement, and they represent skillful human artistry in the face of nearly insuperable rhetorical obstacles.

Volume II is a documentary history in which key rhetorical acts are collected and annotated. The notes explain the historical context, and provide relevant biographical details about the authors. In that volume the ideas of the early movement are presented in the documents through which woman's rights advocates stated their grievances, articulated their ideology, and justified their demands with arguments, evidence, and appeals to basic principles and traditional values. Each document is as complete and authentic as possible, and annotations are designed to make historical references clear to the contemporary reader. These documents are arranged in a roughly chronological order to permit the reader to see development and to discover influences. The two volumes are intended to be read together, texts and analyses working in conjunction to provide a picture of early feminist rhetoric.

No two-volume work could treat the rhetoric of all early feminists.

Three principles guided my selections. First, I focused on the central women's movement rather than examining its branches or movements that worked for related goals, although the special relationships of abolitionism and temperance to woman's rights and woman suffrage have mandated inclusion of speeches from those movements. For this reason, there is no treatment of the rhetoric of those who sought to improve the conditions of women workers, nor of those active in the consumer, settlement house, peace, or birth control movements. Similarly, there is no systematic treatment of the rhetoric of anti-suffragists.

Chapter 10 focuses on rhetoric of Afro-American women activists linking sexism and racism, and thus is an exception to this criterion. The featured Afro-American speakers, Ida B. Wells and Mary Church Terrell, were active supporters of woman's rights and woman suffrage, and Church Terrell was a supporter of the equal rights amendment introduced in 1923. However, their contributions to feminism cannot be understood apart from their concerns as Afro-Americans: to outlaw lynching, to end segregation, and to compel recognition of the special burdens of Afro-American women. They merit inclusion, as well as separate treatment, because they saw the links between discrimination based on race and sex and because, despite their best efforts, they were unable to induce white women to recognize such linkages and to incorporate them into the movement.

Second, I focused on women who were nationally known, slighting many able women speakers whose work was regional. Another project like this one would be needed to incorporate the rhetoric of women such as Laura Clay, Clara Bewick Colby, Abigail Scott Duniway, Helen Jackson Gougar, Jane Gray Swisshelm, and their sisters around the nation.

Third, the accidents of history have compelled me to direct my attention primarily to those who left an extensive rhetorical record. For instance, little can be written about the rhetoric of Lucy Stone because unfortunately only a few texts still exist, and those do not display the great talents she evidently had. Even in the cases of Lucretia Coffin Mott and Angelina Grimké [Weld], assessments of their rhetorical prowess are limited by the small number of texts that remain. By contrast, Elizabeth Cady Stanton and Mary Church Terrell prepared speech texts, retained the manuscripts, and published many of their speeches as essays. As a result, evidence of their intelligence and invention is easy to marshal. The emphasis in this book, then, is not wholly a function of the impact individuals had on the early movement but also of the extant rhetorical evidence.

These rhetorical acts should be available to scholars in many fields because they are the social and historical documents in which the ideology we now call feminism was developed and refined over nearly a century. The works discussed and anthologized in these volumes are basic documents through which to understand the history of what became a large and complex social movement culminating in the enfranchisement of women. Thus my primary goal is simply to make these works available. Of those included in these volumes, only the speeches of Maria W. Miller Stewart (Richardson 1987) and Lucretia Coffin Mott (Greene 1980) are easily accessible in their entirety to contemporary scholars.[2]

I offer this two-volume study to call into question what has become the canon of public address in the United States, a canon that excludes virtually all works by women (Campbell 1985). It is my hope that the analyses of this volume and the texts in volume II will prompt re-examination of U.S. rhetorical literature and the inclusion of some of these works in courses that survey the history of rhetoric and that explore artistic excellence in speaking.

In addition to making texts available and correcting rhetorical history, still another goal of this project is to make it clear that the rhetoric of women must be studied if we are to understand human symbolization in all its variety and to identify touchstones that illustrate the peaks of human symbolic creativity. Rhetorical invention is rarely originality of argument, but rather the selection and adaptation of materials to the occasion, the purpose, and the audience. Early feminist rhetors rose to inventive heights as they sought to overcome the special obstacles they confronted because they were women, and because they were attempting to alter traditional conceptions of gender roles. The relationship between rhetoric and feminism is pertinent to all facets of this study, and the remainder of this chapter explores that special relationship.

STRUGGLING FOR THE RIGHT TO SPEAK

Early woman's rights activists were constrained to be particularly creative because they faced barriers unknown to men. They were a group virtually unique in rhetorical history because a central element in woman's oppression was the denial of her right to speak (Lipking 1983). Quite simply, in nineteenth-century America, femininity and rhetorical action were seen as mutually exclusive. No "true woman" could be a public persuader.

The concept of "true womanhood" (Welter 1976), or the "woman-belle ideal" (Scott 1970), defined females as "other," as suited only for a limited repertoire of gender-based roles, and as the repository of cherished but commercially useless spiritual and human values. These attitudes arose in response to the urbanization and industrialization of the nineteenth century, which separated home and work. As the cult of domesticity was codified in the United States in the early part of the century, two distinct subcultures emerged. Man's place was the world outside the home, the public realm of politics and finance; man's nature was thought to be lustful, amoral, competitive, and ambitious. Woman's place was home, a haven from amoral capitalism and dirty politics, where "the heart was," where the spiritual and emotional needs of husband and children were met by a "ministering angel." Woman's nature was pure, pious, domestic, and submissive (Welter 1976, 21). She was to remain entirely in the private sphere of the home, eschewing any appearance of individuality, leadership, or aggressiveness. Her purity depended on her domesticity; the woman who was compelled by economic need or slavery to work away from her own hearth was tainted. However, woman's alleged moral superiority (Cott 1977, 120, 146-48, 170) generated a conflict out of which the woman's rights movement emerged.

As defined, woman's role contained a contradiction that became apparent as women responded to what they saw as great moral wrongs. Despite their allegedly greater moral sensitivity, women were censured for their efforts against the evils of prostitution and slavery (Berg 1978; Hersh 1978). Women who formed moral reform and abolitionist societies, and who made speeches, held conventions, and published newspapers, entered the public sphere and thereby lost their claims to purity and piety. What became the woman's rights/woman suffrage movement arose out of this contradiction.

Women encountered profound resistance to their efforts for moral reform because rhetorical action of any sort was, as defined by gender roles, a masculine activity. Speakers had to be expert and authoritative; women were submissive. Speakers ventured into the public sphere (the courtroom, the legislature, the pulpit, or the lecture platform); woman's domain was domestic. Speakers called attention to themselves, took stands aggressively, initiated action, and affirmed their expertise; "true women" were retiring and modest, their influence was indirect, and they had no expertise or authority. Because they were thought naturally incapable of reasoning, women were considered unsuited to engage in or to guide public deliberation. The public realm was competitive, driven by ambition; it was a sphere in which the desire to succeed could only be inhibited by humane concerns and spiritual values. Similarly, speaking was competitive, energized by the desire to win a case or persuade others to one's point of view. These were viewed as exclusively masculine traits related to man's allegedly lustful, ruthless, competitive, amoral, and ambitious nature. Activities requiring such qualities were thought to "unsex" women.

The extent of the problem is illustrated by the story of educational pioneer Emma Hart Willard (Scott 1978; Willard 1819). Encouraged by Governor De Witt Clinton in 1819 to present "A Plan for Improving Female Education" to the New York Legislature, Hart Willard presented her proposal to legislators, but carefully remained seated to avoid any hint that she was delivering a speech. In her biography of this influential educator, Alma Lutz writes: "Although this [oral presentation] was very unconventional for a woman, she did not hesitate, so great was her enthusiasm for her *Plan*.... She impressed them not as the much-scorned female politician, but as a noble woman inspired by a great ideal" (Lutz 1931, 28).

In other words, a woman who spoke displayed her "masculinity"; that is, she demonstrated that she possessed qualities traditionally ascribed only to males. When a woman spoke, she enacted her equality, that is, she herself was proof that she was as able as her male counterparts to function in the public sphere. That a woman speaking is such proof explains the outraged reactions to women addressing "promiscuous" audiences of men and women, sharing a platform with male speakers, debating, and preaching, even on such clearly moral issues as slavery, prostitution, and alcohol abuse. The hostility women experienced in reform efforts led them to found female reform organizations and to initiate a movement for woman's rights, at base a movement claiming woman's right to engage in public moral action.

Biology, or rather ignorance of biology, was used to buttress arguments limiting woman's role and excluding her from higher education and political activity. On average, women were smaller than men. As a result, it was assumed that they had smaller brains, and that therefore their brains presumably were too small to sustain the rational deliberation required in politics and business. Moreover, their smaller, and hence more delicate and excitable, nerves could not withstand the pressures of public debate or the marketplace. Menarche, the onset of menstruation, was viewed as a physical cataclysm that rendered women unfit for normal activity. For example, Harvard medical professor Dr. Edward Clarke (1873) argued against higher education for women on the grounds that the blood needed to sustain development of the ovaries and womb would be diverted to the brain, which he believed was a major cause of serious illness.

Because of the conceptions of their nature and the taboos that were part of the cult of domesticity, women who spoke publicly confronted extraordinary obstacles. For example, abolitionist Abby Kelley [Foster]

> faced such continuous and merciless persecution that she earned the title "our Joan of Arc" among her co-workers. Lucy Stone later described Kelley's career as "long, unrelieved, moral torture." . . . Because she often traveled alone, or (worse) with male agents, she was vilified as a "bad" woman. . . . She was further reviled when she continued to appear in public while pregnant. (Hersh 1978, 42-43)

On the one hand, a woman had to meet all the usual requirements of speakers, demonstrating expertise, authority, and rationality in order to show her competence and make herself credible to audiences. However, if that was all she did, she was likely to be judged masculine, unwomanly, aggressive, and cold. As a result, women speakers sometimes searched for ways to legitimate such "unwomanly" behavior and for ways to incorporate evidence of femininity into ordinary rhetorical action. In other instances, their own defiance and outrage overwhelmed their efforts at adaptation. In still other cases, rhetors found womanly ways of persuasion that were self-contradictory, and hence ultimately damaging to their cause. Yet on occasion, extraordinarily skilled women persuaders found symbolic means of responding to these contradictory expectations, and produced masterpieces. The problems women faced as speakers are a recurring theme of this book, a theme that remains relevant for contemporary women who still must struggle to cope with these contradictory expectations, albeit in somewhat modified forms.

FEMININE STYLE

Analysis of persuasion by women indicates that many strategically adopted what might be called a feminine style to cope with the conflicting demands of the podium. That style emerged out of their experiences as women and was adapted to the attitudes and experiences of female audiences. However, it was not, and is not today, a style exclusive to women, either as speakers or as audiences.

Deprived of formal education and confined to the home, a woman learned the crafts of housewifery and motherhood—cooking, cleaning, canning, sewing, childbearing, child-rearing, and the like—from other women through a supervised internship combining expert advice with trial and error. These processes are common to all craft-learning, including carpentry, horse training and plumbing, but craft-related skills cannot be expressed in universal laws; one must learn to apply them contingently, depending upon conditions and materials (McMillan 1982). Learning to adapt to variation is essential to mastery of a craft, and the highly skilled craftsperson is alert to variation, aware of a host of alternatives, and able to read cues related to specific conditions.

If the process of craft-learning is applied to the rhetorical situation (and rhetoric itself is a craft), it produces discourse with certain characteristics. Such discourse will be personal in tone (crafts are learned face-to-face from a mentor), relying heavily on personal experience, anecdotes, and other examples. It will tend to be structured inductively (crafts are learned bit by bit, instance by instance, from which generalizations emerge). It will invite audience participation, including the process of testing generalizations or principles against the experiences of the audience. Audience members will be addressed as peers, with recognition of authority based on experience (more skilled craftspeople are more experienced), and efforts will be made to create identification with the experiences of the audience and those described by the speaker. The goal of such rhetoric is empowerment, a term contemporary feminists have used to refer to the process of persuading listeners that they can act effectively in the world, that they can be "agents of change" (Bitzer 1968). Given the traditional concept of womanhood, which emphasized passivity, submissiveness, and patience, persuading women that they could act was a precondition for other kinds of persuasive efforts.[3]

Many of the qualities of the style just described are also part of the small-group phenomenon known as consciousness-raising, associated with contemporary feminism as well as other social movements, which is a communicative style that can be incorporated into speaking or prose writing (Farrell 1979). Because oppressed groups tend to develop passive personality traits, consciousness-raising is an attractive communication style to people working for social change. Whether in a small group, from the podium, or on the page, consciousness-raising invites audience members to participate in the persuasive process—it empowers them. It is a highly appealing form of discourse, particularly if identification between advocate and audience is facilitated by common values and shared experience.

Based on this description, it should be obvious that while there is nothing inevitably or necessarily female about this rhetorical style, it has been congenial to women because of the acculturation of female speakers and audiences.[4] It can be called "feminine" in this context because it reflects the learning experiences of women who were speakers and audiences in this period, and because, as a less authoritative and aggressive style, it was a less confrontational violation of taboos against public speaking by women.

Because the very act of speaking publicly violated concepts of womanhood, the rhetoric of early woman's rights advocates always had at least two dimensions — presentation of their grievances and justification of woman's right to function in the public sphere, to speak with authority in any area of human life. From the beginnings of the movement, women justified their demands based on what Aileen Kraditor (1965, 43-74) calls the argument from justice and the argument from expediency. The argument from justice was drawn from natural rights philosophy and affirmed the personhood of women and their right to all the civil and political privileges of citizenship.[5] It was a demand for rights affirming that, at least in law and politics, there were no differences between the sexes. By contrast, the argument from expediency presumed that women and men were fundamentally different, so that it would be beneficial, that is, desirable and prudent, to give women rights because of the effect on society. For example, it was argued that if women were educated, they would be better able to fulfill their obligations as wives and mothers; if married women had the right to sue, to enter into contracts, to control their earnings, and to own property, they would be able to protect themselves and their children against profligate husbands, or to fulfill their duties to their children in widowhood. If women were allowed to vote, they would bring to bear on politics their purity, piety, and domestic concerns, and thus purify government and make it more responsive to the needs of the home.

Most woman's rights advocates mixed these arguments, often in a somewhat self-contradictory way. In the earliest period, natural rights arguments predominated, but most advocates still assumed that women were naturally better suited to motherhood and that the aim of a woman's life was wifehood and motherhood. However, even in that period, some argued chiefly from the benefits that increased opportunities or rights would produce for woman's traditional qualities and duties — education would make women more virtuous, increased economic rights for married women would produce better mothers. In the 1870s, arguments from expediency predominated, with emphasis on the societal benefits of the woman's ballot, particularly in fighting the evils of alcohol. Yet as time passed, those who argued from benefits frequently incorporated arguments from natural rights into their rhetoric, and in this later period there were speakers, such as Dr. Anna Howard Shaw, who argued almost exclusively from the natural rights position (Linkugel 1963).

Natural rights arguments were perceived as less feminine. "True women" were unselfish—their efforts were for others, particularly their husbands and children. Women who claimed their rights were seen as selfish, as wanting to abandon their traditional womanly roles to enter the sphere of men, and this made such arguments and advocates particularly unappealing to many women (Camhi 1973, 113). Arguments from benefits were "feminine" in part because they presupposed the qualities of "true womanhood" and in part because they appeared unselfish. Women who argued from expediency did not seek rights for their own sake but only for the good that could be done with them for others. This argument achieved its fullest development in the WCTU's support for woman suffrage as a means to protect the home against the abuses of alcohol.

The obstacles early women persuaders faced persist, although in altered forms, in the present. As a result, my goals in this project are simultaneously scholarly and feminist. As a scholar, I wish to rescue the works of great women speakers from the oblivion to which most have been consigned; above all, I wish to show that the artistry of this rhetoric generated enduring monuments to human thought and creativity.[6] Because early feminists faced obstacles whose residues still haunt contemporary women, their rhetorical efforts are a rich source of illumination. As a feminist, I believe that the works analyzed in this volume and anthologized in volume II represent a particularly abundant mother lode of rhetorical creativity from which contemporary women speakers and activists may draw examples and inspiration.

NOTES

1. Translations of this line vary, but all render *mythos* similarly: "Talking must be men's concern." (1946, 34); "Speech shall be for men." (1935, 11); "Speech shall be the men's care" (1932, 11); and "Speech is man's matter." (1897 rpt. 1967, 20).

2. Even in the six volumes of *History of Woman Suffrage*, hereafter cited as HWS, a source to which beginning scholars frequently turn, nearly all texts are incomplete, sometimes without clear indications of excerpting.

3. Passivity, modesty, patience, and submissiveness were integral parts of "true

womanhood," concepts reinforced by nineteenth-century women's total lack of economic, social, legal, or political power. The impact of such attitudes is apparent in more contemporary studies of women's self-concepts (McClelland 1964). Freeman (1971) cites a study done in the 1950s in which women were asked to pick adjectives to describe themselves: they selected "uncertain, anxious, nervous, hasty, careless, fearful, childish, helpless, sorry, timid, clumsy, stupid, silly, domestic, understanding, tender, sympathetic, pure, generous, affectionate, loving, moral, kind, grateful, and patient" (165). Many of these qualities are at odds with a sense of being capable of effective action.

4. Unlike Farrell (1979, 917n), I do not presume that "feminine" style is rooted in biological differences.

5. Natural rights philosophy grew out of ancient and medieval doctrines of natural law that were modified by an emphasis on the individual in the seventeenth century. Fundamentally, natural rights philosophy took the view that individuals had rights no government could abridge or deny. As a result, the function of government was to protect such rights, requiring plebiscites to determine the consent of the governed and revolution if the government failed in its proper functions. Articulated in the writings of John Locke, natural rights philosophy was elaborated in the United States in the works of Thomas Jefferson, Samuel Adams, and Thomas Paine. Classic expressions of natural rights philosophy are the Declaration of Independence and the Bill of Rights. Concepts of natural rights infused the writings of Mary Wollstonecraft and were central to the Declaration of Sentiments adopted at Seneca Falls in 1848.

6. Rhetoric is not, of course, the only important element in a social movement (Freeman 1975, 1-43).

2

The Struggle for the Right to Speak

It is difficult to determine who initiated women's rhetorical history in the United States. It may have been Deborah Sampson Gannett who, disguised as a male, served in the army in the Revolutionary War and justified her actions subsequently in a series of lectures (Anderson 1984, 135-141). A Scottish woman, Frances Wright, shocked "promiscuous" audiences of men and women in 1824 with her short curly hair, her dress (she wore the free-flowing tunic and pants costume of the utopian New Harmony Community), and her views, which included antislavery, universal education, religious freedom and equality for women (Lane 1972). From that time, women who attempted to speak were labeled "Fanny Wrightists," an epithet intended to frighten away any woman with aspirations to the platform.

Others claim that the earliest U.S. woman to speak publicly to men and women was Maria W. Miller Stewart, an Afro-American who delivered a lecture in Boston's Franklin Hall on September 21, 1832 (Richardson 1987, xii). Her struggle and that of other early feminist-abolitionists, such as Sojourner Truth and Angelina Grimké, dramatically illustrate the nature and extent of taboos against the speech of women, and key examples of their rhetoric will be analyzed in this chapter.[1]

MARIA W. MILLER STEWART

Maria W. Miller Stewart was probably the first woman in the United States to speak publicly to men and women. Her role in the abolitionist and woman's rights movements was relatively limited, but her path-breaking efforts as a speaker may have been a model for other women. She worked for the abolition of slavery and against colonization, and

urged self-help activities to fellow Afro-Americans in Boston. She
addressed an early Afro-American woman's club, and she attended
the first Convention of Anti-Slavery Women held in New York in 1837.
Anticipating the Grimké sisters by five years, Miller Stewart spoke
publicly in Boston's Franklin Hall on September 21, 1832. She spoke
in a high style that, like the 1838 speech of Angelina Grimké [Weld]
discussed below, owed much of its literary quality to the biblical
material she incorporated into her statements.

In that 1832 lecture, she acknowledged resistance to women
speakers: "I have come forward and made myself a hissing and a
reproach among the people" (Stewart 1835, 55). She appealed to
white women, particularly advantaged white women, as would Mary
Church Terrell many years later, for understanding and assistance:

> O, ye fairer sisters, whose hands are never soiled, whose nerves and muscles are
> never strained, go learn by experience! Had we the opportunity that you have
> had, to improve our moral and mental faculties, what would have hindered our
> intellects from being as bright, and our manners from being as dignified as
> yours? . . . Have pity upon us, have pity upon us, O ye who have hearts to feel
> for others' woes. (Stewart 1835, 55)

In a speech to the Afric-American Female Intelligence Society of Boston,
Miller Stewart emphasized woman's civilizing influence, especially on her
children:

> O woman, woman! Upon you I call; for upon your exertions almost entirely
> depends whether the rising generation shall be anything more than we have been
> or not. O woman, woman! Your example is powerful, your influence great; it
> extends over your husbands and your children, and throughout the circle of your
> acquaintance. (Stewart 1987, 55)

Like the Grimkés, she drew on the Bible for support, but her message,
usually directed to those like herself, concerned concrete action in this
world.

In her first speech, Miller Stewart asked: "Why sit ye here and die?"
(Stewart 1835, 51) and in 1831, in a tract entitled "Religion and the
Pure Principles of Morality," she wrote: "It is of no use for us to sit
with our hands folded, hanging our heads like bulrushes, lamenting
our wretched condition; but let us make a mighty effort, and
arise. . . . Do you ask, what can we do? Unite and build a store of your
own" (Stewart 1971, 467-68). Although what she preached differed
little from the sermons of Afro-American ministers, the fact that she
was a woman, especially one who dared speak in public to audiences
of men and women, made her message unacceptable. She encountered

such hostility that she left Boston and ceased public speaking.

In a farewell address of September 21, 1833, anticipating arguments later made by Sarah Grimké and Lucretia Coffin Mott, she defended woman's right to speak based on Scripture:

> What if I am a woman; is not the God of ancient times the God of these modern days? Did he not raise up Deborah to be a mother and a judge in Israel? Did not Queen Esther save the lives of the Jews? And Mary Magdalene first declare the resurrection of Christ from the dead? . . . If such women as are here described have once existed, be no longer astonished then, my brethren and friends, that God at this eventful period should raise up your own females to strive, by their example both in public and private, to assist those who are endeavoring to stop the strong current of prejudice that flows so profusely against us at present. No longer ridicule their efforts, it will be counted for sin. (Stewart 1987, 68-69)

Subsequently, she moved to New York City, attended but did not speak at the Convention of Anti-Slavery Women in 1837, worked as a teacher, and published her speeches and meditations (1835; 1879; Richardson 1987, xiii-xvii, 3-27). Miller Stewart's brief career as a speaker illustrates the inevitable link between any rhetorical effort and the struggle for woman's rights, as well as the centrality of scriptural prohibitions against woman speaking, an issue to be discussed in chapter 3.

SOJOURNER TRUTH

Some Afro-American women were directly involved in the woman's rights/woman suffrage movement, but, in addition, they concerned themselves with the special impact of racism and prejudice on Afro-American women. They responded to the highly negative stereotypes of Afro-American women (Terrell 1898), and, subsequent to Reconstruction, they linked the evils of lynching to conceptions of white women that were an intrinsic part of the "cult of true womanhood" (Wells 1892, 1910).[2]

Afro-American women were active in the effort to abolish slavery, although cooperation between white and Afro-American abolitionists was limited. Like their male counterparts, most white female abolitionists were racists: they believed Afro-Americans were naturally inferior, and they refused to associate with them in secular or religious organizations, and they refused to work for their integration into the economic, political, and social life of the nation before and after the Civil War. The Grimké sisters, discussed below, and Lucretia Coffin Mott, discussed in chapter 3, were rare but noteworthy excep-

tions to this rule. The woman who came to be known as Sojourner
Truth is one of a small group of Afro-Americans involved in efforts
both for the abolition of slavery and for woman's rights
(Davis 1982, 1:427; Hamilton 1978, 40, passim; Terborg-Penn 1977).

Isabella was born a slave in New York State, probably in 1797. Freed
by law in 1828, in 1843 she left New York to preach her view of God
in Massachusetts under her new name, Sojourner Truth. Beginning in
1850 she lectured extensively in western New York and the Midwest
with other distinguished abolitionists. Truth's public work included
speeches for abolitionism, woman's rights, economic assistance for
freed slaves after the war, and for religious causes. Although her
speeches have the unique stamp of her special history, presence, and
character, they reflect the concerns, the arguments, and the rhetorical
strategies typical of early woman's rights rhetoric (Campbell 1986).[3]

Like most other early women speakers, Truth relied heavily on the
Bible, but she felt herself as standing in an unusual relationship to
God, one which she talked about in her speeches, and which she
combined with metaphors of unforgettable vividness. However, she
was also the first woman's rights activist to speak in a colloquial or low
style, heavily laced with humor.[4] Truth's speeches were extemporaneous, if not spontaneous, qualities evident in those which are
extant. On one occasion, for example, when another speaker praised
the U.S. Constitution, she responded:

> Children, I talk to God and God talks to me. . . . [The weevil had destroyed
> thousands of acres of wheat in the West that year.] This morning I was walking
> out, and I got over the fence. I saw the wheat holding up its head, looking very
> big. I go up and take ahold of it. You believe it, there was *no* wheat there? I says,
> God, what *is* the matter with *this* wheat? and he says to me, "Sojourner, there
> is a little weasel [sic] in it." Now I hear talking about the Constitution and the
> rights of man. I comes up and takes hold of the Constitution. It looks *mighty big*,
> and I feels for *my* rights, but there ain't any there. Then I say, God, what *ails*
> this Constitution? He says to me, "Sojourner, there is a little *weasel* in it."
> (Truth 1878, 147)

There survives only a partial text of her most famous speech, delivered at
the Akron, Ohio, Woman's Rights Convention in 1851 (Truth 1878, 133-
35).[5] At its outset, Sojourner Truth acknowledged the potent combination
abolitionism and woman's rights represented for white males: "I think that
'twixt the Negroes of the South and the women of the North, all talking
about rights, the white men will be in a fix pretty soon" (133-34). As a
whole, that speech was a powerful refutation of claims that: (1) women
suffer no ill effects under current laws; (2) women are intellectually

inferior to men, and thus require fewer opportunities; and (3) woman's limited sphere was ordained by God.

Sojourner Truth was herself immediate and dramatic proof of the ills resulting from woman's position, particularly the ills of slave women. Like other poor women, particularly poor slave women, the cult of domesticity took no account of the quality of her life, which had been totally unlike traditional nineteenth-century concepts of womanliness or femininity. "That man over there says that women need to be helped into carriages, and lifted over ditches, and to have the best place everywhere. Nobody ever helps me into carriages, or over mud-puddles, or gives me any best place! And aren't I a woman?" (134). Moreover, her life demonstrated women's physical prowess — she had done the most backbreaking farm work so well that no man could do it better: "I have ploughed and planted, and gathered into barns, and no man could head me! And aren't I a woman?" (134). She called attention to the contradiction at the heart of slavery — the treatment of slave women, which wholly ignored their status as women and mothers, viewing them as chattel, as breeding stock. "I have borne thirteen children, and seen them almost all sold off to slavery, and when I cried out with my mother's grief, none but Jesus heard — and aren't I a woman?" (134). Her response to claims of woman's intellectual inferiority evaded arguments about woman's mental capacity in order to affirm the right to equality of opportunity: "If my cup won't hold but a pint, and yours holds a quart, wouldn't you be mean not to let me have my little half-measure full?" (134). Her response to theological justifications for "woman's place" was equally apt, a dramatic version of the theological notion that Mary's child wiped out Eve's curse: "Then that little man in black [a clergyman] there, he says women can't have as much rights as men, 'cause Christ wasn't a woman! Where did your Christ come from? . . . From God and a woman! Man had nothing to do with Him" (134-35).[6]

Not only did Truth speak for woman's rights, she also emphasized the rights of Afro-American women. At the first annual convention of the American Equal Rights Association, subsequent to the introduction of the Fourteenth Amendment, Truth pointed out: "There is a great stir about colored men getting their rights, but not a word about the colored women; and if colored men get their rights and not colored women get theirs, there will be a bad time about it" (Truth 1867, 3). She also pointed out her unique status: "I suppose I am about the only colored woman that goes about to speak for the rights of the colored woman" (3). She based her claims on natural rights, and she saw those claims as equally applicable to women like herself: "We want to carry the point to one particular thing, and that is woman's rights, for nobody has any business with a right that belongs to her. I can make use of my own right. I want the same use of the same right" (3).

What remains of Truth's rhetoric demonstrates similarities between her speeches and those of other early woman's rights speakers, despite the fact that she was a unique figure. Her colloquial style, her use of humor, and, at times, a maternal, half-joking, half-scolding persona were most unusual, as comparisons to other women activists show. Like many other woman's rights advocates, she relied on biblical authority, personal experience, vivid metaphors, and the power of her presence as immediate proof of her claims. For her, as for many other early women speakers, efforts for the abolition of slavery and woman's rights were intertwined. Sadly, however, on only rare occasions did white activists recognize the relationship between the treatment of Afro-American slave women and woman's rights (Grimké 1836; Stanton 1860).

THE GRIMKÉ SISTERS

The Grimké sisters were among the earliest major figures in United States women's rhetorical history, and their efforts to speak out against slavery reveal dramatically the force and character of the prohibitions against rhetorical action by women. Sarah and Angelina Grimké were the daughters of a prosperous South Carolina slaveowner (Birney 1885; Lerner 1967; Lumpkin 1974). Each in turn rejected the system of slavery, traveled north to Philadelphia, joined the Society of Quakers, and believed she was called to be a minister.[7] In 1835 Angelina wrote a letter to William Lloyd Garrison, the radical abolitionist, founder of the American Anti-Slavery Society, and editor of the *Liberator*, responding to the stories in that paper telling of the abuse of abolitionist speakers. Garrison published her eloquent testimony about the evils of slavery, and although severely criticized by the Quakers and her sister Sarah for writing the letter and incurring public exposure, Angelina became committed to that struggle.

In 1836 Elizur Wright, secretary of the American Anti-Slavery Society, invited Angelina to come to New York under the society's sponsorship to speak to women in sewing circles and private parlors on the subject of slavery. She was already engaged in writing her *Appeal to the Christian Women of the Southern States*. The arguments she developed there were grounded in natural rights philosophy, and she took the position that women could be effective agents of change — they could read, pray, speak, and act. She urged them to private persuasion: "Speak to your relatives, friends, acquaintances, be not afraid . . . to let your sentiments be known. . . . Try to persuade your husband, father, brothers and sons that slavery is a crime *against God and man*" (Grimké 1836, 16-18; Lerner 1967, 139). She urged women who owned slaves to set them free and pay them wages; or, at the very least, to educate them, and, if the law forbade it, to suffer the penalty. The pamphlet was unique as an appeal by a Southern abolitionist woman to Southern women and as an appeal to Southern white women to identify with their slave sisters.

Despite expressions of disapproval from her sister and the Philadelphia Quakers, Angelina accepted Wright's invitation, specifying that she and Sarah, who agreed to accompany her, would accept no pay and would bear their own expenses. Accepting remuneration would have been too blatant a violation of society's norms. The sisters from South Carolina had become the first female abolitionist "apostles" (called agents) in the United States. They attended an agents' convention, led by Theodore Weld, designed to train newly recruited speakers, at which every objection raised by the public to abolitionism was presented, discussed, and refuted, and at which they heard model speeches by Weld and others.

Their work began with "parlor talks" presented under the auspices of the Female Anti-Slavery Society. So many women were eager to hear them, however, that no private parlor was large enough; a minister offered them the session room in his church. The announcement of their first meeting caused consternation; the idea of women lecturing in a church was shocking. Abolitionist leader Gerrit Smith advised them to cancel the meeting, but Weld urged them to proceed, which they did. Some three hundred women gathered; the meeting opened with a prayer and a greeting, after which the clergymen who had delivered them departed. The lectures continued during the next two months, and soon session rooms were too small to contain the audience, so they moved into church sanctuaries. They had broken the first major barrier: women were now speaking in public places.

In May of 1837, Sarah and Angelina attended the Anti-Slavery Convention of American Women in New York City. In the speeches they gave there, they insisted that race prejudice must be fought in the North as well as in the South. Angelina's speech was published by the convention as *An Appeal to the Women of the Nominally Free States*, Sarah's as an *Address to Free Colored Americans*.

Immediately afterward they began a series of lectures in Massachusetts, lectures noteworthy for the fact that many were given to large audiences of men and women. Husbands whose wives came home to tell of the Grimké sisters' testimony and eloquence slipped into the backs of churches to hear for themselves, and slowly this came to be accepted. Sarah and Angelina had broken a second barrier; they were now speaking to audiences that included men.

However, opposition surfaced. Ministers refused them churches, disapproving of them both as abolitionists and as women. Finally, at Amesbury, Massachusetts, two young men challenged Angelina's statements and a heated dispute ensued. Based on their experience in the South, these men contended that the conditions of the slaves were "no worse than those of the yeomen and manufacturers of the North" (Lerner 1967, 178). By public request, Angelina agreed to debate these men at a subsequent meeting in Amesbury, a debate that so scandalized a local newspaper editor that he declared it "too indelicate" for publication (Lerner 1967, 179). Now they had broken through still another barrier: a woman had dared to share a platform with men as their equal, and she had engaged them in a logical, argumentative form deemed unsuitable to woman's nature.

Catharine Beecher was deeply perturbed by Angelina's activities and published a pamphlet addressed to Angelina, *An Essay on Slavery and Abolition with Reference to the Duty of American Females*, to attack and counter her views (Beecher 1837). During her speaking tour in Massachusetts, Angelina responded by writing a series of *Letters to Catharine Beecher*, which were published in the anti-slavery press and then reprinted as a pamphlet (Grimké 1838).

On July 28, 1837, irritation with the Grimkés as embodiments of woman's rights issues and as abolitionists emerged in a "Pastoral Letter of the General Association of Massachusetts to the Congregational Churches under Their Care." Without naming them directly, the letter warned all churches against "the dangers which at present seem to threaten the female character with widespread and permanent injury." Women were charged to perform their "appropriate duties . . . as clearly stated in the New Testament." Woman's strength, the letter asserted, was her weakness and dependence; "but when she assumes the place and tone of man as a public reformer, our care and protection of her seem unnecessary . . . and her character becomes unnatural. If the vine, whose strength and beauty is to lean upon the trelliswork, and half conceal its clusters, thinks to assume the independence and the overshadowing nature of the elm, it will not only cease to bear fruit, but fall in shame and dishonor into the dust" (HWS 1:81).

Sarah responded with a series of *Letters on the Equality of the Sexes* (1838). She held that the Scriptures reflected the patriarchal society that had produced them, and argued that woman had been created by God as man's companion and equal. These letters were the first serious discussion of woman's rights by an American woman, and they influenced Lucretia Coffin Mott (Cromwell 1958, 29), discussed in chapter 3. Angelina took a similar position. In a letter to Theodore Weld, she wrote: "We are placed very unexpectedly in a very trying situation, in the forefront of an entirely new contest — a contest for the *rights of woman* as a moral, intelligent and responsible being" (Barnes and Dumond 1934, 1:415). In a letter to Weld and John Greenleaf Whittier, she added: "If we surrender the right to *speak* to the public this year, we must surrender the right to petition the next year and the right to *write* the year after and so on. What *then* can *woman* do for the slave when she is herself under the feet of man and shamed into *silence*?" (Barnes and Dumond 1934, 1:430).

The setting for two major speeches by women, one composed and adopted by delegates from numerous female anti-slavery societies, the other authored by Angelina Grimké, was Pennsylvania Hall. Refused the use of churches and denied the right to rent halls for their meetings, abolitionists in Philadelphia formed an association, sold shares, and raised $40,000 to build a hall to be used for free speech "on any and every subject not of an immoral character" (Birney 1885, 234). Public reaction to the hall — to meetings of radical abolitionists, to meetings of mixed race, and to speeches by female abolitionists before audiences of mixed sex and race — was intensely hostile. The mayor of Philadelphia suggested that black and white women cease meeting together in order to reduce tensions in the city, but they refused (Bacon, 1986; 107). The *History of Pennsylvania Hall* ([Webb] 1838) reports that the Anti-Slavery Convention of American Women began meeting on Tuesday, May 15, 1838; on the afternoon of May 17, Sara T. Smith, on behalf of the Business Committee, presented an address to the Anti-Slavery Convention of American Women (*History* 1838, 131-34). Angelina had spoken on the evening of May 16 at a general meeting of male and female abolitionists that was part of ceremonies dedicating the hall, which was the first meeting at which "men and women acted together as moral beings" (Birney 1885, 24). This joining of the American and Female Anti-Slavery Societies was a rare and transient moment of abolitionist unity and triumph in their new hall.

These two speeches are not about woman's rights as such; what they illustrate is the link between abolitionism and the birth of a woman's rights movement. These two rhetorical acts are juxtaposed in the analysis that follows because one, as the creation of delegates from many female anti-slavery societies addressed to all abolitionists, including males, provides strong evidence of their general concerns and of the lines of argument female abolitionists appropriated. It is also an explicit defense of a woman's right to be active in the abolitionist movement. The other, a masterpiece of rhetorical invention, illustrates the creative skills of a woman confronting the most severe rhetorical obstacles. The text is incomplete, but its quality and coherence belie the introductory remarks in the *History of Pennsylvania Hall*: "All we have attempted to do is to furnish an outline of the *ideas*, wishing the reader to understand that the chaste, yet forcible language in which they were clothed, could not be given" (123). It is a finished work of rhetorical artistry.

The address on behalf of the Anti-Slavery Convention of American Women responded to proscriptions against women speaking and agitating for the abolition of slavery by linking woman's rights and abolitionism. Sara T. Smith, speaking for the Convention, said:

> We fear not censure for going beyond the circle which has been drawn around us by physical force, by mental usurpation, by the usages of ages — not any one of which, can we admit, gives the right to prescribe [sic] it; else might . . . the chains we are now seeking to break continue riveted on the neck of the slave. (*History* 1838, 131)

The speech also responded to the idea that because slavery was a political question, it lay outside women's concerns or, as they phrased it, that "we are 'stepping out of our sphere' when we take part in its discussion" (131). The women argued that slavery, however political, was a moral and religious issue. They exploited the contradiction implicit in woman's allegedly natural piety, asking: "Must woman necessarily be less gentle because her heart is open to the claims of humanity, or less modest because she feels for the degradation of her enslaved sisters, and would stretch forth her hand for their rescue?" (132). They also argued that even if slavery were an entirely political question, the public and private spheres could not be so neatly separated. If war came, they asked: "Will it be easy to convince them [women] that it is no concern of theirs, that their homes are rendered desolate, and their habitations the abodes of wretchedness?" (132).

The speech, adopted by the convention of women, was designed to show other women that they could act effectively, but it also addressed male abolitionists. Membership in an anti-slavery society released no one from "individual action"; all were to use their special talents: "To some among us may be given the head to devise, to others the hand to execute; one may have time to devote, another money; let each give liberally of that which he or she possesses. . . . Let the aged counsel, the young execute; plead not inability" (132). Each person had a special work of self-education to perform by reading anti-slavery publications, a position they affirmed by citing the authority of editors of abolitionist publications. Like others affected by the Enlightenment, the authors of this speech believed that knowledge was power, not only for them but for former slaves, and they urged the formation of schools to educate "colored children." They asked the male and female abolitionists they addressed to practice what they preached in their personal lives — for example, not to buy goods produced by slaves, an action clearly open to women, even if it meant the loss of the "sensual gratifications" of sugar and cotton clothing.

The plea for consistency of behavior took on a more controversial hue in the final paragraphs of the women's address. Their tone shifted; they urged their brethren to thoughtful deliberation. They began by attempting to avoid misinterpretation: "We would not be understood as wishing to identify the anti-slavery cause with that of peace" (133). Like other radical abolitionists, they understood that their efforts might result in war. They were deeply concerned about the methods used by abolitionist agents in advancing their cause, and they raised the pacifist issue in its most extreme form — that under no condition was violence permissible. They said:

We would only suggest to you, the importance of carefully examining how far abolitionists are restrained from the use of such methods of defence [violence], by their declaration of sentiments, issued at the time of the formation of the American Anti-Slavery Society; and what the influence of its use would probably be upon our cause. From these two positions only, do we feel at liberty to present the subject. (133)

The argument that followed was stylistically conciliatory but rigorously deductive, grounded in the *Declaration of Sentiments* adopted at the founding of the American Anti-Slavery Society in 1833. They quoted from the *Declaration* (published in 1835) to contrast abolitionist principles to those of the nation's founders:

Their [the nation's founders'] principles led them to wage war against their oppressors, and to spill human blood, like water, in order to be free. *Ours* forbid the doing of evil that good may come, and lead us to reject and entreat the oppressed to reject, the use of all carnal weapons for deliverance from bondage; relying solely upon those which are spiritual, and mighty, through God, to the pulling down of strong holds.

Their measures were physical resistance—the marshalling in arms—the hostile array—the mortal encounter. *Ours* shall be such only as the opposition of moral purity to moral corruption—the destruction of error by the potency of truth. (134; *Declaration* 1835, 3)

The address was logically consistent, drawing conclusions entailed in the *Declaration*, but its authors lessened the impact of their logic and the temerity of giving advice to their male counterparts by phrasing their position as a question: "Are we not, by them [constitutions of many Anti-Slavery Societies that incorporate similar sentiments], bound utterly to reject the use of weapons of physical resistance, in our efforts to promote the emancipation of the slave?" (134). They acknowledged the right of individual choice in this matter, but emphasized the implications of such actions for their cause. They reinforced their plea for thoughtful consideration of this matter with biblical authority, inviting male abolitionists to "prove all things" (134; 1 Thess. 5:21).

Remembering that the immediate audience was composed of women, but that the address would be conveyed to all abolitionists, including their male counterparts, one may note the pronouns used. Earlier in the speech they spoke of "he and she"; here they seem to have been addressing males. Earlier in the speech they had claimed the right to speak and act; here they presumed to advise their fellows. Moreover, they did not assert their moral authority to argue against violence on principle. The women's convention rejected violent self-defense on the pragmatic grounds that it could only injure their cause, and they supported their claim with the actual experiences of abolitionist speakers. Theirs was a plea for the efficacy of creative nonviolence as a tool for social change. It "heaps coals of fire on the head" of the enemy, they said, appropriating Paul's advice to the Roman church (Rom. 12:20). They also affirmed "a universally admitted truth, that opposition strengthens human purpose" to justify their view that self-defense benefited their opponents (134).

As these comments indicate, the address presented women abolitionists acting as rhetors and as moral agents and, in so doing, violated somewhat the limits of woman's traditional role. The address was in a middle style: calm, reasoned, and firmly stated. Women had a right to act against slavery, the authors said, because, although political and public, this issue affected woman's place. However, like many other early women persuaders, they bolstered their authority by invoking the Bible, they invited thoughtful deliberation rather than asserting their views too strongly, and they appealed to the experiences of their audience in support of their conclusions. Both rhetorically and historically, this speech was important because, as a carefully prepared, authentic text, it allows a general understanding of female abolitionist rhetoric at the time of Angelina Grimké [Weld]'s speech.

Angelina's speech stands in striking contrast to the address adopted by the women's convention. The style of her speech was high, that is, literary, biblical, extremely formal, and varied—it thundered and it courted. Its delivery on the evening of May 16 was a moment of high drama in the history of women's rhetoric, indeed in the history of women. An unruly mob had gathered outside Pennsylvania Hall. William Lloyd Garrison opened the meeting; Maria W. Chapman spoke, then Angelina. Her speech was followed by addresses by Abby Kelley and Lucretia Coffin Mott.

Angelina's speech was a rhetorical masterwork. She heartened those in the hall, urging them to further action by showing them that their past action had been effective. Moreover, there were no frail, helpless women among those she addressed. The occasion was extremely threatening: there was a mob milling and shouting outside which would return to burn the new hall down the following evening. Angelina was highly unconventional and inventive in adapting to the terror and violence of the immediate scene and in selecting a rhetorical persona for herself that would overcome resistance to her as a woman speaker.

In this extraordinary situation, Angelina began by taking the high ground, from which point she at once challenged the audience. In her first sentence she asked, "What came ye out for to see? A reed shaken with the wind?" (*History* 1838, 123). With these words she set the tone of the entire speech. The quotation is from Matthew 11:7, and with it she rebuked her audience spiritually while challenging the mob outside. "Is it curiosity merely, or a deep sympathy with the perishing slave, that has brought this large audience together?" (123) she asked, testing the meeting's commitment to abolitionism. Her question was followed, according to the contemporary witnesses who compiled the *History*, by "a yell from the mob without the building." In response, she said: "Do you ask, 'what has the North to do with slavery?' Hear it—hear it. Those voices without tell us that the spirit of slavery is *here*" (123). The anger of the mob demonstrated both the need for their work and its effectiveness, "for surely liberty would not foam and tear herself with rage, because her friends are multiplied daily" (123).

The sounds rang out again, and again the interruption was transmuted into evidence. She put their worst fears into words and challenged them to compare their transitory terror to the life of the slave:

> What if the mob should now burst in upon us, break up our meeting and commit violence upon our persons — would this be anything compared with what the slaves endure? No, no: and we do not remember them "as bound with them" [Heb. 13:3], if we shrink in the time of peril, or feel unwilling to sacrifice ourselves, if need be, for their sake. (124)

The scene became an occasion to experience imaginatively what it was to be a slave and to understand the biblical injunction to identify with the slave. But the mob's behavior proved more. She said: "I thank the Lord that there is yet left life enough to feel the truth, even though it rages at it — that conscience is not so completely seared as to be unmoved by the truth of the living God" (124). The fury of the mob demonstrated that the abolitionists' cause was a painful appeal to conscience, and the howls were proof that these sinners could yet be saved. Mob behavior was "but an evidence that our efforts are the best that could have been adopted" and proof of their success: "If the arm of the North had not caused the Bastille of slavery to totter to its foundation, you would not hear those cries. A few years ago, and the South felt secure, and with a contemptuous sneer asked, 'Who are the abolitionists?' " (125). The shouts of the mob demonstrated that the anti-slavery groups were doing the Lord's work and doing it effectively.

It would be hard to imagine a speech further removed from the stereotype of the modest, unassertive woman, and Angelina Grimké found a striking method for transcending that role. By using the howls of the mob to her own ends and by relying on biblical allusion and authority, Angelina was able to enact the role of prophet. On the simplest level, biblical language reflected the general abolitionist view of slavery as a sin, a view that transformed abolitionism into a holy cause, sanctioned by God, that must succeed. But biblical materials did much more here, because these materials cast her in a different role.

With the mob screaming outside — throwing rocks and breaking windows, threatening all who heard her — Angelina began by quoting the words of Jesus addressed to the multitudes concerning John the Baptist (Matt. 11:7). This biblical reference associated her with the prophet and herald, John, and with the messianic role of Jesus. It invested this opening moment of her speech with special significance. She underscored her prophetic role a sentence later by referring to the mob as "Deluded beings! 'they know not what they do,' " thus appropriating Christ's words from the cross (Luke 23:34). She then paraphrased the Sermon on the Mount (Matt. 7:5) in telling the abolitionists what they must do: "Do you ask, then, 'what has the North to do?' I answer, cast out first the spirit of slavery from your own hearts, and then lend your aid to convert the South" (123). Again, her words placed her in a messianic, prophetic position. A more explicit defense of her role came in words drawn from Paul's Epistle to the Corinthians: "He hath chosen the foolish things of the world to confound the wise, and the weak to overcome the mighty" (1 Cor. 1:27). The ambiguity of these allusions is part of their strength: on the one hand, they apply to abolitionists as a group and to their mission, but they also have particular relevance to the work of women like herself.

Evidence that Angelina appropriated a prophetic role runs through the entire speech. As part of her testimony as a former slaveholding Southerner, she told of the sad time in the South when none shared her feelings about slavery, when "no voice in the wilderness was heard calling on the people to repent and do works meet for repentance," another allusion to biblical descriptions of a messianic forerunner (124; Isa. 40:3, Matt. 3:3). She described her feelings during this pre-abolitionist period with the words of an Old Testament prophet: "The language of my soul was, 'Oh tell it not in Gath, publish it not in the streets of Askelon' " (125; 2 Sam. 1:20). This allusion drew an analogy between conditions in Israel, that must not be broadcast lest the heathen rejoice, and the shame of American slavery, which violated both religious and republican principles. Her purpose as a speaker and a moral agent found expression in the words of the prophet Isaiah: "I will lift up my voice like a trumpet, and show this people their transgression" (125; Isa. 58:1). And she specifically referred to herself as being "in the midst of temptation" as a Southern woman (124).

In this speech, Angelina created a rhetorical persona, a role that legitimized her as a female rhetor, which was a strategy she had used on other occasions (Japp 1985). Here she was no mere woman speaking; she was a prophet, the voice of God (Berg and Berry 1981; Mack 1982). To reject her and her words was to deny prophecy. The choice was a conscious one: even though Quakers believed that preaching was an intuitive gift consistent with the nature of woman, Angelina consistently refused to use her Quakerism as a justification for speaking. In 1837 she wrote: "If it is wrong for woman to lecture or preach then let the Quakers give up their false views, and let other sects refuse to hear their women, but if it is *right* then let *all* women who have gifts, 'mind their calling' and enjoy 'the liberty wherewith

Christ hath made them free', in that declaration of Paul, 'in Christ Jesus there is neither male nor female' " (Barnes and Dumond 1934, 1:416; Gal. 3:28). She wrote of her great fear of speaking, then added: "but the Lord is at my right hand, I lean on the arm of my beloved and he sustains me and fills my mouth as soon as I open it" (Barnes and Dumond 1934, 1:416-17). Earlier she had used the concept of a prophetic role to attack contemporary clergy who criticized what she did, and to argue for women in the clergy: "The Church is built *not* upon the priests at all but upon the *prophets* and *apostles*, Jesus Christ being the chief corner stone.... As there were *prophetesses* as well as prophets, so there *ought* to be now *female* as well as male ministers" (Barnes and Dumond 1934, 1:431-32). In her speech in Pennsylvania Hall, however, Angelina did not argue this position; she simply assumed the prophetic role through language and allusion and answered biblically based attacks on female speakers indirectly. This, in fact, was a strategy Theodore Weld had urged in an earlier exchange of letters (Barnes and Dumond 1934, 1:415-27).

Angelina Grimké empowered her audience. She inbued abolitionists with a sense of the rightness of their cause, of their mission in the North, and of the effectiveness of their work by appropriating evidence from the immediate scene; she then singled out her sister abolitionists. She entreated the women of Philadelphia, "as a Southern woman, with much attachment to the land of my birth" (126), to use their superior moral power to cleanse her beloved land of its sin. She argued that women can be effective agents of change, while recognizing their legal and political disabilities: "It is only through petitions that you can reach the Legislature. It is therefore peculiarly *your* duty to petition. Do you say, 'It does no good?' The South already turns pale at the number sent" (126). She transformed limitation into opportunity and obligation, and the struggle over the gag rule prohibiting petitions to the Congress into evidence of efficacy. She addressed the issue of resistance to women's activities directly: "They deny our right to petition and to remonstrate against abuses of our sex and of our kind. We have these rights, however, from our God. Only let us exercise them" (126). She appealed to woman's peculiar capacity for empathy. Male hostility to such moral action, which was consistent with their natures as traditionally conceived, was juxtaposed against women's God-given rights. As natural rights, these need not be requested, only exercised. Action was a moral duty, and based on the effect of petitions by Englishwomen, such action would be effective. Finally, she appealed by saying, "that while the slaves continue to suffer, and when they shout deliverance, we may feel the satisfaction of *having done what we could*" (126).

CONCLUSION

Maria W. Miller Stewart played only a small role in the abolitionist and woman's rights movements, but she was among the first if not the first U.S. woman whose speeches showed the inevitable link between public protest and woman's rights. After losing her teaching position in New York City she moved to Baltimore, then to Washington, D.C., where she worked as a matron in the Freedmen's Hospital and opened a Sunday school for poor and destitute children. The pension she was granted as a widow of the War of 1812 was used in part to finance publication of a second edition of her speeches and writings (1879). Miller Stewart's speeches are moving jeremiads, exhorting Afro-Americans facing prejudice and discrimination to self-help, speeches that manifest the special role that Afro-American women have played in fighting against the burdens of racism, poverty, and sexism that afflict them and their families.

Sojourner Truth's role in the reform movements of her day has been called "relatively minor," but she stands as a unique and vivid reminder of the relationship between woman's rights and the abolition of slavery, because she "captured the imagination of many" (Redding 1971, 3:481; Stowe 1863). Although the record of her speeches is scanty and incomplete, her rhetoric provides glimpses of what Northrop Frye calls "high style in ordinary speech . . . heard whenever a speaker is honestly struggling to express what his [sic] society, as a society, is trying to be and do" (1963, 45). Sojourner Truth's most famous speech dramatically links the issues of sex, race, and class, to show that slave women were not seen as women or as mothers. Her extraordinary rhetorical skill proved that some Afro-Americans were so talented that even slavery and illiteracy could not extinguish their abilities.

All of the speeches analyzed in this chapter illustrate the force of prohibitions against women speaking, the creativity with which they responded to such proscriptions, and the rhetorical link between efforts for the abolition of slavery and the rise of a movement for the rights of woman; there were also non-rhetorical links (Bacon 1986, 108-9). The speech of the Anti-Slavery Convention of American Women in 1838 articulates common lines of argument: the speech exploits the contradiction implicit in woman's role and rejects rigid distinctions between the public and private sphere. Like the speeches of Miller Stewart, it illustrates the willingness of women to take positions and to direct advice to their brethren. Finally, it demonstrates women's skill in using a softened style that violates traditional norms as little as possible.

Angelina Grimké's 1838 speech reflects some traditional con-cerns — the need to convince members of a fledgling movement of the rightness of their cause, and the need to persuade women with little power and few resources that they can be effective in working for social change. It is a particularly eloquent and explicit example of a speaker seeking to empower the women in her audience. More important, however, it illustrates the remarkable rhetorical skill of a woman who could exploit a terrorizing mob as evidence for her claims and who could subtly appropriate the language of the Bible in order to assume a persona that transcended male-female roles and legitimated her rhetorical action. Angelina's assumption of the prophetic role created dissonance in her highly religious audience. Audience members had to choose between two conflicting but scripturally based beliefs — that women were to remain silent in public, even on moral matters, and that God sent prophets, who were sometimes female, as His mouth-pieces. Her use of this sophisticated strategy enriches critical under-standing of the role of character in persuasion, because it illustrates the relevance of social role relationships and of the dramatic concept of personae in explaining how influence occurs.

Both 1838 addresses are significant as they are part of what have been called the "precipitating events" that bring a social movement into existence. Such events are moments in which key individuals, usually potential leaders, come to perceive that their experiences are not isolated acts of discrimination or oppression but part of a pattern that is endemic to the social system. They experience "structural strain" — the conflict between themselves and society — and realize that systemic change is required in order to remove the barriers they confront. Many early woman's rights leaders had these experiences in abolitionism. Female abolitionist societies constituted a network that woman's rights advocates could use to spread their concerns. Others had their consciousness raised by experiences in other reform move-ments; some had repeated experiences in a variety of causes. In short, contemporary protest efforts provided a vital crucible for the develop-ment of a woman's rights movement.

Sarah and Angelina Grimké were like comets that soared briefly to signal the beginnings of the woman's rights movement. During the twenty-three weeks they spent in New England, "they spoke before at least 88 meetings in 67 towns. . . . [They] reached, face to face, a minimum of 40,500 people in meetings" (Lerner 1967, 227). Two years after Seneca Falls, Angelina became interested in woman's rights activity and carried on an active correspondence with its leaders. She sent stirring letters to the national conventions in Worcester in 1851 and Syracuse in 1852, and although absent was elected to serve on the Central Committee of both conventions. During the Civil War she became vice president of the Woman's National Loyal League, a group active in gathering petitions to urge passage of an amendment abolishing slavery. In 1863, when the league called a convention in New York City, she spoke from the floor, made a platform speech, and then, at the direction of the convention, prepared and presented a stirring "Address to the Soldiers" (Lumpkin 1974, 201, 206, 218; Anderson 1984, 77-79). Angelina's disappearance as a speaker is something of a mystery.[8] There is no record of further rhetorical activity by Sarah. The Grimké sisters lit the way for woman's rights; others would have to take up the torch.

NOTES

1. Because the founders of Quakerism strongly believed in woman's capacity to preach and prophesy, which were gifts of the spirit consistent with woman's nature, some Quaker women, such as Lucretia Coffin Mott, gained experience speaking to mixed audiences in their meetings. However, because they lacked reason, Quaker women might not join in making the rules that governed their meetings (Bacon 1986; Giele 1961).

2. Historian Ann Firor Scott links the cult of true womanhood to slavery (1970).

3. The textual materials that remain are stenographic reports of her spontaneous utterances and are usually incomplete (Truth 1878; Fauset 1938). Two apparently complete texts of speeches delivered at the first annual meeting of the American Equal Rights Association exist (Truth 1867, 3), but these also have the associative structure of spontaneous utterances.

4. Northrop Frye describes "low" or colloquial style as "a separate rhetorical style, appropriate for some situations and not for others. With all its anti-grammatical forms, it has its own vocabulary, its own syntax, its own rhythm, its own imagery and humor" (1963, 41). The rhetoric of the Rev. Dr. Anna Howard Shaw is also in low or colloquial style and, like Truth, stenographic texts of her speeches reflect the fact that she spoke extemporaneously.

5. Since Truth grew up speaking Dutch in upstate New York and had no contact with Southerners until her teens, there is little reason to believe that she spoke in substandard Southern dialect, the form in which this speech was originally recorded. As a result, I have rendered the text in standard English.

6. This theological view interprets the material in Genesis 3:15 to mean that the

curse placed on Eve for succumbing to the blandishments of the serpent will be expunged by Mary's child, whose sacrificial death redeems the sins of all humans (Gal. 3:13; Rev. 22:3).

7. Both George Fox, the founder of Quakerism, and Margaret Askew Fell, later his wife, wrote treatises defending woman's right to speak and preach. Fox's work, *The Woman Learning in Silence*, appeared originally in London in 1656; Margaret Fell's work, *Womens* [sic] *Speaking Justified*, originally appeared in London in 1667 (rpt. 1979). A further declaration, probably by Margaret Fell's daughter Sarah, has been transcribed and reprinted with headnotes (1975). Janet Zollinger Giele comments: "Only the Quakers and Unitarians were more or less consistent in their tolerance of women's early public activity" (Giele 1961, 82).

8. By 1838, Sarah's speaking career was ending, primarily because she was eclipsed by Angelina. Angelina married Theodore Weld two days before delivering her speech in Pennsylvania Hall. After the speech, Sarah, Angelina, and Theodore retreated to a shared home and confined their efforts to writing. Biographers have offered different explanations for Angelina's departure from the lecture platform. Birney (1885), her contemporary, hints at a debilitating physical or nervous ailment. Lerner (1967) surmises that the problem was a prolapsed uterus. Lumpkin (1974) rejects these to posit a psychological explanation based on Theodore Weld's intense concern with the sin of pride (which led him to end his speaking career), Sarah's jealousy of Angelina's successes as a speaker, and Angelina's fear that Sarah would replace her in her children's affections if she traveled to speak.

3

Responding to Opposition Based on Theology: Proposing a Single Moral Standard

The most troublesome ideological obstacle to woman's rights was the theological tenet that woman's distinctive role was part of God's plan. Many activists attempted to refute this belief in their speeches, one of which is the centerpiece of this chapter. In her study of the woman suffrage movement, Aileen Kraditor identifies three rationales used to justify denying women the franchise: the theological view that God had ordained it, the biological view that anatomy was destiny, and the sociological argument that woman was part of the fundamental unit of society, the family, which was to be represented publicly by the man of the house (Kraditor 1965, 43-74). These rationales were not limited to the suffrage question, but were basic arguments used to justify the cult of true womanhood that confined woman to the private and domestic sphere.

Although all three were interrelated, the theological rationale was not only the most fundamental, but it also emerged earliest, and the religious authority on which it rested made it particularly difficult to refute. However, many women responded to it. As noted in the last chapter, Maria W. Miller Stewart, among the first women in the United States to speak publicly to men and women, justified her right to speak on biblical grounds in her farewell address (Richardson 1987, xiii), and Sarah Grimké made an extended scriptural defense of woman's right to speak and agitate (1838). Antoinette Brown [Blackwell], the first American woman to be ordained as a minister, also made an early defense (1849).[1] The most infamous defense, the *Woman's Bible* (Stanton et al. 1892, 1895), appeared much later and was repudiated by the National American Woman Suffrage Association, despite the public efforts of its president, Susan B. Anthony (Harper 1898-1908, 2:853-54). Many other women contributed to the refutation of the theological rationale for the oppression of women, including the religiously conservative Frances Willard (1889) and the radical anticlericalist Matilda Joslyn Gage (1890). Although these other efforts were significant, this chapter concerns a relatively early effort, the *Discourse on Woman*, a speech given in Philadelphia in 1849 by Lucretia Coffin Mott, and published the following year.

Coffin Mott's speech merits close attention on several grounds. First, she was a skilled speaker whose career preceded both the abolitionist and woman's rights movements, beginning instead within Quakerism, which from its inception had permitted women to prophesy and preach. As a result, the speech provides an opportunity to examine the rhetorical invention of a talented and successful woman speaker in a period when such achievement was extremely rare. Second, unlike other women who spoke out, Coffin Mott had religious authority. From age twenty-eight, she had been recognized as a Quaker minister and, in the tradition of that denomination, was a careful and analytical student of the Bible (Bacon 1986; Mack 1986). Third, the speech includes sophisticated and original responses, both direct and indirect, to arguments based on Scripture against woman's rights.

Coffin Mott's *Discourse on Woman* came into being as a response to a lecture delivered by Richard Henry Dana, Sr., a poet and essayist. No text of this lecture exists, and there is only one contemporary account of it, as delivered on a later occasion. According to that account, published in the *Literary World* of New York in 1850, "Mr. Dana is not at all of the modern school who affect to make Woman what she is not, never has been, and never can be, man and woman both, or perhaps we should rather say, simply man for the unsexing philosophy ignores the woman altogether" (Mr. Dana's Lecture, 1850). The *History of Woman Suffrage*, published many years afterward, reported:

> Richard H. Dana of Boston gave a lecture on womanhood throughout the country in which he ridiculed the demands for civil and political rights, and for a larger sphere of action and eulogized Shakespeare's women, especially Desdemona, Ophelia, and Juliet and recommended them to his countrywomen as models of innocence, tenderness and confiding love in man for their study and imitation. (HWS 1:367-68)

According to this account, Coffin Mott was in the audience at Philadelphia and went up to him afterward to say that she could not accept his views of woman's true character and destiny; he is supposed to have replied, "I am very sorry," while hurriedly departing.

To offset the effect of his lecture, some liberal Philadelphians approached Coffin Mott with the request that she answer Dana. That she was considered worthy to respond to Dana, himself a noted lecturer, is evidence of her rhetorical skill and reputation.

REFUTING THEOLOGICAL ARGUMENTS

Discourse on Woman was a classic example of middle style, neither ornate and formal nor conversational and casual. It began almost diffidently, particularly when compared with the speeches discussed in the last chapter. Moreover, Coffin Mott averred that she had "no prepared address," which would explain the much simpler style. But an absence of preparation is not believable, despite the rambling organization of the speech. This is an extemporaneous speech, that is, a speech drawn from a storehouse of material that the speaker had used before on numerous occasions. There was no prepared text from which she spoke, but as she pointed out, this was a subject that had claimed her "earnest interest for many years" (Mott 1850, 3).

A theological rationale undergirded the concept of "true womanhood" and the "woman-belle ideal" of this period. The specific prohibition against speaking was grounded in two key passages of Scripture. The most frequently cited was Paul's injunction:

> Let your women keep silence in the churches: for it is not permitted unto them to speak; but they are commanded to be under obedience, as also saith the law. And if they will learn anything, let them ask their husbands at home: for it is a shame for women to speak in church. (1 Cor. 14:34-35)

Another Pauline text was of nearly equal force:

> Let the women learn in silence with all subjection. But I suffer not a woman to teach, nor to usurp authority over the man, but to be in silence. For Adam was first formed, then Eve. And Adam was not deceived, but the woman being deceived was in the transgression. (1 Tim. 2:11-14)

From the brief accounts of Dana's lecture, it is unclear just how he used this theological rationale, but Coffin Mott began by responding to it directly.

Coffin Mott's argument rested on the Protestant idea of the priesthood of all believers who could read and interpret for themselves. It was also hermeneutical; it did not challenge the authority of Scripture but rather its traditional translation, interpretation, and application. She began, as did all who responded to the theological rationale, with

the creation story, but she reminded the audience of the version told
in the first chapter of Genesis, a story of simultaneous and equal
creation that is usually forgotten:

> In the beginning, man and woman were created equal. "Male and female
> created he them, and blessed them, and called their name Adam." He gave
> dominion to both over the lower animals, but not to one over the other.
> (4; Gen. 1:27)

Just as Dana had relied on Shakespeare and Sir Philip Sidney, Coffin
Mott, too, buttressed her views with by quoting from the *Task*:

> Man o'er woman
> He made not lord, such title to himself
> Reserving, human left from human free (4; Cowper 1835, 1:403)

Her response to the creation story in Genesis 2 and 3 was brief to the point
of being laconic, an assertion that the curse placed on woman after the
fall ("thy desire shall be to thy husband, and he shall rule over thee,"
Gen. 3:16) merely indicated that in the aftermath of the fall, woman had
been removed from what was originally her rightful equal place.
More generally, she argued:

> The laws given on Mount Sinai for the government of man and woman were
> equal, the precepts of Jesus make no distinction. Those who read the Scriptures,
> and judge for themselves, not resting satisfied with the perverted application of
> the text, do not find the distinction that theology and ecclesiastical authorities
> have made, in the condition of the sexes. (5)

These claims rested on a close reading of biblical texts and appealed to
those who accepted a priesthood of believers and the Quaker notion of
an "inner light" (Bacon 1969, 122). Coffin Mott's speech is one more
reminder of the strong debt the ideology of the woman's rights movement
owed to Protestantism.

She followed with a survey of biblical texts that presented models
for women, including the stories of Miriam, sister of Moses and Aaron,
and Deborah, a judge and military leader. She noted women who were
prophets, such as Huldah and Anna, even mentioning the denunciation of false women prophets in Ezekiel 14:17. Likewise she recalled
women in the early church. Here her examples were augmented by a
hermeneutical argument. She said: "Phebe is mentioned as a *servant*
of Christ, and commended as such to the brethren. It is worthy of note,
that the word *servant*, when applied to Tychicus, is rendered *minister*.
Women *professing* godliness, should be translated *preaching*" (6). A

little later, addressing herself to the Pauline text cited earlier, she said:

> The epistle to the Corinthian church, where the supposed apostolic prohibition against women's preaching is found, contains express directions how woman shall appear, when she prayeth or prophesyeth. Judge then whether this admonition, relative to *speaking* and asking questions, in the excited state of that church, should be regarded as a standing injunction on woman's *preaching*, when that word was not used by the apostle? Where is the Scripture authority for the advice given to the early church, under peculiar circumstances, being binding on the church of the present day? Ecclesiastical history informs us, that for two or three hundred years, female ministers suffered martyrdom, in company with their brethren. (6)

Again Coffin Mott used the hermeneutical method: she asked what a term meant as used in the original text, compared texts and translations for consistency, and challenged generalizations drawn from advice given under special historical conditions.

Such arguments were not common at this period in the United States. Protestant Germany was the home of this "higher" biblical criticism, which reached its heyday in the nineteenth century, traveling first to England and then to America. Throughout the 1880s and 1890s, books and journals were published that approached the Scriptures historically. The movement gained momentum from the appearance of the Revised Version of the New Testament in 1881 and of the Old Testament in 1885, which helped to undermine faith in infallibility and literalism (Kraditor 1965, 76).[2] Coffin Mott's arguments reflected the beginnings of "higher criticism" in the United States, and they would have been particularly appealing to liberal Protestants and Quakers.

Coffin Mott's contentions were powerful because they accepted the authority of Scripture, while claiming that there had been mistranslation and misinterpretation, and they called on individuals to read and study the text and decide for themselves. Her examples of women in the Bible demonstrated that an active, public role for women was consistent with theology and moral purity. As she remarked later in the speech, "We would admit all the difference, that our great and beneficent Creator has made, in the relation of man and woman, nor would we seek to disturb this relation; but we deny that the present position of woman is her true sphere of usefulness" (7). As these quoted passages illustrate, Coffin Mott's tone was restrained; when she confronted her audience, she never did so with the blazing directness of Grimké [Weld]'s speech, but always subtly and gently, yet firmly and deliberately.

A UNISEXUAL MORAL STANDARD

From biblical models that affirm woman's ability to act for good in the public sphere, Coffin Mott turned to the crux of Dana's argument, that women are "desexed" or corrupted by the woman's rights movement. The theological rationale had become so fundamental precisely because it held that only if woman remains domestic can she remain pure. Coffin Mott's refutation now became more direct: she said that her opponent's view made woman "fear to exercise her reason, and her noblest powers, lest these should be thought to 'attempt to act the man' " (Mott 1850, 7). She then developed the argument for woman's rights through a strategy of definitions and examples. Turning the tables on Dana, who had condemned "the announcement of women's achievements" as "a gross innovation upon the obscurity of female life," she countered: "So far from her 'ambition leading her to attempt to act the man,' she needs all the encouragement she can receive, by the removal of obstacles from her path, in order that she may become a 'true woman' " (7-8). She then rejected the established view of true womanhood and proposed an alternative conception.

In order to establish a single standard for moral behavior by both sexes, Coffin Mott described extremes of masculinity and femininity, both of which she rejected on moral grounds—a radical move, particularly for that period.[3] She proclaimed:

> As it is desirable that man should act a manly and generous part, not "mannish," so let woman be urged to exercise a dignified and womanly bearing, not womanish. Let her cultivate all the graces and proper accomplishments of her sex, but let not these degenerate into a kind of effeminacy, in which she is satisfied to be the mere plaything or toy of society, content with her outward adornings, and with the tone of flattery and fulsome adulation too often addressed to her. (8)

This was an attack on the morality implicit in "true womanhood." That conception was "degrading," "a kind of effeminacy," in which woman became a "mere plaything or toy" satisfied with "outward adorning," "flattery," and "fulsome adulation" (8). Under its weight, she described women, in the words of the highly respected educator Catharine Beecher, as "sinking down into almost useless inactivity" (9), insinuating that it corrupted woman's work ethic (Lerner 1969, 5), and tainted men as well. If woman was allowed to bring all her powers to use, she said, "The energies of men need not then be wholly devoted to the counting house and common business of life, in order that women in fashionable society may be supported in their daily promenades and nightly visits to the theatre and ball room" (8). Presumably, men would then have time to tend to spiritual matters.

Coffin Mott combined this ethical attack with examples designed to illustrate the unisexual criterion she advocated. The examples denied that women must be unsexed by public speaking and action for moral reform, and showed men and women engaged in a struggle against evil. For instance, she asked:

> Did Elizabeth Fry lose any of her feminine qualities by the public walk into which she was called? Having performed the duties of a mother to a large family, feeling that she owed a labor of love to the poor prisoner, she was empowered by Him who sent her forth, to go to kings and crowned heads of the earth, and ask audience of these; and it was granted her. Did she lose the delicacy of woman by her acts? No. Her retiring modesty was characteristic of her to the latest period of her life. . . . Is Dorothea Dix throwing off her womanly nature and appearance in the course she is pursuing? . . . To use the contemptuous word applied in the lecture alluded to, is she becoming "mannish?" Is she compromising her womanly dignity in going forth to seek to better the condition of the insane and afflicted? Is not a beautiful mind and retiring modesty still conspicuous in her? Indeed, I would ask, if this modesty is not attractive also, when manifested in the other sex? It was strikingly marked in Horace Mann when presiding over the late National Education Convention in this city. The retiring modesty of William Ellery Channing, was beautiful. (10-11)

Coffin Mott also refuted the view advanced by Dana, whom she identified only as "the lecturer," that men and women "were opposite, if not somewhat antagonistic; and required a union, as in chemistry, to form a perfect whole." She labeled that a "simile" and responded: "It is the union of similar, not opposite affections, which are necessary for the perfection of the marriage bond" (12). She impugned the evidence for such a view: "The contrast drawn seemed a fallacy, as has much, very much that has been presented, in the sickly sentimental strains of the poet, from age to age" (12). Once again she was ready to violate gender roles by imputing sentimentality to a male and appropriating reason for herself. She summarized the "customs" surrounding marriage ceremonies, and condemned them, saying: "There are large Christian denominations who [sic] do not recognize such degrading relations of husband and wife" (13). She went on to describe the simple Quaker ceremony in which a man and a woman married each other before the meeting, without benefit of clergy or any vows implying the woman's inferiority.

Coffin Mott attacked the cult of true womanhood on moral grounds and used examples to show that a single standard could be applied to the characters and accomplishments of both male and female human beings. Moreover, she argued that the changes advocated by woman's rights advocates would make the world more, not less, moral. The argument for a unisexual criterion for moral judgment was buttressed by an appeal to the principles of natural rights. Coffin Mott responded to the query, "What does woman want, more than she enjoys?" in this way: "I answer, she asks nothing as favor, but as right, she wants to be acknowledged a moral, responsible being" (12). Coffin Mott's vision of an ideal world, articulated in her conclusion, reflected these ideas:

> Let woman then go on — not asking as favor, but claiming as right, the removal of all the hindrances to her elevation in the scale of being — let her receive encouragement for the proper cultivation of all her powers, so that she may enter profitably into the active business of life; employing her own hands, in ministering to her necessities, strengthening her physical being by proper exercise, and observance of the laws of health. (19)

This is a vision of utopia informed by natural rights principles. As such, it harnesses her new conception of woman to fundamental political principles.

COFFIN MOTT'S RHETORICAL ACHIEVEMENT

Coffin Mott's speech is interesting not only for its unusual hermeneutical approach to theology and for its systematically androgynous view of human character, but also because it permits us to understand why Lucretia Coffin Mott was such a successful speaker.

We know little of the immediate effect of this speech, other than its publication record. One biographer reports that it "was well received" (Bacon 1980, 136). Much more is known about Coffin Mott's speaking career as a whole, although relatively few speech texts are extant (Greene 1980). From 1818 on she was well known as a lecturer for temperance, peace, the rights of workers, and the abolition of slavery. In 1821, at age twenty-eight, she was recognized officially as a minister (Bacon 1969, 105). In 1840 she spoke to the state legislatures of Delaware, New Jersey and Pennsylvania on the slavery issue, a remarkable feat given the fact that the first speech by a woman to a state legislature had been delivered by Angelina Grimké only two years before (Bacon 1980, 91; Lerner 1967, 1). Moreover, her biographer notes:

> although the Motts were unable to gain a hearing for Lucretia at the U.S. House of Representatives, it was arranged that she preach in the Unitarian Church in the District in January of 1843, and over forty members of Congress were

present to hear her, as well as a large audience of government officials and journalists. Referring to that speech, Ralph Waldo Emerson wrote to his wife that "it was like the rumble of an earthquake — the sensation that attended the speech, and no man would have done so much and come away alive." (Bacon 1980, 104-5)

In sum, Lucretia Coffin Mott was recognized as a highly effective speaker by Quakers and non-Quakers, by men and women, by those who favored social change and those who were part of the establishment. Given the period in which she spoke and the intensity of its resistance to women speakers, how did she manage to succeed?

The answer is that she embodied the androgynous moral standard she espoused; she was living proof that women are not unsexed by speaking or by working for reform, even in the most controversial areas. Moreover, she incorporated the androgynous standard into the style of her speech. She adopted a gender-free persona; she avoided egregious violations of taboos against female rhetorical aggressiveness, especially avoiding any appearance of debating; she invited audience participation by addressing her listeners as peers capable of sensible deliberation; she directed her attention particularly to the impact of views about women upon the young; and she used male authorities to condemn women's legal position. She attacked woman's traditional role indirectly; however, she developed convincing arguments, took strong stands, and blithely accused her male opponent of both sentimentality and a lack of logic.

Coffin Mott's persona in this speech was that of the minister, as understood by Quakers. One became a Quaker minister as a result of repeated demonstrations, tested by the members of one's meeting, that one had experienced the indwelling of the inner light. Because such indwellings were inspired and the message intuited, women as well as men could become ministers. Hence, the ministerial role as perceived within the Quaker community was unisexual, not gender-bound. Whatever convictions came to an individual through the inner light were tested by the community in discussion and in light of personal experience. This precisely was the purpose of *Discourse on Woman* as Coffin Mott herself described it. In fact, she quoted Jesus' legitimation of free discussion, "He that doeth truth cometh to the light, that his deeds may be made manifest, that they are wrought in God" (4; John 3:21); those words were a powerful justification for her speech.

There are many indications that Coffin Mott was aware of the obstacles she faced as a woman speaker. She had agreed to speak in order to offset the impact of Dana's lecture, but she understood the perils of being perceived as engaging in debate with him. She denied what in fact she did, saying: "I have not come here with a view of answering any particular parts of the lecture alluded to, in order to point out the fallacy of its reasoning" (Mott 1850, 4). She praised the lecture for its "intellectual vigor and beauty" (3), but almost immediately added that the lecturer "did not profess to offer anything like argument on that occasion, but rather a *sentiment*" (4). She expressed regret that, as a result, its "sentiments" would be "likely to ensnare the young" (3), here and elsewhere emphasizing the view that her ministry was directed to the young, a ministry most congenial to a "true woman." She described her purpose as wishing "to offer some views for your consideration . . . which may lead to such reflection and discussion as will present the subject in a true light" (4), a purpose that avoided claims of personal authority and made her the leader in a more cooperative process.

Coffin Mott did not avoid controversial stands or moral judgments. She took a broad view of woman's rights that included equal education, voting rights, and modification of marriage laws. Moreover, she attacked traditional gender roles, though only on moral grounds. She found ways to lessen negative reactions to herself as a woman speaking. For example, she cited male authorities to voice the most severe condemnations of woman's status: Judge Elisha Hurlbut and jurist and law professor Timothy Walker had attacked the legal position of women in harsh, blunt terms; journalist and popular writer Nathaniel Willis had articulated the view that woman's rights efforts were not immoral but instead called women to a higher destiny; William Cowper was the poetic voice who attacked ills treated as sacred through custom; and Lord Brougham had praised the quality of English author Harriet Martineau's works on political economy.

Only in the religious area did Coffin Mott rely on her own authority and that of Scripture, consistent with her beliefs about the "inner light." She affirmed woman's role as helpmeet and nurturer of the young; she linked woman's rights to morality and the Puritan work ethic. She claimed that woman's rights was a quest for *true* womanhood, and in her view, "By proper education, she [a wife] understands her duties, physical, intellectual and moral; and fulfilling these, she is a help meet, in the true sense of the word" (13). She admitted all differences between the sexes that were "God-given," while calling for a society in which women could "use all their powers." The models of womanhood she used as examples included many women who, like her, had combined public activism with traditional roles. Near the end of the speech, she described the new woman: "No fear that she will then transcend the proper limits of female delicacy. True modesty will be as fully preserved, in acting out those important vocations to which she may be called, as in the nursery or at the fireside, *ministering to man's self-indulgence*" (emphasis added; 20), a vivid reiteration of her moral attack on the current relationship between men and women.

Coffin Mott feminized her rhetorical role and reinforced her androgynous view of human beings by addressing her audience as peers, by seeking audience participation through questions, by espousing a philosophical position which encouraged thought, by developing her ideas inductively through examples and personal experience, and by inviting the audience to test her conclusions. By speaking, arguing, presenting evidence, and drawing conclusions in a matter-of-fact way, she fulfilled traditional rhetorical requirements, usually perceived as outside the capability of females. As a result, her *Discourse* incorporated qualities associated with both genders.

CONCLUSION

Coffin Mott used Dana's lecture as an occasion to respond to the theological rationale that underlay his views. She made a hermeneutical argument against the scriptural basis of the rationale, she made a moral attack on the concept of "true womanhood" and the sexual relationships it created, and she enacted the unisexual standard for moral judgment, which she espoused. Above all, as an individual, she embodied her claims. She was an educated social reformer and minister, who was also a wife and mother. She herself was the proof, along with the examples she presented, that women could move into the public sphere and retain their moral character and their commitment to humane values (Bacon 1980; Cromwell 1958; Hallowell 1884). Other women would find ways to avoid the typical dilemma of the female rhetor, but she did so in ways that were more complex than those of most other movement speakers.

During its earliest phase, Coffin Mott was one of the foremost figures in the woman's rights movement. She exemplified the links between abolitionism and woman's rights, and her established reputation as a reformer and speaker enabled her to attract large audiences to conventions. Throughout her life she was a lecturer for temperance, peace, and the rights of workers, as well as for abolitionism and woman's rights. She met Elizabeth Cady Stanton in London in 1840, when Coffin Mott and Henry Stanton were delegates to the World Anti-Slavery Convention that refused to seat delegates from female anti-slavery societies. That meeting laid the foundation out of which the Seneca Falls convention grew; Coffin Mott's speech at that convention was the attraction featured in the convention call. She signed the calls for and spoke at national woman's rights conventions held prior to the Civil War, and she continued her agitation for the rights of freed slaves and of women until her death in 1880.

NOTES

1. "Exegesis of I Corinthians, XIV, 34, 34; and II Timothy, 11, 12," refuting the biblical argument that woman should not speak in public, was subsequently presented as a speech at the National Woman's Rights Convention, Worcester, Massachusetts, 1850 ([Blackwell] 1849; Cazden 1983, 57).

2. As early as 1764, a Quaker named Andrew Purver had published, in two folio volumes, *A New and Literal Translation of all the Books of the Old and New Testament; with Notes, Critical and Explanatory* (Jones 1920, 671).

3. She developed a similar position at the Cleveland Woman's Rights Convention in 1853:

It has sometimes been said that if women were associated with men in their efforts, there would not be as much immorality as now exists, in Congress, for instance, and other places. But we ought, I think, to claim no more for woman than for man, we ought to put woman on a par with man, not invest her with power, or claim her superiority over her brother. If we do she is just as likely to become a tyrant as man is; as with Catherine the Second. It is always unsafe to invest man with power over his fellow being. "Call no man master"—that is a true doctrine. But, be sure that there would be a better rule than now, the elements which belong to woman as such and to man as such would be beautifully and harmoniously blended. It is to be hoped that there would be less of war, injustice, and intolerance in the world than now. (Greene 1980, 218)

4

Woman's Rights Conventions: Ideological Crucibles

> We have often been asked, "What is the use of Conventions? Why talk? Why not go to work?" Just as if the thought did not precede the act! Those who act without previously thinking, are not good for much. Thought is first required, then the expression of it, and that leads to action; and action based upon thought never needs to be reversed; it is lasti..g and profitable, and produces the desired effect.
> — Ernestine Potowski Rose, 1860 (HWS 1:693)

Individual women continued the tradition begun by the Grimké sisters, Maria W. Miller Stewart, and others in struggling for the right to speak, but such individual efforts could not, by themselves, create a social movement. The foundations for a movement were laid in the series of woman's rights conventions that began in 1848 at Seneca Falls, occurred yearly on a national level from 1850 to 1860 (except for 1857), and resumed after the war in 1866 to culminate in a national organization, the American Equal Rights Association.

Woman's rights conventions were not meetings of organizations but substitutes for them. In fact, a proposal to form a national organization was considered and rejected in 1852. Opposition to such a move was practical and ideological. Women activists had found abolitionist organizations oppressive and conflict-filled; moreover, many believed that political and religious organizations were prime causes of female oppression (Phillips 1985, 86-87; HWS 1:540-41).

In addition to substituting for a formal organization, holding conventions contributed to the development of a movement in several ways. They raised morale and increased commitment to the cause by regularly gathering together like-minded women and men. They were public forums in which "values, norms, and structure emerged" (Phillips 1985, 8-9), creating a stable movement ideology and making woman's rights part of public discourse. Because famous people, such as Lucretia Coffin Mott, Ernestine Potowski Rose, Ralph Waldo Emerson, and Wendell Phillips, were featured speakers, conventions attracted a broad range of potential supporters; this exposure was supplemented by publishing the proceedings of the conventions of 1851–1854, 1856, 1859, and 1860.

Initially the conventions were small. The 1848 Seneca Falls convention attracted some 300 people; 263 people met at the first national convention in 1850 at Worcester, Massachusetts; 3,000 people were present at sessions of the New York City convention of 1853 (Phillips 1985, 118; Wagner 1978, 299). Numerous reports of opposition speakers and heckling attest to the range of opinion represented on the platform and in the audience. Hence, the conventions were an ideal forum for the testing and formulation of an ideology. Because the conventions were forums for the debate of movement ideas, their published proceedings are a good source of information about movement ideology and the rhetorical processes by which women were persuaded to become active supporters of this cause.

The development of ideology is a process by which a movement acquires coherence, as members decide just what they are about. Early movement rhetoric, addressed primarily to sympathizers, must energize listeners so that sympathizers become activists, a process complicated in this case by the fact that those addressed were women acculturated to passivity and submission. This chapter analyzes the movement's manifesto, the Declaration of Sentiments adopted at Seneca Falls in 1848, and summarizes convention resolutions from 1848 to 1860 in order to assess ideological consistency. It also analyzes two early speeches, one from 1848 by Elizabeth Cady Stanton and one by Ernestine Potowski Rose from 1851, in order to show how women attempted to persuade other women to violate the norms of true womanhood and to become activists for woman's rights.

The two speeches were chosen because of the importance of these two women in the early movement and because each speech is a significant ideological statement. Elizabeth Cady Stanton was the moving force behind the first convention: she suggested the form of the Declaration of Sentiments, and, with the other organizers, authored the resolutions of the convention, demanding the inclusion of suffrage. As a result, the major address she delivered at the convention is a rich source of ideological information as well as the first effort in a major rhetorical career. Ernestine Potowski Rose was a Polish woman who emigrated at age sixteen, traveled throughout Europe, and married the English William E. Rose, a follower of Robert Owen. She came to the United States in 1836 to begin a career lecturing on the evils of the existing social system, arguing for the abolition of slavery and for the rights of woman. Over some thirty years, she lectured in at least twenty-three states, and her early speeches helped to prepare the way for the nascent movement; she was a major speaker and ideologist at the early woman's rights conventions (Suhl 1959). Newspapers described her as "liberal, eloquent, and witty"; the biographical sketch of her in the movement history described her as "pointed, logical and impassioned" (HWS 1:98, 100). Her speech at the 1851 convention was a major early statement of the movement's fundamental ideological principles.

Seneca Falls was not the first convention to gather women, but it was the first convention to focus its attention on woman's rights.[1] Two weeks later a similar convention was held in Rochester, New York. No formal meetings occurred for the next year and a half, but as word of the Seneca Falls convention spread, women around the nation became politically aroused. In 1850 local conventions were held in Ohio, followed in the same year by the first national convention in Worcester. This convention drew many, such as Lucy Stone, who had previously been working alone. The call to the convention was signed by eighty-nine prominent men and women. Eleven states were represented, and provision was made for a second national convention the following year, also to be held in Worcester. The third national convention, in Syracuse in 1852, was the largest to date with 2,000 delegates from eight states and Canada, and was Susan B. Anthony's formal introduction to the movement. Subsequent national conventions were held in Cleveland (1853), Philadelphia (1854), Cincinnati (1855), and New York City (1856, 1860); regional conventions were held in numerous locations (HWS 1, passim). In the years before the Civil War, these conventions constituted the woman's rights movement. Because the convention at Seneca Falls initiated the movement, and because it produced such important rhetorical acts, it provided an ideological key to the conventions that followed.

THE SENECA FALLS CONVENTION

On July 14, 1848, a call for a convention, signed by Elizabeth Cady Stanton, Lucretia Coffin Mott, Martha Coffin Wright, and Mary Ann McClintock, appeared in the *Seneca County Courier*:

Woman's Rights Convention

A convention to discuss the social, civil, and religious condition and rights of women will be held in the Wesleyan Chapel, at Seneca Falls, New York, on Wednesday and Thursday, the 19th and 20th of July current; commencing at 10 o'clock A.M. During the first day the meeting will be exclusively for women who are earnestly invited to attend. The public generally are invited to be present on the second day, when Lucretia Mott, of Philadelphia, and other ladies and gentlemen, will address the convention. (Lutz 1940, 44-45)[2]

Some three hundred people appeared, including forty men, who were admitted. James Mott served as chair, and his wife spoke to explain the purpose of the convention. Elizabeth Cady Stanton presented the Declaration of Sentiments and a set of resolutions prepared by the four women who had called the convention; she then made a speech, followed by general discussion.

In imitation of the Declaration of Sentiments adopted in 1833 to express the abolitionist principles of the members of the American Anti-Slavery Society (1835), the sponsors of the Seneca Falls convention wished to present a manifesto to the convention for consideration. They cast about for an appropriate and symbolically potent form in which to express their grievances and state their demands, and happened upon the idea of composing a parody of the Declaration of Independence. The choice was inspired and highly strategic (Lucas 1988).

The Declaration of Independence is a key document articulating the principles underlying the nation. In addition, the 1776 Declaration encapsulates the ideas that cohere to form natural rights philosophy. As a result it evokes all the patriotic sentiments associated with the founding of the nation, and it expresses in the most forceful and least controversial form the radical notion that all human beings have certain fundamental rights as humans, that the function of government is to protect those rights from encroachment, and that when and if government does not perform that duty, revolutionary change is appropriate. No document provides a better formal blueprint for articulating an ideological manifesto to Americans, because it links social change to patriotism and to the ideas underlying the Constitution of the United States.

Not only is the Declaration of Independence infused with patriotic connotations, but its form is ideally suited to the rhetoric of a manifesto, attested to by its appropriation by revolutionary groups in France, several South American nations, Vietnam, and the United States civil rights movement, among others. As a declaration, it is rhetorical in two ways: it addresses an audience, and it provides justifications. As had the authors of the 1776 Declaration, the 1848 authors stated, "a decent respect to the opinions of mankind requires that they should declare the causes which impel them" to such a course (*Proceedings* 1870, 5). Such a statement expresses respect for public opinion and obligates the speaker to present his or her case. In both declarations, that statement was followed by an assertion of the principles guiding the authors' actions and a list of specific grievances. In other words, after stating their purpose, the authors of both documents laid out the premises from which arguments were to be made, premises which, in turn, were followed by the specifics that, measured against the principles, mandated action.

The 1848 Declaration of Sentiments was persuasive and startling precisely because small changes in wording made its audience aware of assumptions underlying the Declaration of Independence. For example, the 1848 authors' assertion, "We hold these truths to be self-evident: that all men and women are created equal" was startling because it implicitly questioned the meaning of "men" in the original document (5). Without the parody, the original usage appeared to be generic; in light of the parody and of the legal and social disabilities of women, it became clear that "men" referred only to one gender, and the founding document became, not a universal affirmation of human rights, but an assertion of male prerogatives (Basch 1986; Kerber 1980).

The process of raising doubts about the meaning of the 1776 Declaration continued with the bill of particulars.[3] The grievances included denial of the franchise, an inherent element of natural rights; the legal disabilities of married women; and the discrimination women encountered in gaining access to education, employment, and in religious observance. The list was a dramatic, forceful reminder of the discrepancy between the principles of natural rights as articulated in the founding documents and their application to women (Janeway 1971, 99-100).

The list of grievances encapsulated what social movement scholars term structural strain, the fundamental areas of conflict between a particular group and the dominant culture, conflicts that must persist until social change occurs. As presented in the 1848 Declaration, these fall into four areas: (1) violations of natural rights; (2) disabilities of married women; (3) religious discrimination; and (4) denials of opportunity for individual development. As subsequent convention resolutions demonstrate, these four categories encompass the major concerns of the woman's rights movement prior to the Civil War.

Grievances related to natural rights included denial of the franchise, being compelled to submit to laws in whose formation women had had no voice, and taxation without representation. As the Declaration makes clear, the authors considered themselves United States citizens entitled to and demanding of "immediate admission to all the rights and privileges which belong to them as citizens of the United States" (7). Moreover, they expressed their indignation that fundamental rights were withheld from them while being extended "to the most ignorant and degraded men — both natives and foreigners" (6).

Married women's disabilities were summed up in several grievances. Marriage law rendered women civilly dead, a status with significant legal and economic implications, three of which were detailed: first, a wife was deprived of all rights to property, including her own wages. Second, she was considered morally incompetent: the husband was deemed responsible for any crime committed by his wife in his presence, because marriage made him her master, requiring her to promise obedience to him, and permitting him to deprive her of her liberty and to administer chastisement. Third, divorce laws had been enacted by men without regard for women in terms of causes, guardianship of children, and the like (6).

Interestingly, these grievances made no reference to a significant event that had occurred in April of that year — passage of the first New York State Married Woman's Property Act. As Peggy Rabkin's work has demonstrated, debate over married women's property laws contributed significantly to the development of the woman's rights movement (1975; 1980). Rabkin details a process of statutory revision in New York State, begun in 1828, by which commercial relations were "defeudalized," thus simplifying commercial transactions, particularly those involving land. This process left social relations between the sexes untouched, but it was recognized by many that the revisions should extend to women. In 1837, Judge Thomas Herttell introduced a bill in the New York State Assembly for the protection and preservation of the rights and property of married women, and, after its defeat, he published the arguments in support of his bill in a widely read pamphlet (Herttell 1839).

The process of ordering the status of married women in ways consistent with other changes began with the 1848 Married Woman's Property Act, and continued with amendments to that act in 1849, 1860, 1862, and 1896 (Rabkin 1975, 230). Rabkin argues that these legal changes and the forces underlying them created a context in the state hospitable to the woman's rights movement (230). She points out that, in her autobiography, Cady Stanton wrote that the 1848 bill "[gave] rise to some discussion of woman's rights" and that it was useful that "the demands made in the [Seneca Falls] convention were not entirely new to the reading and thinking public of New York" (Stanton 1898, 150-51; Rabkin 1975, 317). The only new demand, in fact, was suffrage. These recent legal advances explain why Cady Stanton would say in her convention speech that it was the right time for women to demand their rights.

Three clauses in the Declaration of Sentiments treated religious discrimination. One pointed to woman's subordinate position in the church and exclusion from the ministry; a second pointed to the effects of a double standard of morality, the creation of a false public sentiment created by "giving to the world a different code of morals for men and women"; and a third accused man of the crime of Lucifer, of usurping "the prerogative of Jehovah himself, claiming it as his right to assign for her a sphere of action, when that belongs to her conscience and to her God" (7). These accusations all rested on the Protestant principle of the priesthood of all believers. According to this tenet, it was a sin to interpose anyone or anything between a woman and her God, to deny a woman's right to act on her faith, and to propagate two standards of morality. These charges are reminders of the importance of religious motivation in early woman's rights agitation and of the resentment women felt about the role of the organized church in perpetuating woman's oppression.[4]

Finally, the grievances concerning the denial of individual development were derivative of natural rights principles found in the Declaration of Independence, namely the individual's "unalienable" right to "life, liberty, and the pursuit of happiness." Woman had been denied education, the authors charged; man had monopolized all profitable employments and had closed to her all avenues of wealth and distinction. The grievances concluded with the general accusation that man had "endeavored, in every way that he could, to destroy her confidence in her own powers, to lessen her self-respect, and to make her willing to lead a dependent and abject life" (7). In other words, not only had men enacted legal prohibitions restricting woman, they had also made active efforts to destroy woman's motivation to develop her powers.

What the 1848 grievances reveal are the debt this movement owed to natural rights philosophy, and to principles ultimately deriving from the Protestant Reformation. They also identify prime sources of resentment: marriage laws, the practices of most churches, and barriers that were particularly frustrating to middle-class white women, such as denial of higher education, of the opportunity to practice a profession or to do business, and denial of the right to own and handle property. According to this document, protesting women wanted to be treated as citizens, as persons in the sight of the law, and as individuals capable of the full range of human possibilities.

The ideology of the nascent movement can be identified more precisely by once again contrasting the Declaration of Sentiments to the Declaration of Independence. In 1776, the nation's founders found it necessary "to dissolve the political bonds which have connected them, . . . and to assume . . . [a] separate and equal station." By contrast, in 1848, woman's rights activists found it necessary "to assume . . . a position different from that which they have hitherto occupied" and to insist upon "immediate admission to all the rights and privileges which belong to them as citizens" (7). In 1776, male colonists defended their right "to alter or abolish" a government that did not secure their inalienable rights. In 1848, woman's rights activists "refuse[d] allegiance . . . and . . . insist[ed] upon the institution of a new government" (5). In 1776, the founders reported on the failure of their past efforts to petition for redress of their grievances and, in light of that, declared "these colonies free and independent . . . [with] full Power to levy War." In 1848, woman's rights activists "anticipated no small amount of misconception, misrepresentation, and ridicule," and pledged to "employ agents, circulate tracts, petition the state and national legislatures, and endeavor to enlist the pulpit and the press in our behalf" (7). They signed the document, "Firmly relying upon the final triumph of the Right and True," rather than by pledging to one another, as did the founders, their "Lives, . . . Fortunes, and . . . sacred Honor" (7).

These differences are noteworthy. Instead of separation, women demanded admission. Instead of dissolution enforced by war, women promised to use legal and persuasive means to achieve their ends, including, if possible, the pulpit they had condemned. Instead of relying on themselves and their resources, women relied on the impersonal forces of the Right and the True for their final triumph. These differences indicate that, despite the radical character of individual demands, the supporters of the Declaration of Sentiments perceived theirs to be a reformist, not a revolutionary movement. In fact, in response to hostile press coverage of the convention, most signers asked to have their names removed (Stanton 1898, 149). They did not wish to abolish the nation's government, they wanted to participate in it. They did not wish to separate, but to be admitted. They did not propose to use civil disobedience to achieve their ends.[5] Of course, in this sense, the form these women adopted was inappropriate, because it leads inexorably to the declaration of a separate independent entity, and they did not want to arrive at such a conclusion.

The Seneca Falls convention resolutions (HWS 1:71-73), like the Declaration of Sentiments, were grounded in natural rights philosophy, Protestantism, and the concept of moral evolution. The resolutions of subsequent conventions present a remarkably similar picture. However, resolutions adopted by the conventions and debate over them present a slightly different picture of movement concerns: the debate emphasizes for us the significance of rhetoric for the early movement, and demarcates points of disagreement.

At Seneca Falls, twelve resolutions were adopted. They were preceded by a clause which invoked the authority of Blackstone's *Commentaries* in order to claim that a law of Nature bound all human beings and gave all human laws their force and validity. Based on that natural rights premise, the resolutions declared invalid all laws conflicting with the true and substantial happiness*of woman. They resolved that, in the eyes of the Creator as well as under the law of Nature, woman was man's equal, and that the highest good of the race demanded that she be recognized as such. Moreover, they affirmed that "equality of rights results necessarily from the fact of the identity of the race in capabilities and responsibilities."

More particularly, the resolutions emphasized woman's right to speak and the importance of persuading men of the rightness of their cause. The resolutions remarked that males did not accord woman the moral superiority that she was supposed naturally to possess. Noting this contradiction, they resolved that it was "pre-eminently [man's] duty to encourage her to speak, and teach, as she has opportunity, in all religious assemblies." They also remarked the contradiction in condemning "woman when she addresses a public audience," while encouraging by their attendance "her appearance on the stage, in the concert, or in feats of the circus." The emphasis on rhetorical action was particularly clear in the final resolution, which affirmed that

---

* "Happiness" does not here have its ordinary contemporary meaning of "pleasure, joy, contentment." Its meaning is that found in the phrase "life, liberty, and the pursuit of happiness," referring to the right to develop oneself in whatever directions one's inclinations and capabilities lead. As such, it refers to equality of opportunity to develop as an individual.

"especially in regard to the great subjects of morals and religion, it is self-evidently her right to participate with her brother in teaching them, both in private and in public, by writing and by speaking, . . . in any assemblies proper to be held."

Clearly, gaining acceptance of woman's right to speak was one of the movement's highest priorities. The importance of educating women was also emphasized. One resolution called for women "to be enlightened in regard to the laws under which they live, that they may no longer publish their degradation by declaring themselves satisfied with their present position, nor their ignorance, by asserting that they have all the rights they want." Presumably, if women were informed of their disadvantaged status, they would assent to the ideas embodied in these documents. In effect, those who signed the Declaration and voted for the resolutions declared themselves a vanguard that would promulgate woman's rights. The convention voted on the Declaration of Sentiments and resolutions on the second day; both were supported unanimously except for the resolution advocating woman suffrage, which passed by a narrow margin after a speech of support by Frederick Douglass (HWS 1:73).

A survey of resolutions adopted at woman's rights conventions prior to the Civil War explains why the 1848 Declaration of Sentiments remained an enduring statement of the issues underlying the woman's rights movement. That document not only encompassed the major concerns, but its tone reflected both the patriotic, reformist spirit and the radical demands for full equality that typified the movement in this period.[6]

Resolutions adopted at conventions throughout the 1850s affirmed natural rights principles (HWS 1:361, 707, 808, 816, 817, 820, 821, 825, 834). Some resolutions dealt with organizational concerns, for example whether a national organization should be formed (HWS 1:540-42) and whether a newspaper should be made the national organ of the movement (HWS 1:378). Still others condemned church opposition and moral double standards (HWS 1:707). Some conventions reaffirmed woman's right to varied opportunities, particularly in education and employment (HWS 1:361, 673, 708, 817, 818, 820, 821, 827). Many resolutions called for an end to married women's disabilities (HWS 1:361, 673, 708, 817, 818, 820, 821, 827). On rare occasions, the conventions set priorities: for example, the national convention of 1851 resolved that "the Right of Suffrage for Women is, in our opinion, the corner-stone of this enterprise, since we do not seek to protect woman, but to place her in a position to protect herself" (HWS 1:825). Religious issues, particularly the extent to which Scripture supported woman's rights, generated lively debate at national conventions in 1852 (HWS 1:535-40) and 1853 (HWS 1:133-40), as would views about the movement's role in marriage and divorce reform in 1860, to be discussed in the next chapter.

Many convention speeches of the prewar period are of considerable rhetorical interest. Some illustrate the special genius of individuals, such as that of Sojourner Truth in 1851. Some speeches illustrate rather unusual perspectives, such as that of Antoinette Brown [Blackwell] in 1850 on religion. Some are significant ideological statements, such as Amy Preston's 1852 address at Westchester, Pennsylvania, that was "adopted as an exposition of the principles and purposes of the Convention" (HWS 1:360). However, two speeches from early conventions not only illuminate movement ideology, but also embody rhetorical efforts to reach out to women and persuade them to support the cause. The first of these is Elizabeth Cady Stanton's speech at Seneca Falls; the second is Ernestine Potowski Rose's speech at the second national convention in Worcester in 1851. Cady Stanton was making her first public speech; Potowski Rose was an experienced public speaker who had begun agitating for woman's rights in 1836. Cady Stanton focused her attention on objections to woman suffrage; Potowski Rose emphasized the persuasive force of law. However, both speeches responded to major arguments against woman's rights demands, explained why women were essential to this reform, and provided justifications for women's activism.

CADY STANTON'S SPEECH

This first speech by Elizabeth Cady Stanton constitutes a radical shift from those analyzed previously (*Proceedings* 1870, 3-19).[7] It is the first speech considered whose content was feminist in modern terms. Moreover, it was cast in high style, its tone was defiant, and its claims were strongly asserted. It took radical positions: for example, it included white racism among male sins, and it refused to concede male superiority on even the physical level. It was a long speech, rambling at points, but remarkable for setting in place so many key issues, including responses to the three major rationales (theological, biological, and sociological) for woman's limited sphere. It included, among other major arguments, a world history of the subjugation of women, a treatment of the myth of man's natural superiority, a description of the cultural barriers to woman's intellectual development, a depiction

of Adam as a creature of emotion rather than reason, the assertion
that female virtues are also male virtues, and the recognition that
assertions of difference between the sexes always end up affirming
male superiority.

Cady Stanton began by explaining why, despite prohibitions against
women speaking, she was willing to violate the traditional female role.
She said:

> I should feel exceedingly diffident to appear before you at this time, having never
> before spoken in public, were I not nerved by a sense of right and duty, did I
> not feel the time had fully come for the question of woman's wrongs to be laid
> before the public, did I not believe that woman herself must do this work; for
> woman alone can understand the height, the depth, the length, and the breadth
> of her own degradation. (3)

In 1848, any woman who spoke in public was likely to be hesitant. In
acknowledging such feelings, Cady Stanton evinced her understanding of
the norms of femininity. Her present willingness to violate the taboo was
justified by moral principles, by a sense of timeliness, and by a belief that
only women could effect the changes required. Her moral principles, the
"sense of right and duty," would be the basis of her refutation. Her sense
of advantageous timing grew out of the recent enactment of married
woman's property acts. Her claim that women alone could perform this
work of social change was reinforced in the next part of the speech.

Cady Stanton showed why men were incapable of working for
woman's rights. She laid down a principle: "Moral beings can only
judge of others by themselves." She did not argue that the sexes had
different natures, but asserted that man "had been educated to believe
that she differs from him so materially that he cannot judge of her
thoughts, feelings, and opinions by his own" (3). The problem was
male socialization, an explanation which allowed her to affirm
woman's vital role in this movement while remaining true to natural
rights principles. She then described male socialization, using
evidence from around the world.

Cady Stanton proceeded to attack spurious claims of male intellectual, moral, and physical superiority. She argued that until women had
equal opportunities educationally and professionally, the relative intellectual abilities of men and women could not be ascertained. She
attacked male moral superiority by pointing to male behavior, such as
the "bitterness, envy, hatred and malice" of clergymen of contending
sects, backbiting among physicians, and riots at the polls. Once again,
she ended with a reversal of conventional wisdom, claiming that man

had become woman's moral inferior, "not by nature, but made so by a false education" (7). Woman had been schooled to self-denial and suffering, permitting males to exploit her virtues in order to become selfish and to excuse their selfishness by saying that "God made woman more self-denying than men" (7). Here, instead of assenting to traditional views of woman's natural moral superiority, Cady Stanton attributed moral differences in the sexes to acculturation, and thus remained true to natural rights principles.

Male physical superiority was explained by women's lack of opportunity for physical education, but Cady Stanton also produced examples from around the world demonstrating women's physical prowess, and invoked the principle that use "produces growth and development" (9). She also noted that the power of mind was, in such noteworthy examples as ex-President John Quincy Adams, unrelated to the power of the body.

Cady Stanton responded particularly to objections to women's new and radical demand for the vote. She claimed suffrage as a natural right of women as citizens, and her scathing denunciation of the logic of male superiority provided justification for this claim even as it revealed the intensity of her feelings:

> We need not prove ourselves equal to Daniel Webster to enjoy this privilege, for the ignorant Irishman in the ditch has all the civil rights he has. We need not prove our muscular power equal to this same Irishman to enjoy this privilege, for the most tiny, weak, ill-shaped stripling of twenty-one, has all the civil rights of the Irishman. We have no objection to discussing the question of equality, . . . but we wish the question of equality kept distinct from the question of rights, for the proof of the one does not determine the truth of the other. All white men in this country have the same rights, however they may differ in mind, body or estate. The right is ours. (10)

This was a strong reaffirmation of the ballot as an integral part of a person's natural rights, regardless of capacity or situation, but it also revealed the indignation she and others like her felt at being at a disadvantage to those men whom they saw as their intellectual and moral inferiors.

She then responded to common arguments against woman suffrage: for example, if the polls were places women should not frequent, then their presence at the polls was needed to make them safe for their sires and their sons. Cady Stanton commented that if women were already represented by their fathers, husbands, brothers, and sons (which was the basis of sociological arguments against woman's rights), one could judge the quality of that representation by the gross inadequacy of the current statutes. To objections that woman's rights would destroy domestic harmony, she hinted at issues more common to contemporary feminism. For example, she alluded to women who "stand silent witnesses of the cruel infliction of blows and stripes from angry fathers on the trembling forms of helpless infancy. It is a mother's sacred duty to shield her children from violence, from whatever source it may come" (15). In contrast, she claimed that the "only happy households we now see are those in which husband and wife share equally in counsel and government" (16).

The speech demonstrated Cady Stanton's skill in answering arguments against expanded rights for women and revealed some of the motives energizing white, middle-class activists. It also revealed both her disappointment and her pride in her own sex. At one point she said: "The most discouraging, the most lamentable aspect our case wears is the indifference, indeed, the contempt with which women themselves regard the movement" (12). She explained such attitudes as a result of socialization. She reported evidence collected by British author Harriet Martineau that Turkish women shut in harems were not only satisfied with their position, but "think us strangely neglected in being left so free, and boast of their spy system and imprisonment as tokens of the value in which they are held" (12). That extreme case demonstrated that women who were enslaved could be socialized to accept, even defend, their oppressed status. Obviously, a movement to make women aware of their condition was required.

Pride in her sex infused Cady Stanton's extended conclusion. She produced a long list of outstanding women, beginning with great queens and ending with Joan of Arc, whose story became a model for the women of the movement:

> She had a full faith in herself and inspired all those who saw her with the same. Let us cultivate like faith, like enthusiasm, and we, too, shall impress all who see and hear us with the same confidence we ourselves feel in our final success. . . . "Voices" were the visitors and advisers of Joan of Arc. Do not "voices" come to us daily from the haunts of poverty, sorrow, degradation and despair, already too long unheeded. Now is the time for the women of this country, if they would save our free institutions, to defend the right, to buckle on the armor that can best resist the keenest weapons of the enemy—contempt and ridicule. The same religious enthusiasm that nerved Joan of Arc to her work nerves us to ours. In every generation God calls some men and women for the utterance of truth, a heroic action, and our work today is the fulfilling of what has long since been foretold by the Prophet—Joel 2:28: "And it shall come to pass afterward, that I will pour out my spirit upon all flesh, and your sons and your daughters shall prophesy." (18-19)

The image was extreme and dramatic, reflecting the speaker's perception of the power of the taboos women faced and the courage women needed in order to act. Like Joan, women had to do this work because men had failed at it. Like Joan, women had to be nerved by a sense of right and duty to violate the limits of the traditional female role. Like Joan, they had to heed the voices of their sisters who were calling on them for help. Like Joan, they would face hostility, contempt, and ridicule, but they would be doing what was foretold for women — assuming moral leadership. The work of woman's rights thus became heroic, a moral crusade. Indeed, Cady Stanton was herself, like Joan of Arc, a model for this crusade. Buoyed by a sense of right and duty she overcame her diffidence to speak. She did so because she believed the time was ripe for action which only women could perform. In a superb moment of enactment, Cady Stanton said to the women she addressed, do as I have done.

When considered in relation to the speeches of Angelina Grimké [Weld] and Lucretia Coffin Mott, it is apparent that Cady Stanton's first speech was far more assertive in tone. She violated woman's traditional role, and made little or no effort to render that violation less offensive to her audience. There was no gentleness or ambiguity, as in Coffin Mott's speech, and no special persona was used to legitimate her right to speak. She was her own person: Henry Stanton left town while the convention met after she refused to remove the demand for suffrage from the convention's Declaration and resolutions. She made no apologies, and spoke her mind with considerable directness. Moreover, the scope of the speech was so large that it covered much of what would be discussed and debated in the prewar period. It is the most encompassing of the speeches considered in this volume, rivaled perhaps only by Susan B. Anthony's sweeping defense of the woman citizen's right to vote. Because Cady Stanton was so important to the movement, I shall defer a general assessment of her role until chapter 9. As is already apparent, she played a central role in the founding of the movement and in developing its early ideology. Because of her obligations as a mother, Cady Stanton attended no other woman's rights conventions until 1860, although she often sent messages to be read by others. However, she spoke at a Woman's State Temperance meeting in Rochester in 1852 and to the New York legislature in 1854.

POTOWSKI ROSE'S 1851 SPEECH

In 1851 Ernestine Potowski Rose was already an experienced speaker and dedicated woman's rights activist. A contemporary observer, Paulina Wright Davis, wrote that Potowski Rose "made an address of an hour in length, which has never been surpassed" (Davis 1871, 19). Her speech was short, less than one third the length of Cady Stanton's; it was also more tightly focused, less elevated in style, and even fiercer in tone (*Proceedings* 1851, 36-47).

Like the movement manifesto and Cady Stanton's convention speech, Potowski Rose's arguments were grounded in natural rights principles. For example, she asked:

> Is she [woman] then not included in that [1776] declaration? Answer, ye wise men of the nation, and answer truly; add not hypocrisy to oppression! . . . But . . . you dare not so libel and insult humanity as to say, that she is not included in that declaration; and if she is, then what right has man, except that of might, to deprive woman of the rights and privileges he claims for himself? (36-37)

Even a brief excerpt reflects Potowski Rose's self-confidence and her mastery of nineteenth-century oratorical style. The speech was dramatic and included pointed, sarcastic attacks.

Whereas Cady Stanton discussed marriage only briefly, Potowski Rose devoted a major portion of her speech to marriage laws. She commented: "But it will be said that the husband provides for the wife. . . . Yes! he *keeps* her, and so he does a favorite horse; by law they are both considered his property" (37-38). She discussed wives' total loss of identity, their suffering due to wastrels, their treatment as animals, and the cultural acceptance of wife beating. She asserted that any kind feeling in husbands was due to the influence of their mothers and sisters, and she demanded an end to the wife's merger with the husband. Moreover, she emphasized the persuasive force of law, claiming that it was a strong element "in forming public opinion," that "bad and unjust laws must in the nature of things make man so too" (38). Many of her examples, like that cited above, were drawn from marital relations.

Potowski Rose is interesting because although her case rested on natural rights, she also argued from expediency, that is, made claims based on the benefits to be derived from change. For instance, she stated: "Yes, in addition to the principle of right, this is one of the reasons, drawn from expediency, why woman should participate in all the important duties of life; for, with all due respect to the other sex, she is the true civilizer of man" (42). Such arguments ordinarily contradict those based on natural rights because they presume that woman's nature is distinctive and that her influence will improve whatever sphere she enters. These two kinds of argument were both prevalent throughout the early women's movement, and the contradictions between them bedeviled movement ideology.

Like Cady Stanton, Potowski Rose argued that women must take up their own cause because education had made men incapable of understanding woman or legislating for her. Potowski Rose pointed to many women of achievement to demonstrate the fallacy of male intellectual superiority. Moreover, she attacked claims of male physical superiority by noting that "the inmates of the forest are his superior" (44) and by alleging that woman was what man had made her.

> Do you not yet understand what has made woman what she is? Then see what the sickly taste and perverted judgment of man now admires in woman. Not physical and mental vigor, but a pale, delicate face; hands too small to grasp a broom, . . . a voice so sentimental and depressed, that what she says can be learned only by the moving of her half parted lips and above all, that nervous sensibility which sees a ghost in every passing shadow, that beautiful diffidence which dares not take a step without the protecting arm of man to support her tender frame, and that shrinking mock-modesty that faints at the mention of a leg of a table. (45)

She linked this line of argument to the issue of woman's moral superiority by quoting a famous clergyman who implied that a woman's character could not withstand public exposure. She responded: "In his benighted mind, the modesty and virtue of woman is of so fragile a nature, that when it is in contact with the atmosphere, it evaporates like chloroform" (45). She showed how "degrading" such an opinion of female moral character was to women.

Male ignorance and prejudice became reasons for women to undertake the work of reform and bases for believing that efforts to persuade men could be successful. Woman's capacity for great works was attested to by the achievements of Mary Wollstonecraft, Margaret Fuller, Harriet Martineau, and many others. It was also demonstrated by an image that reversed traditional conceptions of femininity, such as that found in the "Pastoral Letter" condemning the speaking of Angelina and Sarah Grimké. Potowski Rose said: "She, like the tender ivy plant, bent yet unbroken by the storms of life, not only upholds her own hopeful courage, but clings around the tempest-fallen oak, to speak hope to his faltering spirit, and shelter him from the returning blast of the storm" (44).

Like Cady Stanton, Potowski Rose suggested that the woman's rights movement was a moral crusade to uplift all humankind. Reflecting views that would be made more familiar by the work of Friedrich

Engels (1884), she said: "The race is elevated in excellence and power, or kept back in progression, in accordance with the scale of woman's position in society" (46). As a result, the woman's rights movement was part of humanity's evolutionary progress. It was also a crusade, based on individual conscience, that would go far beyond legal change:

> We have a crusade before us, far holier and more righteous than led warriors to Palestine—a crusade, not to deprive any one of his rights, but to claim our own. . . . To achieve this glorious victory of right over might, woman has much to do. Man may remove her legal shackles, and recognize her as his equal, which will greatly aid in her elevation; but the law cannot compel her to cultivate her mind and take an independent stand as a free being. . . . She must act according to her best convictions, irrespective of any other voice than that of right and duty. (47)

Potowski Rose's speech demonstrates that she understood the persuasive force of legal reform as well as its limitation. Altering woman's legal status was now the focus of the movement, but its larger purpose for the future was to change woman's self-conception and motivate her to strive to become all that she could be. However, Potowski Rose did not address the conflicts between individual development and pressures for marriage and motherhood, conflicts that would begin to be treated only in modern feminism.

When compared to other speeches of the early movement, those of Cady Stanton and Potowski Rose were much more florid and ornate. As noted earlier, Cady Stanton made no attempt to modify the traditionally masculine role of rhetor and, with some frequency, was defiant and even scornful of male ideas and actions. Still fiercer in tone than Cady Stanton, Potowski Rose made speakers like Grimké [Weld] and Coffin Mott seem even gentler by comparison. Potowski Rose shared with Grimké [Weld] a sense of drama, but the drama did not arise out of the situation, as with the Pennsylvania Hall speech, but was provided by the speaker herself.

Ernestine Potowski Rose's speeches, and her efforts to obtain passage of a married woman's property act in New York State in 1836, contributed to creating a climate in which the woman's rights movement could develop. Potowski Rose remained active in the movement prior to the Civil War, speaking at many early conventions. During the war she joined Anthony and Cady Stanton in the Woman's National Loyal League, gathering signatures in support of a federal amendment abolishing slavery. In 1869, together with Anthony and Cady Stanton, she founded the National Woman Suffrage Association. She returned to England permanently in 1873 due to ill health, and died in 1892.

CONCLUSION

As the Declaration of Sentiments of Seneca Falls and the resolutions of the prewar conventions demonstrate, those who participated in the incipient movement came to share an understanding of the ideas underlying their cause. Even the initially radical demand for suffrage came to be acceptable because it was grounded in the principles of natural rights. Conceptions of a woman's right to develop as an individual were treated as a logical outgrowth of natural rights; at least in the convention rhetoric, no conflict was seen between woman's role as wife and mother and her personal development. Many activists were deeply religious, yet they disagreed about the degree to which movement ideology should be grounded in Scripture; all agreed that the organized church had been a major force for women's oppression. The legal disabilities of married women were deplored and their removal was seen as an urgent priority. In some convention debates, suffrage was seen as a priority because it was fundamental to the protection of other rights, but the ballot had not yet emerged as the focus of the movement.

Despite excellent attendance, Seneca Falls was a small, local convention. Press reaction, however, transformed it into a national event and thus precipitated a social movement. Most newspaper editors were so outraged by the convention that they gave it the kind of publicity of which press agents dream. Headlines trumpeted an "Insurrection Among Women," "The Reign of Petticoats," "Bolting Among the Ladies," and "Petticoats vs. Boots." Stories described the convention sponsors as "a rebellious group of aged spinsters, crossed in love, trying to avenge themselves by making others more miserable than themselves," and accused them of "wishing to wear men's clothes" and "aiming to put men in the kitchen while they swaggered about the world" (Lutz 1940, 52).

Horace Greeley, editor of the *New York Tribune*, was somewhat sympathetic to the movement. He pointed out that most women did not desire these rights but acknowledged that "however unwise and mistaken the demand, it is but the assertion of a natural right and as such must be conceded" (Gurko 1976, 104). Other editorials, though, called the convention "the most shocking and unnatural incident ever recorded in the history of womanity" and said that equal rights would "demoralize and degrade" women and "prove a monstrous injury to all mankind" (Gurko 1976, 103). The contempt and ridicule foretold in the Declaration of Sentiments and in Cady Stanton's speech were so withering that, as noted above, most signers of the Declaration of Sentiments and Resolutions asked to have their names withdrawn.

Press reaction to later conventions was equally hostile. The first national convention in Worcester was called a "hen convention"; a "hybrid, mongrel, piebald, crackbrained, pitiful, disgusting and ridiculous assemblage"; and "a gathering of crazy old women" who wanted to abolish both the Bible and the Constitution (Gurko 1976, 139). In 1853, after the *New York Herald* had called the women "unsexed in mind" and "barren fools" and theirs a "Woman's Wrong Convention," Horace Greeley shrewdly commented: "Nothing is so good for a weak and popular movement as this sort of opposition. . . . The mass of people throughout the country who might otherwise not know of its existence, will have their attention called and their sympathies enlisted in its behalf" (Gurko 1976, 165-66).

Indeed, press reaction to these early conventions vividly illustrates the value of opposition for a movement. For example, in an attempt to discredit the 1848 convention, James Gordon Bennett, editor of the *New York Herald*, printed the entire Declaration of Sentiments, and by so doing disseminated woman's rights ideas throughout the nation. Press attacks ensured that a wide public learned of the conventions and, when editors printed key speeches or documents, the coverage ensured that readers would understand the grounds underlying women's demands. As a result, these conventions reached a large audience and, in conjunction with early woman's rights journals, such as Amelia Bloomer's *Lily* (1849-1859), started as a result of the Seneca Falls convention, Paulina Wright Davis's *Una* (1853-1856), and other publications (Jerry 1986), created a constituency of interested and knowledgeable women and men out of which a social movement could grow.

The Seneca Falls convention was important not only because hostile press coverage publicized early organizational efforts that others were moved to emulate, but because the Declaration of Sentiments was a manifesto that accurately reflected the principles underlying the entire movement and that enunciated fundamental grievances about which movement activists came to agree. The Declaration was not immediately recognized as such. As noted above, at subsequent conventions there was talk about generating a document to supercede it, but such discussion inevitably led to defenses of its forcefulness and its clear statement of grievances. Many commentators have criticized the early movement for producing no clear ideological statement. The Declaration of Sentiments was defective — it violated the form it appropriated, because, as comparison reveals, it was no declaration of independence. Unlike its 1776 model, the Seneca Falls document sought assimilation and amalgamation, and it sought these ends through persuasion, not rebellion. But this was not an ideological defect, because the Declaration accurately reflected the views of those whose principles it expressed. This was a movement grounded in natural rights philosophy whose adherents sought to extend natural rights to women. They wanted reform, not revolution. They demanded legal changes, but equally strongly they desired changes in attitudes and beliefs, changes that would enlarge woman's sphere and enable her to enter realms that had been the exclusive domain of males. In espousing natural rights principles, woman's rights advocates reaffirmed their commitment to the values of the nation, and as the movement developed, they saw themselves as perfecting, not overthrowing, the democratic republic they loved as Americans.

NOTES

1. Anti-Slavery Conventions of American Women were held in New York in 1837 and in Philadelphia in 1837 and 1839 (*Proceedings* 1837, 1839, *History of Pennsylvania Hall*, 1838).

2. The call also appeared in Frederick Douglass's paper, the *North Star*, published in Rochester, New York (Foner 1976, 12).

3. This process is analogous to consciousness-raising in the contemporary feminist movement and to feminist literary criticism which treats classic works in a special way. In the words of Wayne C. Booth, these texts are "not thrown out, not censored, not burned, but thrown into controversy" (1982, 74). In 1853, William Lloyd Garrison defended the Declaration of Sentiments from the attack that a parody could never be taken seriously, arguing that it performed just this critical function (HWS 1:136).

4. For example, Lucretia Coffin Mott's speech at the 1854 national convention began: "It is not Christianity, but priestcraft that has subjected woman as we find her" (HWS 1:380-381).

5. Occasionally early activists, such as physician Harriot Hunt, refused to pay their taxes and faced the economic consequences.

6. Whether or not it typified the movement for a longer period is a more difficult question. Interestingly, in an interview published in 1974, Alice Paul reported that it was to the 1848 Declaration of Sentiments that the National Woman's Party Convention in 1920 looked for guidance in determining the next step in the woman's rights struggle (cited in Ford 1984, 5).

7. Lois Banner's biography of Cady Stanton indicates that she gave an earlier speech on temperance in Johnstown, New York (1980, 29); Elisabeth Griffith's biography refers to a first speech on temperance made in Seneca Falls in 1841 (1984, 41), but in her text Cady Stanton said this Seneca Falls speech was her first.

5

A Movement in Transition: The Debate of 1860

The resolutions and speeches of the early conventions show that the legal status of married women was a central grievance motivating woman's rights activists. The newly organized movement struggled mightily over how controversial facets of marriage law, particularly divorce, were to be addressed. That struggle is the subject of this chapter.

Relations between spouses, like all facets of women's lives, had been affected by the growth of the cult of domesticity; conceptions of true womanhood included changed conceptions of marriage. In his study of divorce in the United States, William O'Neill notes that the modern conjugal or nuclear family began to emerge in the sixteenth and seventeenth centuries as perceptions of the child altered. Family life came to be oriented toward children and child-rearing as the industrial revolution altered patterns of work, and the family lost its public character as an economic institution to become increasingly private and domestic. Divorce became essential, because "when families become the center of social organization, their intimacy can become suffocating, their demands unbearable, and their expectations too high to be easily realizable. Divorce then becomes the safety valve that makes the system workable" (O'Neill 1967, 6-7).

In 1860 and 1861, legislation was introduced to liberalize New York's restrictive divorce laws.[1] That effort prompted an exchange at the 1860 national woman's rights convention in New York City which displayed movement views of marriage and exposed internal conflicts about the movement's future. Subsequent discussion of marriage and divorce was inhibited by political events of the postwar era, which focused movement attention on suffrage, and by the Beecher-Tilton scandal of 1872. This drama with its public accusations of adultery against Henry Ward Beecher, one of America's foremost ministers, and his subsequent trial, together with its "free love" overtones, would make discussions of marriage and divorce too perilous for a small movement that was highly controversial in its own right (Blake 1962, ch. 8; Pleck 1983, 457-58). As a result, the "divorce debate" of 1860 is a rare source of evidence of movement views of marriage and divorce.

Progress toward major goals of the movement was evident by the time of the 1860 convention. In March of that year, New York had amended its Married Woman's Property Act, mentioned above in chapter 4. These amendments gave a wife control over the property she accrued after marriage as well as the property she brought to it. The law also gave her the right to buy and sell such property on her "sole and separate account" (*Laws of the State of New York* 1860, 157-159), to bargain and make contracts, and to sue and be sued in her own name; it made her joint guardian of her children and guaranteed her control of at least some of her husband's property in the event of his death.[2] Other states, including Indiana, Maine, Missouri, and Ohio, were also broadening married women's property rights. In addition, Matthew Vassar had recently donated $400,000 to establish a woman's college in Poughkeepsie, New York (Gurko 1976, 202).

Although the woman's rights movement had persisted for twelve years and had contributed to legal and economic advances for women, in 1860 it was still young and structurally fragile. No local or national organizations existed; no stable, official organ publicized movement activities; and membership, measured by convention attendance and involvement, was small. The precise destination of the movement was still to be decided, despite the ideological agreement expressed in early convention resolutions, especially the 1848 Declaration of Sentiments. Now, in the midst of rejoicing over the progress in woman's rights, Elizabeth Cady Stanton introduced a series of resolutions on divorce, prompting an exchange that not only disclosed early activists' views of marriage but also exposed fundamental conflicts within the movement.

VIEWS OF MARRIAGE AND DIVORCE

The 1860 convention resolutions and speeches had their roots in past public debate. Cady Stanton had urged divorce on the grounds of habitual drunkenness at the New York State Woman's Temperance Convention of 1852 (HWS 1:482, 485). Conflicting views of divorce had been aired in New York newspapers between November 1852, and February 1853 (James 1853), and again in March 1860

(Greeley 1860). As argued in print, the issues were religious, political, and feminist. The religious issue was the nature of marriage—was it a sacrament or a contract? The political issue was the role of government in the life of the individual—was its function to assure the moral quality of the community or to protect the freedom of individual moral decision? The feminist issue was more recent and concerned the impact of current marriage and divorce law on wives and children: "Whereas divorce in earlier periods of history had been primarily a prerogative demanded by men to rid themselves of unwanted wives and open the way for new marriages, nineteenth-century American divorce was becoming more and more a right demanded by women on humanitarian grounds. The day was passing when wives would meekly submit to all kinds of abuse from brutal husbands" (Blake, 95).

As the law existed in New York in 1860, divorce was granted only on grounds of adultery; legal separations were permitted for cruel and inhuman treatment, for conduct threatening the safety of the wife, for abandonment by the husband, and for his refusal or neglect to provide for her. Public debate, however, focused attention on the liberal law in Indiana, which provided for divorce on grounds of adultery, impotency, abandonment for one year, cruel treatment of either party by the other, habitual drunkenness of either party, failure of the husband to make reasonable provision for his family, the conviction of either party of an infamous crime, and "any other cause for which the Court shall deem it proper that a divorce should be granted" (Greeley 1860, 189, appendix).

As earlier conventions had recognized, marriage was the most important and potentially the most oppressive relationship into which nineteenth-century women entered. For economic and social reasons, women were compelled to marry, and the depersonalizing character of "woman's place" was magnified in marriage, which made wives nonpersons. The changes in marriage laws demanded by woman's rights activists were representative of the changes women wanted in society. At base, all were demands for natural rights; that is, they were demands for the legal, political, and social rights belonging to all human beings.

Paulina Wright Davis, instrumental in organizing the first national woman's rights convention in 1850, reflected the early movement's view of marriage when she said:

> Marriage, as it now exists, is only a name, a form without a soul, a bondage, legal and therefore honorable. . . . Make marriage what it should be, a union of soul

> with soul, a blending of two in one, without masterdom or helpless dependence, and it is then as God designed it to be. (*Proceedings . . . 1852* 1852, 61; HWS 1:534-35)

The status of a wife as civilly dead, as the property of her husband, was symbolic of woman's status in society. In 1851, Cady Stanton explained: "Many people consider this [the status of wife] a very small matter; but it is the symbol of the most cursed monopoly on this footstool; a monopoly by man of all rights, the life, liberty, and happiness of one-half of the human family—all womankind" (*Proceedings . . . 1851* 1852, 89). On the same occasion, Potowski Rose described woman's married state with bitter eloquence:

> At marriage, she loses her identity, and her being is said to have become merged in her husband. Has nature thus merged it? Has she ceased to exist and feel pleasure and pain? When she violates the laws of her being, does her husband pay the penalty? When she breaks the moral law, does he suffer the punishment? And when at his nightly orgies . . . he squanders the means she helped . . . to accumulate, and she awakens to penury and destitution, will it supply the wants of her children to tell them, that owing to the superiority of the man, she had no redress by law; and that as her being was merged in his, so also ought theirs to be? (*Proceedings . . . 1851* 1852, 37).[3]

Because marriage was so central to the lives of nineteenth-century women, the demand for recognition of woman's natural rights implied recognition of her personhood in marriage; exactly what such recognition would entail was central to the 1860 convention debate.

At that convention, Elizabeth Cady Stanton introduced ten resolutions and spoke in support of them. Antoinette Brown [Blackwell] then offered thirteen resolutions and spoke for them. Ernestine Potowski Rose spoke next, supporting Cady Stanton. These speeches, opening the evening session of May 11, have been labeled the "divorce debate," and some historians have concluded from them that the movement's internal conflict concerned marriage and divorce (Gurko 1976, 201-205; Smith 1970, 164).[4] However, their shared assumptions were as important as their differences. A more contentious debate, also significant for the future of the movement, took place subsequently between these three women, supported by Susan B. Anthony, and Wendell Phillips, supported by William Lloyd Garrison, and is discussed later in this chapter.

The resolutions and speeches presented by Elizabeth Cady Stanton and Antoinette Brown [Blackwell] displayed differing styles as well as differing conceptions of marriage. First, Cady Stanton's speech is in high style, and is even more polished than her speech at Seneca Falls.

The first half is composed of a series of lengthy, ornate apostrophes, a rhetorical device by which a speaker addresses an absent or imaginary person. There is much less defiance than in the earlier speech, largely because the apostrophes are a form of indirect address.

Cady Stanton viewed marriage as an institution that, like government, could be changed, and as a contract that, like others, must meet certain requirements to be valid. As an institution, it should be judged in terms of how well it promoted "the highest good of the individual" (*Proceedings* 1860, 67). Her seventh resolution asserted that "an unfortunate or ill-assorted marriage is ever a calamity, . . . and when society or government, by its laws or customs, compels its continuance . . . it usurps an authority never delegated to man, nor exercised by God himself" (66). Liberalized divorce would be moral progress, because it would preserve the home as a true sanctuary and eliminate legal separation, which was "disgraceful" and "beset with many temptations to lead a false, unreal life" (71). She rejected religious views of marriage as sacred, contending that "all God's arrangements are perfect, harmonious, and complete" (68). Current marriage laws and customs forced wives into relationships robbing them of human dignity and of natural rights, including the right to love. Marriages became institutions of legalized prostitution from which women could escape only through suicide, murder, or infidelity (69-70).

However, Cady Stanton also made comments about marriage that echoed traditional ideals of true womanhood. For example, she said that "nothing is sacred in the family and home, but just so far as it is built up and anchored in love" (70). She affirmed that home was woman's sphere and promised men freedom from further aggravation if demands for liberalized divorce were met: "Leave us to make these laws that govern the inner sanctuary of our own homes, and faithful satellites we will ever be to the dinnerpot, the cradle, and the old arm-chair" (70). Moreover, she concluded:

> If in marriage either party claims the right to stand supreme, to woman, the mother of the race, belongs the scepter and the crown. Her life is one long sacrifice for man. . . . For you we gladly pour out our heart's blood and die . . . knowing that from our suffering comes forth a new and more glorious resurrection of thought and life. (73)

Cady Stanton argued for legal equality within marriage and in divorce, but she did not conceive of a new institution of marriage or of changes in the relationship of men and women within it.

Antoinette Brown [Blackwell], by contrast, spoke in a much simpler, more extemporaneous style, and although her speech included some direct refutation of Cady Stanton, she did not respond directly on major issues. She saw marriage as "the voluntary alliance of two persons . . . as permanent as the life of the parties" (Resolution 1; *Proceedings* 1860, 73). She conceived of marriage as an ideal, a "union of equals" in which "two persons . . . covenant to work together, to uphold each other in all excellence, and to mutually blend their lives and interests into a common harmony" (79). In this definition of marriage, each partner had a permanent moral obligation to the other, "no matter how profligate that other's conduct may be" (Res. 3; 74). She recognized that existing marriage laws mandated the personal subjection of the wife to the husband, which she called "a false relation" (75); however, she went beyond Cady Stanton to espouse a radical individualism which made the wife responsible for her oppression, claiming that "she consents to this subjection, I do insist that she consents to degradation; that this is a sin, and it is impossible to make it other than sin" (75). Despite such a permanent obligation, "legal divorce may be necessary for personal and family protection" (76). Nevertheless, even after divorce, the moral bonds implicit in a voluntary alliance between equals remained.

Permitting divorce under such rare and extreme conditions was contrasted with "easy divorce." Unlike a house, which might be vacated on grounds of inconvenience, marriage required women to pledge themselves to the goal of "perfecting . . . all the interests arising from those relations" (78). Unless both partners accepted such a moral obligation, Brown [Blackwell] said, all marriages would be defective, and no marriage could lead to the perfection of its partners. Women sometimes entered marriage prematurely, later to realize that their decision had been foolish, but because the situation was of their own making, they were responsible for attempting to create the conditions for a true union. Brown [Blackwell] evoked the resolve of an unhappy wife:

> "Now that I see my mistake, I will commence being true to myself, I will become a true unit, strong and noble in myself; and if I can never make our union a true one, I will work toward that good result, I will live for this great work — for truth and all its interests." Let me tell you, if she is not great enough to do this, she is not great enough to enter into any union! (77)

Individualism and marriage were reconciled by resolving that "the great duty of every human being is to secure his [sic] own highest moral development" (Res. 6; 74), and that "the permanence and indissolubility of marriage tend more directly than any thing else towards this result [the creation of perfect individual units]" (Res. 13; 74). For Brown [Blackwell], legal divorce should be possible under some few conditions, but moral divorce could never occur.

Brown [Blackwell]'s resolutions and speech revealed great ambivalence about the institution of marriage. For example, she said marital problems were "all individual. We have few men or women fit to be married" (76). Yet she acknowledged underlying structural problems: "So long as society is constituted in such a way that woman is expected to do nothing if she have a father, brother, or husband, able to support her, there is no salvation for her, in or out of marriage" (81). In other words, "as long as you make women helpless, inefficient beings, who never expect to earn a farthing in their lives, who never expect to do any thing outside of the family, but to be cared for and protected by others throughout life, you cannot have true marriages" (80). The cure was "not in dissolving marriage, but it is in giving to the married her own natural independence and self-sovereignty, by which she can maintain herself" (80). Brown [Blackwell] claimed that marriage was voluntary and that a wife was morally responsible for entering a flawed union, but she also acknowledged that women's training was inadequate to prepare them to be units in a true marriage.

Brown [Blackwell]'s resolutions and speech contained radical contradictions. She said that marriage was permanent, but that divorce and legal separation had to be permitted under some circumstances. While "our first duty is to ourselves" (74), even after divorce a woman "is never to forget that in the sight of God and her own soul, she is his wife . . . [and] that to work for his redemption is her highest social obligation" (76). Still more disturbing, she said that women were not to submit to subjugation, but she gave no indication of how they were to escape it. She recognized that marriage laws in nearly all states oppressed women, but argued that an oppressed wife had a duty to flee to some unnamed state that permitted divorce (75). To escape from oppression, she noted, a woman may be obliged to live on another continent, but she still owed her husband "the wife's loyalty"; what did the husband owe? It was a wife's duty to redeem her erring spouse, just as she would a drunkard in the gutter, but, if so, what was the nature of the special marriage relationship? Brown [Blackwell] did not make claims about the real world, but expressed a set of semi-religious views of what moral behavior in marriage should be; she ascribed to women alone the heavy moral responsibilities within marriage, despite passing references to man's similar duties. In her ambivalence about woman's role and responsibility in the marital relationship she recognized, perhaps subconsciously, the conflict between a woman's obligations to a husband and children and to herself.

Potowski Rose responded to Brown [Blackwell]'s resolutions and speech by supporting the views of Cady Stanton. She spoke in a simple style appropriate to extemporaneous remarks, but her speech involved very direct and forceful refutation of Brown [Blackwell]'s main points. In contrast to the ideal union envisioned by Brown [Blackwell], Potowski Rose described marriages in which "the husband holds the iron heel of legal oppression on the subjugate neck of the wife until every spark of womanhood is crushed out" (82). She denied the evils of easy divorce by reversing Brown [Blackwell]'s analogy: "We are a good deal the creatures of habit, but we will not be forced. We live (I speak from experience) in uncomfortable houses for years, rather than move . . . but force any one to live for life in one house, and he would run away from it, though it were a palace" (84). She argued that a woman better met her obligations to her children through divorce than by keeping them in a home where "father and mother despise and hate each other, and still live together as husband and wife" (84).

However, Potowski Rose, too, linked marriage and love, defending divorce by saying that "love must be free, or it ceases to be love" (81). She described marriage as an "institution, called out by the needs of social, affectional human nature, for human purposes, its objects are, first, the happiness of the parties immediately concerned, and secondly, the welfare of society" (83). Divorce was a means to the preservation of marriage. She pointed out that free love "acknowledges no marriage, and therefore requires no divorce. I believe in true marriages, and therefore I ask for a law to free men and women from false ones" (84). She linked woman's rights efforts to the creation of true marriage by pointing out that economic dependence contributed to unhappy marriage: "Educate woman, to enable her to promote her independence, and she will not be obliged to marry for a home and a subsistence. Give the wife an equal right with the husband in the property acquired after marriage, and it will be a bond of union between them" (84).

Both Cady Stanton and Potowski Rose advocated more liberal divorce laws to give married women an escape from their oppression. Despite her reservations, Brown [Blackwell] also accepted divorce in some extreme circumstances, but unlike them, she believed that marriage was an indissoluble union entailing lifelong moral obligations. The major disagreement in this exchange was that Cady Stanton and

Potowski Rose spoke about marriage in the real world, whereas Brown [Blackwell] propounded an extreme individualism that incorporated a wildly idealistic concept of marriage. Yet despite these differences, the speeches of Cady Stanton, Brown [Blackwell], and Potowski Rose were grounded in a number of common ideological principles. All three proposed that laws and customs regarding marriage should establish and support an institution recognizing and protecting the selfhood of each spouse. Cady Stanton and Potowski Rose argued that because existing laws did not create such marriages, either husband or wife should be able to end the relationship if his or her selfhood was being violated. Brown [Blackwell] argued that divorce should be a last resort available only after the spouses had fulfilled their moral obligation to each other, namely to reform the marriage so as to ensure the selfhood of both partners.

All three speakers grounded their views in individualism, an emphasis that counterbalanced the traditional marital function of child-rearing. All three celebrated marriage. Potowski Rose and Cady Stanton treated marriage as an entirely human, legal entity, whereas Brown [Blackwell] saw it as a sacred, moral union. None of them addressed the way a woman should handle her obligations to her husband and children in relation to her obligations to herself. Brown [Blackwell], in her ambivalence, hinted at the possibility of conflict between a woman's role in marriage and her development as an individual. But none of the speakers suggested that if marriage were to be an institution in which spouses and children developed to their fullest, traditional spousal roles might have to change. According to all three, if women were educated to self-sufficiency, trained to expect a partnership of equals, and made equals with their spouses in law, then marriage would be an institution in which women would and could grow as individuals. From the viewpoint of contemporary feminism, their views of the institution were romantic, and their analysis of the institution and its impact on women was nonexistent.[5]

In this debate, Cady Stanton's style was more ornate, and she was less defiant and scornful of males than in speeches considered in previous chapters. Potowski Rose spoke in a middle style appropriate to the extemporaneous character of debate, and although she directly refuted Brown [Blackwell]'s remarks, her speech had none of the fierce tone of her 1851 convention address. Brown [Blackwell] singled women out for a special burden of responsibility and spoke with a romanticism so extreme as to undermine her credibility: in effect, she claimed that men were women's burden. However, none of the three women appeared to make an effort to transform the rhetor's role in the way that Grimké [Weld] or Coffin Mott did in their speeches.

Antoinette Brown [Blackwell]'s life stretches across the entirety of the early woman's rights movement. She attended Oberlin and completed its theological course in 1850, but was refused a license to preach. She began a successful career as a lecturer, speaking on woman's rights, anti-slavery, and temperance. In 1853 she was ordained as minister of the First Congregational Church in Butler and Savannah, New York, becoming the first woman ordained in a recognized denomination. In 1856 she married Samuel Blackwell and left the lecture platform. In 1875, however, she published *Sexes Throughout Nature*, a refutation of the use of the works of Charles Darwin and Herbert Spencer to reject woman's emancipation. She returned to the lecture platform in 1878 and contributed columns to the *Woman's Journal*. She faithfully attended conventions prior to the Civil War and, later, suffrage meetings all over the country. In 1920, at the age of ninety-five, she was the only member of the early group of woman's rights activists still alive to exercise her right to vote.

INTERNAL CONFLICT

Wendell Phillips responded to the resolutions and speeches of Cady Stanton, Brown [Blackwell], and Potowski Rose by saying: "I would move to lay them [the divorce resolutions] on the table; but my conviction that they are out of order is so emphatic, that I wish to go further than that, and move that they do not appear on the journals of this Convention" (*Proceedings* 1860, 85). The speeches and resolutions presupposed a link between the issue of woman's natural rights and the need to reform marriage and divorce law. Phillips took a different position. He insisted:

[Woman's rights conventions] have nothing to do with them [questions of marriage and divorce], any more than with the question of Intemperance, or Kansas, in my opinion. This Convention is no Marriage Convention — if it were, the subject would be in order; but this Convention, if I understand it, assembles to discuss the laws that rest unequally upon women, not those that rest equally upon men and women. It is the laws that make distinctions between the sexes. Now, whether a man and a woman are married for a year or a life is a question which affects the man just as much as the woman. . . . We have nothing to do with a question which affects both sexes equally. Therefore, it seems to me we have nothing to do with the theory of Marriage, which is the basis, as Mrs. Rose has very clearly shown, of Divorce. (85)

Phillips's view of the movement was supported by other convention participants. His motion was seconded by a Mrs. Abby Gibbons, and his brief speech was interrupted by applause eight times. William Lloyd Garrison spoke in support of the motion; he felt that "this question of Marriage came in as at least incidental to the main question of the equal rights of woman" (88), and he agreed that all mention of the topic should be omitted from the convention record.

Phillips's views on marriage became clear early in his speech. After commenting that "there are cases where men are bound to women carcasses as well as where women are bound to men carcasses" (a comment greeted with laughter and applause by the audience), Phillips admitted that he knew, "as every body else does, that the results of marriage, in the present condition of society, are often more disastrous to woman than to man" (85). Phillips's rationale for exorcising discussions of marriage and divorce from the convention proceedings revealed the pressures working to effect a narrowing of movement concerns:

> The reason why I object so emphatically to the introduction of the question here is because it is a question which admits of so many theories . . . that it is large enough for a movement of its own. Our question is only unnecessarily burdened with it. . . . No question — Anti-Slavery, Temperance, Woman's Rights — can move forward efficiently, unless it keeps its platform separate and unmixed with extraneous issues, unmixed with discussions which carry us into endless realms of debate. (85-86)

According to Phillips, they had to be realistic: only a distinct, relatively narrow movement had a chance to succeed. Movement aims had to be purified of all extraneous elements if they were to be made clear to the public. As Phillips saw it, the sole objective of the woman's rights movement was "to deal with the simple question which we propose — how to make the statute-book look upon woman exactly as it does upon man" (86).

As he continued, he narrowed the objectives still further. He prophesied: "In a few years more, I do not know but we shall disband, and watch these women to the ballot-box, to see that they do their duty" (87). Garrison agreed. He said that "in a government like this, that they had nothing more to do than put the ballot into the hand of the woman, as it was in the hand of the man" (88). In both speeches, the demand for woman's natural rights was replaced by the suffragist demand for the ballot, and in both speeches, the rationale for limiting movement goals was a pragmatic need to adapt ideology to society.

In response to a request for clarification from Antoinette Brown [Blackwell], Phillips explained that his motion was a response to both sets of resolutions. In rejoinder, Brown [Blackwell] stated what she saw as the point in contention:

> Now, does this question [divorce] grow legitimately out of the great question of woman's equality? The world says, marriage is not an alliance between equals in human rights. My whole argument was based on the position that it is. If this question is not legitimate, what is? . . . It *must* come upon this platform, for at present it is a relation which legally and socially bears unequally upon woman. (89)

Susan B. Anthony entered the dispute to support Brown [Blackwell]:

> And as to the point that this question does not belong to this platform, — from that I totally dissent. Marriage has ever and always been a one-sided matter, resting most unequally upon the sexes. By it, man gains all — woman loses all; tyrant law and lust reign supreme with him — meek submission, and cheerful, ready obedience alone befit her. Woman has never been consulted; her wish has never at all been taken into consideration. . . . Woman has never been thought of other than as a piece of property, to be disposed of at the will and pleasure of man. (90)

In other words, women as wives lost their selfhood; hence, marriage and divorce were inextricably bound up with woman's rights, and their discussion was appropriate to any assembly gathered to consider woman's rights. Finally, Cady Stanton's public reaction to Phillips and Garrison came in the form of a letter to the editor published in the *New York Tribune* in which she addressed herself to Phillips's motion and offered a detailed refutation of his arguments about the issues that the movement should not address, arguing that the disabilities of married women were central to the movement (95-97).[6] She did not mention disagreements over divorce law provisions.

The convention failed to vote on the resolutions proposed by either Cady Stanton or Brown [Blackwell], but Phillips's motion came to a vote and was rejected (90). The vote suggests that convention delegates saw the important issue as the relevance of marriage and divorce to the woman's rights movement, rather than the specific provisions of a divorce law as set forth in the resolutions.[7]

Wendell Phillips, abolitionist and orator, followed William Lloyd Garrison, editor of the *Liberator* and founder of the American Anti-Slavery Society, into the woman's rights movement. He was named as one of the trustees of the Charles F. Hovey fund, which was established to support anti-slavery and woman's rights activism, and which sometimes provided support for the work of Susan B. Anthony. He became part of the group that, following the Civil War, argued that woman suffrage should be deferred to give suffrage to freed male slaves. He allied himself with the more conservative, Boston-based American Woman Suffrage Association.

Like Phillips, William Lloyd Garrison played a relatively minor role in the early women's movement. Like many women during this period, his life illustrated the links between abolitionism and woman's rights; indeed, in 1835, he was dragged through the streets on a rope and narrowly escaped with his life after addressing the Boston Female Anti-Slavery Society. With Phillips, he signed the call to the first national woman's rights convention, regularly attended prewar conventions, and was affiliated with the American Woman Suffrage Association.

CONCLUSION

Social movements are organisms that change and grow. Two processes stimulate that change: conflict between movement members and conflict between the movement and the surrounding society. As a result, movement ideologists face a dilemma—whether to maintain the movement's ideological purity or to politicize demands to make them more palatable to outsiders. Speakers may choose to purify movement ideology, creating a more unified, exclusive, and homogeneous movement while intensifying conflict between the movement and society. Alternatively, they may choose to sacrifice ideological purity and risk internal conflict in order to attract a wider membership and increase the chance that desired goals will be achieved (Simons 1970).

Like any social movement, woman's rights contained the potential for internal conflict. Because of its roots in other protest movements, it was a coalition of people who had been or who continued to be active in a variety of reform efforts, particularly abolitionism and temperance. These coalitions proved fragile. Political disagreements with former abolitionist allies would dominate the postwar period, and alliances with temperance forces in the 1880s would broaden support for and arouse opposition to suffrage while diluting movement ideology. The movement was a coalition in still another sense, as it included men as well as women.[8] Both the 1860 convention debate and postwar conflicts demonstrated that male supporters tended to be less committed to movement goals, whether broadly conceived as woman's rights or more narrowly construed as woman suffrage.

Prior to the 1860 debate, there was little evidence of internal conflict in the early woman's rights movement, but this would change abruptly after the Civil War.[9] The 1860 meeting was the last of the national woman's rights conventions for six years. During the Civil War, woman's rights activism ceased. The movement re-emerged in 1866 to organize formally under a new name and with different goals; but the American Equal Rights Association (AERA) dissolved over the issue of whether or not suffrage for former slaves and suffrage for women would be pursued simultaneously. The decision by former abolitionist and Republican allies that this was "the Negro's hour," meaning that woman suffrage should be deferred to a more propitious moment, ended in schism. In 1869 two competing organizations were formed: the National Woman Suffrage Association (NWSA), led by Elizabeth Cady Stanton, Susan B. Anthony, and Matilda Joslyn Gage; and the American Woman Suffrage Association (AWSA), led by Lucy Stone, Henry Blackwell, Julia Ward Howe, and Wendell Phillips, among others. Forces outside the movement contributed substantially to the split; however, as the 1860 debate demonstrated, divisive forces were at work within the movement even before the Civil War.

By 1870 the status of the suffrage issue within movement ideology had shifted dramatically. More conservative and pragmatic activists looked back at prewar convention rhetoric to comment that "the early days of the discussion about woman's position was a period of great agitation in regard to all social problems" (Higginson 1870, 361). In remarks at the annual meeting of the AWSA in 1870, Thomas Wentworth Higginson summed up these conservative attitudes:

> Early in the movement in behalf of women the broad platform of "woman's rights" was adopted. This was all proper and right then, but the progress of reform has developed the fact that suffrage for woman is the key that will unlock to her the doors of social and political equality. (Higginson 1870b, 378)

Higginson's views were reiterated in numerous articles by Henry Blackwell, one of the *Woman's Journal*'s editors (1870a, 1870b, 1870c, 1870d, 1871).

Statements by Elizabeth Cady Stanton in 1848 and 1866 reflect the shift that had occurred. In her first public speech, she eloquently expressed the broad concerns of the woman's rights movement: "woman stands by the side of man, his equal, placed here by her God, to enjoy with him the beautiful earth, which is her home as it is his, having the same sense of right and wrong and looking to the same Being for guidance and support" (*Proceedings* 1870, 3-4). At the

AERA convention in 1866, however, she flatly stated: "we have assembled today to discuss the right and duty of woman to claim and use the ballot" (*Proceedings* 1866, 5).

Movement leaders urged this narrow concentration on woman suffrage on pragmatic grounds. For example, women active in the temperance movement in the 1870s were told to forego support for the Prohibition Party. Fearing that "by espousing Prohibition, Suffragists would array their cause against the immense material forces of money, appetite, and passion" (Blackwell 1875), leaders warned against linking their cause to any political party. Advocates of free love faced blistering attacks from the *Woman's Journal* writers because their ideas "distort[ed] the nature of the movement," provided "ammunition" for anti-suffragists, and "have hindered progress toward enfranchisement" (Blackwell 1873). Less controversial deviations from the demand for suffrage met less extreme, but essentially similar reactions. Movement activists were counseled not to make comments on any topic that might distract attention from the call for the woman's ballot.

In the debate at the national convention in 1860, the forces that would transform the woman's rights movement into a movement for woman suffrage first became visible. If all the speeches are taken into account, it is clear that there was disagreement, but that it did not concern marriage and divorce. The real issue was the nature and direction of the movement itself. The central conflict at this convention was ideological. One faction argued that any issue relevant to the denial of woman's selfhood was appropriate for discussion at a woman's rights convention. Another faction argued that pragmatic concerns should determine movement ideology. When read alone, the speeches of Cady Stanton, Potowski Rose, and Brown [Blackwell] seem to indicate that woman's rights activists held widely differing views of marriage and divorce. However, when the entire debate is considered, disagreements over specific provisions of marriage and divorce laws become minor when compared to the three speakers' agreement regarding the application of natural rights principles to women. The centrality of natural rights ideology in the early woman's rights movement is evident in these three speeches; it was challenged by the narrow pragmatism of Phillips, Garrison, and their supporters. This internal conflict at the 1860 convention foreshadowed the process by which the woman's rights movement would become the woman suffrage movement.

NOTES

1. In 1860, Elizabeth Cady Stanton was invited to address the senate judiciary committee on behalf of the bill; she spoke before an assembly chamber full of curious legislators. Ideologically, the views presented there were identical to those of her speech at the 1860 convention (Stanton 1861). New York changed its laws to permit divorce on grounds other than adultery in 1966.

2. In 1862 the act was amended to lessen women's economic rights, and in 1871, mothers lost the right to joint guardianship of their children (HWS 1:747-749).

3. Potowski Rose made a similar statement at the 1853 convention (HWS 1:579).

4. Some recent scholarship sees the postwar conflict over "the Negro's hour" as having its roots in the 1860 debate (Goodman 1985).

5. Their views are echoed in the rhetoric of Frances E. Willard, discussed in chapter 8. Even the most radical group in the early movement, the National Woman's Party, "failed to analyze carefully the institution which they so instinctively feared, and made no constructive suggestions about how to transform marriage into an 'outlet' for women. . . . Certainly there were feminists within the NWP and outside it in the twenties and thirties who had given these problems serious consideration. But they were isolated from the NWP consensus on the priority of legal and economic goals" (Becker 1975, 440).

6. In her autobiography she wrote:

I was surprised and humiliated to find myself under the ban of his [Phillips's] disapprobation. My face was scarlet, and I trembled with mingled feelings of doubt and fear—doubt as to the wisdom of my position and fear lest the convention should repudiate the whole discussion (Stanton 1898, 218-219).

On 28 May 1860, she wrote to Susan B. Anthony:

With all his excellence and nobility, Wendell Phillips is a man. His words, tone, and manner came down on me like a clap of thunder. We are right, however. . . . Woman's degradation is in man's idea of his sexual rights. Our religion, laws, customs, are all founded on the belief that woman was made for man. Come what will, my whole soul rejoices in the truth that I have uttered. (Stanton and Blatch 1922, 2:79)

7. I am indebted to Charles Conrad (1978; 1981) for this analysis. Phillips's and Garrison's speeches are incomplete in the debate as reprinted in HWS 1:716-740.

8. Sociologists refer to two types of movement constituencies: those who will benefit directly from change, in this case women, are the beneficiary constituency; those who benefit only indirectly, if at all, in this case men, are the conscience constituency. Those distinctions are complicated here because arguably the changes demanded by the woman's rights movement entailed economic and social costs for males (Phillips 1985, 149).

9. There were disagreements, particularly at the national conventions of 1852 and 1853, regarding the extent to which Scripture was the basis for woman's rights and the church the source of her wrongs (HWS 1:535-540, 133-146).

6

Adapting to Males: Addressing State Legislators

Rhetoric addressed primarily to sympathizers at woman's rights conventions was paralleled by efforts to persuade those outside the movement, particularly state legislators, to make the changes sought by movement activists. The speeches of women to state legislatures offer an opportunity to examine how women created a public forum for their cause and how they appealed to males to legislate change.

Direct appeals to state legislators were a natural outcome of early movement activities. Once women in local and national conventions began to define the problems that motivated them to seek change, they realized the significance of the legal disabilities of married women; attempts to obtain legal and economic rights from state legislatures were a logical next step. Such efforts are rhetorically significant because they reveal how women approached those who would not benefit directly from desired changes, and because they indicate how inclusively advocates defined their movement. Also, the need to persuade powerful male politicians in a conspicuous, assertive manner stirred up conflicts among early activists over woman's proper role.

As indicated earlier, the central issue was whether or not women are different from men in some fundamental way, and, consequently, whether legislation should be grounded in such biological or cultural differences, or in a view of women as human beings, identical to their male counterparts. This conflict has pervaded the movement, surfacing not only in the early period but also in the 1920s, as reframed by the equal rights amendment, and in the 1980s, as raised in lawsuits to determine whether employers can be required to offer women employees maternal leave. Both views of woman's nature have had considerable force, but they are not easily combined. As a result, attempts to persuade male legislators compelled women activists to clarify their ideological positions. Like many contemporary feminists, early advocates revealed considerable ambivalence. They argued from woman's femininity — for example, her maternal instincts and her modesty — and, simultaneously, they appealed to natural rights principles to justify demands for women's basic legal rights.

Although many women spoke to state legislatures in support of woman's rights, few texts have survived.[1] For instance, Ernestine Potowski Rose addressed the New York legislature several times, but none of her speeches is extant. Clarina Howard Nichols spoke to legislatures in Vermont and Kansas; only a synopsis of the former speech still exists (Woman's Rights and Wrongs 1852).[2] The lack of surviving texts is easily explained. Some of these speeches were extemporaneous, hence no texts remained in the possession of their authors; moreover, such speeches were delivered in special sessions for which there were no published proceedings. However, the texts that remain are significant because they show a nascent movement struggling to be credible to outsiders, defining its parameters, and seeking to justify limited albeit fundamental reforms. Clarina Howard Nichols's speech of 1852 to the Vermont legislature and Elizabeth Cady Stanton's speeches of 1854 and 1860 to the New York legislature reveal the nature and limits of the rhetorical strategies adopted by influential figures in the woman's rights effort.

Women did not gain access to these important male audiences easily. Typically, the vehicle was a set of petitions demonstrating significant public support for a bill before the legislature. When on December 2, 1852, Clarina Howard Nichols stood before a packed chamber of the Vermont legislature, her presence there was a result of petitions directed to the legislature's education committee. The petitions were signed by more than two hundred prominent businessmen of her town, Brattleboro, supporting passage of a law permitting women to vote in local school district elections. Because the committee chairperson strongly opposed the bill and threatened to table it, a legislator friend persuaded other legislators to pass a resolution of invitation that she come to "present the whole subject of Woman's Rights" (HWS 1:173; Christiansen 1987, 92-98). Similarly, when Elizabeth Cady Stanton spoke to the joint judiciary committees of the New York legislature in 1854, she was there because of ten weeks of petitioning by sixty women, who gathered 5,931 signatures in support of legislation for women's legal rights and 4,164 signatures for woman suffrage. This evidence of public support was the basis on which the legislature permitted her to speak (Gurko 1976, 175-76; HWS 1:612).

Both women faced intense hostility at this intrusion into the exclusively male public sphere. A newspaper editor, with whom Clarina Howard Nichols competed as editor of the *Windham County* (Vermont) *Democrat*, promised to present her with a suit of men's clothing because of what he took to be her "scramble for the breeches" (HWS 1:173). When Judge Cady, Elizabeth's father, discovered that she was to speak before the state legislature, he ordered her not to deliver the speech, threatening to cut her out of his will if she persisted (Lutz 1940, 90, 96). He relented when she read the speech to him, though, and even assisted her with additional legal illustrations for her arguments (Stanton 1898, 187-89).

Both women failed to obtain immediate enactment of the reforms they supported. However, Howard Nichols believed the favorable impression she created was "a great triumph for woman's rights" (HWS 1:174). Similarly, despite the 1854 defeat, in 1860 Cady Stanton spoke to the legislature for a second time, an event followed by legislation improving married women's legal status significantly (HWS 1:686-88). But her subsequent failure to persuade the New York legislature to permit women to vote for delegates to the 1867 state constitutional convention, along with the failure of that convention to give New York women the vote, embittered Cady Stanton, and these failures were one factor in the train of events leading to the movement's schism in 1869 (Stanton 1867).

Like most speeches addressed to legislators, these three addresses were previewed before woman's rights conventions. Howard Nichols had spoken in similar terms at the national woman's rights convention in 1851 in Worcester, Massachusetts (1853); Stanton's 1854 speech was previewed only days before at the woman's rights convention, strategically convened in Albany. After the convention, Susan B. Anthony had 50,000 copies of the speech printed, deposited a copy on the desk of each legislator, and distributed the remainder as pamphlets throughout the state (HWS 1:595). By contrast, Cady Stanton's 1860 speech was delivered to the national woman's rights convention of 1860 several months after it had been delivered before legislators.

Rhetoric has been described as a process "*of adjusting ideas to people and of people to ideas*" (Bryant 1953, 413). The speeches of Clarina Howard Nichols and Elizabeth Cady Stanton illuminate the strategies by which woman's rights advocates appealed to men outside the movement, and the anger and outrage that was evident in what they said despite their attempts at adaptation.

CLARINA HOWARD NICHOLS

Clarina Howard Nichols began her speaking career at the national woman's rights convention in Worcester, Massachusetts, on October 15, 1851. Prior to her first speech she had edited the *Windham County Democrat*. In 1854 she traveled to Kansas, then considered the far West. Her influence on the state's constitutional convention of 1859 was such that Kansas entered the union in 1861 with the most liberal laws relating to women of any state (Gambone 1973, 12-13).

The speech she delivered at the 1851 convention, *The Responsibilities of Woman*, was so well received that it was reprinted as part of the Woman's Rights Tract Series. In its report, the *New York Daily Tribune* commented that she "was altogether the most *womanly* speaker at the Convention" (17 October 1851, 7-8). No text of her 1852 address to the Vermont legislature exists, but Howard Nichols's reminiscences suggest similarities between it and the 1851 convention speech (HWS 1:172). Therefore, the earlier speech can be used to flesh out the relatively brief synopsis which remains from the later speech (Christiansen 1987, 65-88), even though such a procedure is rather risky.

The Responsibilities of Woman is a long, complicated speech. It is noteworthy on several grounds. First, it reversed the issues entirely by talking of "responsibilities" instead of "rights," but it did this so cleverly that rights inevitably entered along with responsibilities. Second, although the speaker claimed to speak extemporaneously, the speech developed so smoothly and gracefully that the claim is suspect — there is much evidence of artistry in its style and argument. Third, the extended examples or short narratives that are the primary form of evidence are of such power that they can properly be called inflammatory; Howard Nichols offered a gentle recitation of tales of vicious abuse. Her provocative use of these extended examples as a way to feminize her role as speaker is another clever reversal.

Although the speech was delivered at a woman's rights convention, it is likely that Howard Nichols addressed an audience that included hostile males (Phillips 1985, 71, 84, 89, 103-06; Wagner 1978, 299, 439). Nearly all woman's rights conventions included a mixture of clergymen and reporters, among whom were committed opponents, some of whom spoke in opposition. Moreover, some treated the activities of these conventions, like other speechmaking, as a source of entertainment and did not hesitate to heckle the speakers and disrupt the meetings. Women who attended also represented a broad range of opinion.

Howard Nichols adapted to hostile and conservative elements in her audience in very complicated ways. First, and most simply, her demands were reformist. She advocated that women educate themselves; she rejected general suffrage for women, but her demands for property rights and joint guardianship of children involved substantial and significant change. These demands were mitigated by a strategic linkage of woman's rights and woman's responsibilities.

Howard Nichols strategically argued that women needed legal rights in order to fulfill their responsibilities as wives and mothers. The crux of that argument was expressed in an analogy drawn from the Bible. This can be seen as a deliberate ploy, because it presents women as helpless and in need of male protection:

> If we are not fitted to be capable wives and mothers, — as contended by a gentlemen on the stand yesterday, — if we make poor brick, it is because our brother man has stolen our straw. Give us back our straw, brothers, — there is plenty of it, — and we will make you *good* brick. Brick we must make — men say so; then *give* us our straw, — we cannot *take* it. (Nichols 1853, 11)

This allusion to the Israelite slaves, whose rations of straw were eliminated by the Egyptians, but who were still required to produce the same amount of brick and were beaten when they could not, was ideal for expressing her reformist position. Women, she said, have responsibilities as wives and mothers; give them the means to fulfill those responsibilities. The analogy also appealed to the commonsensical notion that something cannot be made from nothing; it invoked biblical authority, but indirectly it also called woman's traditional role into question. After all, Jehovah sent Moses to lead the Israelite slaves out of captivity and slavery to independence in the promised land.

These substantive moves were buttressed by her persona as a speaker. She feminized that role to present herself as a traditional woman, with traditional concepts of woman's role, repeatedly reminding her audience that she was "a wife, a mother, a sister, a daughter" (2). She used male authorities and biblical allusions as evidence to support her claims. Numerous examples combining male authority with personal experience attested to the legal problems women faced. Logically, a legal problem that affects one woman can affect any woman. This combination thus served the end of logical argument, while supporting the notion that women learn through personal experience as interpreted by male experts. On another level, she presented extended examples of male behavior so vicious and depraved that the sheer, calm recitation of them amounted to a deadly attack on males. In short, she used a feminized rhetorical role in a highly aggressive way. Under the strategic window dressing of femininity came a thundering denunciation of male treatment of women.

In this speech, Howard Nichols adopted a particularly complex method of appealing to a hostile audience. She abandoned the natural rights position, albeit with some hints of ambivalence, in order to ground her arguments in woman's traditional role. In effect, woman's rights demands became agitation for the means to be good wives and mothers. The changes she advocated were moderately reformist; she presented herself as an advocate of change who nevertheless reaffirmed the traditional female role. At the same time, however, she used evidence drawn from her personal experience to confront the audience with horrifying evidence of the extent of the problem.

Like the 1851 convention speech, her address to the Vermont legislature concerned married women's rights. There was one new element in the second speech that is of interest. According to the synopsis, Howard Nichols argued as follows:

> The holding of property is ranked by our republican governments among inalienable rights, and the reason for so ranking it is to be found in the necessities and responsibilities of the human being, which absorb the entire means created by average energies — in their proper and honorable discharge. In the marriage relation, as proved by actual life, the responsibilities of the parties are equal, though dissimilar; and if the father prove recreant or incompetent, the support and training of the children naturally devolve upon the mother; thus establishing beyond question, her equal right to hold and control means. (Woman's Rights and Wrongs 1852, 4)

In effect, she argued that the right to property was an inalienable right because of the responsibilities faced by all human beings, and she specified as one of those responsibilities that of the mother for her children. She argued that marriage did not deprive women of their necessities and responsibilities as persons, it trebled them. As a result, married women should have property rights, and extending such rights would be beneficial in protecting widows and in providing the means by which women could take over the care of their children when circumstances made it necessary. The synopsis suggests a strong reformist emphasis: Howard Nichols appears to have concentrated on this double argument regarding both the responsibilities of women and the benefits to the community of giving women the means to fulfill their responsibilities under all conditions.

Howard Nichols's synthesis of these two, somewhat contradictory grounds for argument was quite skillful. While affirming that, contrary to the law, women continued to be persons after marriage, she mitigated the force of that claim by arguing that conditions could easily force women to assume responsibilities as heads of households. The frequency with which such conditions had occurred, she continued, and the experiences of women in those circumstances, mandated legal changes protecting a woman's right to fulfill her responsibilities, particularly to her children. It is likely that Howard Nichols was personally ambivalent as well as realistic about the persuasiveness of her arguments. Her personal ambivalence was reflected in her early opposition to woman suffrage; her strategic realism was apparent in the tactics she used in newspaper editorials supporting woman's rights (Christiansen 1987, 69-70).

As seen through the prism of Howard Nichols's speeches, woman's rights advocates defined their movement inclusively: it involved all women and, through their families, all persons. They adapted to outsiders by taking a reformist stance and by appealing for change on the grounds of women's traditional role. They buttressed this with rhetorical efforts to feminize their arguments and appeals; at other times they used material so powerful that its very utterance demanded radical change.

ELIZABETH CADY STANTON

Elizabeth Cady Stanton spoke to committees of the New York legislature in 1854 and 1860 in support of broadening the rights of married women. In 1861 she spoke to legislators in support of increasing the grounds for divorce; in 1867 she urged that women be permitted to vote for delegates to a convention to revise the New York state constitution and that the constitution be altered to give women the franchise. The speeches of 1854, 1861, and 1867 reveal her persuasive skills, but in them she also confronted her hostile audience with blunt truths. On these occasions she spoke on behalf of what were almost surely hopeless causes. In 1860, however, Cady Stanton not only retained her philosophical integrity but moderated somewhat her appeals to legislators, and in that year, the New York legislature passed laws removing the major disabilities of married women. Quite possibly Cady Stanton felt that when she faced intense hostility, prudence was wasted and agitation the order of the day but that when the prize was almost within her grasp, skillful adjustments were appropriate. In any event, there are important contrasts between the speeches she made in 1854 and 1860 regarding the legal disabilities of married women.

Elizabeth Cady Stanton's 1854 speech was a complex mixture of adaptation and confrontation (HWS 1:595-605). On the one hand, she adapted to the legal character of the issues and to the legal training of her audience in order to demonstrate her mastery of the subject, and she adapted to traditional notions of woman to link her cause to women's domestic responsibilities. In these ways her speech resembles those of Clarina Howard Nichols. However, she also pointed to the misogyny lurking behind the statutes defining the legal position of married women, and the tone of her speech revealed the intensity of women's dissatisfaction with their current condition.

Cady Stanton demonstrated her command of the conventions of nineteenth-century oratory by her elevated, dramatic style, including the use of amplification, personification, classical and biblical allusions, parallelism, and metaphor. Her speech began with the flourishes typical of much rhetoric of the period. After quoting an epigram extolling progress, she drew a dramatic picture:

> The tyrant, Custom, has been summoned before the bar of Common Sense. His Majesty no longer awes the multitude — his scepter is broken — his crown is trampled in the dust — the sentence of death is pronounced upon him. All nations, ranks and classes have, in turn, questioned and repudiated his authority; and now, that the monster is chained and caged, timid woman, on tiptoe, comes to look him in the face, and to demand of her brave sires and sons who have struck stout blows for liberty, if, in this change of dynasty, she, too, shall find relief. (595)

She thus portrayed woman's rights as part of an agon, a conflict expressed in dramatic terms. The scene was a courtroom. Custom, personified as a tyrant, has been overthrown. Now that he has been mastered by males, "timid woman" dares petition her male champions for relief.

Cady Stanton's casting of the issue in these dramatic terms was a careful strategic maneuver. The force of evil was Custom, not husbands, fathers, legislators, or males in general. The bar was Common Sense, an appeal to rationality. Those who overthrew the tyrant were males, and woman, in her traditional submissive and modest role, was asking men, in their traditional aggressive, dominant position, for relief, not equality. Cady Stanton's use of drama and personification prepared the audience for logical appeals and suggested that the demands to be made would be modest ones, addressed to the male audience in their traditional roles by a woman in her traditional role.

The speech began vividly in high style, and Cady Stanton's language throughout was consistently elevated. Her first major argument, analyzing the position of woman as woman, developed through an extended parallelism in which each point was made in the parallel form of "we are . . . and yet." A pathetic appeal based on the legal status of widows began, "Behold in yonder humble house a married pair." She amplified her ideas through enumeration of detail; she cited Shakespeare's *Taming of the Shrew*, Plato's *Symposium*, and the Bible as evidence, and she concluded her speech with a brilliant and lofty metaphor.

However, Cady Stanton also recognized that the issue was a legal one and that the committee members were lawyers trained to demand a certain kind of argument and evidence. For that reason, her speech was replete with specific legal citations from the Bill of Rights, the New York state constitution, legal sourcebooks, and other legal authorities. She took no chance that the audience would question her mastery of the details of the issue. She combined this evidence with a rehearsal of the history of the American legal tradition and the principles that underlie it. She recalled the principles energizing the American Revolution and pointed to contradictions in the American system, such as the fact that women were taxed but had no right to vote. She appealed for the right to trial by a jury of one's peers, and traced the history of that right back to rights claimed by Charles I of England.

Cady Stanton appealed to her audience's knowledge of human nature, asking: "Who ever saw a human being that would not abuse unlimited power?" She ended her argument by positing a dilemma. On the one hand, she said, "Admit a radical difference in sex and you demand different spheres — water for fish, air for birds." She followed that with a cruel analogy:

> It is impossible to make the southern planter believe that his slave feels and reasons just as he does. . . . If you can force on his unwilling vision a vivid picture of the negro's wrongs and for a moment touch his soul, his logic brings him instant consolation. He says, the slave does not feel this as I would. Here, gentlemen, is our difficulty: When we plead our cause before the law makers and *savants* of the republic, they cannot take in the idea that men and women are alike. (603-04)[3]

This was the other horn of the dilemma: "But if, gentlemen, you take the ground that the sexes are alike, and, therefore, you are our faithful representatives — then why all these special laws for woman? . . . 'Do unto others as you would have others do unto you.' This, men and brethren, is all we ask at your hands" (604). She thus linked logic, legal and historical evidence, and the Judeo-Christian tradition to make a case for woman's rights.

Adaptation to the audience was evident in the structure of the speech, which was organized in terms of woman's traditional roles — woman as woman (or as person and citizen, the most radical of the categories); then, as wife, widow, and mother. Except for an appeal for woman's rights as citizen and voter, Cady Stanton's efforts, like those of Clarina Howard Nichols, were directed toward legal changes that would enable women to fulfill their duties as wives and mothers more fully and to avoid living out their lives in penury as widows.

Cady Stanton justified more radical appeals in terms of woman's nature as traditionally defined. For instance, appeals for fundamental civil rights, such as the right to trial by a jury of her peers, were linked to women's modesty. She asked, "Shall an erring woman be dragged before a bar of grim-visaged judges, lawyers, and jurors, there to be grossly questioned in public on subjects which women scarce breathe in secret to one another?" (597). She appealed to traditional notions of women's special feelings, of their maternal instincts, even of their special nature. She asked, "Shall laws which come from the logical brain of man take cognizance of violence done to the moral and affectional nature which predominates, as is said, in woman?" (598). She even suggested the desirability of "woman's moral power . . . speak[ing] through the ballot-box" (603).

Such appeals were dangerous because they reinforced the conventional rationales used to justify woman's special sphere and the laws that bound her to it. On the other hand, the appeals exemplify the seductive stratagems that the oppressed are constrained to use when they lack the legal, political, and economic power to effect change. In Cady Stanton's day, only men could vote; only men could enact new laws; only men controlled property and earnings. Male agents of change had to be persuaded to empower women, and such appeals asked them to act in traditional ways to protect traditional womanhood, to act as women's champions to save them from peril and to protect them from evil.

The conclusion of the speech was a masterpiece that fused all her strategies of adaptation while responding to a significant problem the movement faced. Cady Stanton declared: "You may say that the mass of women of this state do not make the demand; it comes from a few sour, disappointed old maids and childless women. You are mistaken; the mass speak through us" (604). Cady Stanton was married with children, and she exploited her "motherly image" throughout her career in order to counteract such charges (Griffith 1984). In addition, she argued systematically and logically that most women contributed to their own and their children's support and, in some instances, to that of their husbands as well. The evidence she pointed to was the numbers of drunkards and vagrants to be found in every village and town, a problem she obviously believed was known and familiar to her audience.

She also asked the legislators to put themselves in the place of married women: "Now, do you *candidly* think these wives do not wish to control the wages they earn — to own the land they buy — the houses they build? to have at their disposal their own children, without being subject to the constant interference and tyranny of an idle, worthless profligate?" (605). Identification of that sort presumed the ability to see women as humans with needs and motives like their own. She asserted that woman's rights advocates spoke not only for the wives of drunkards but also for any woman "who has worked hard all her days," for "the mother, whose only child is bound out for a term of years, against her expressed wishes"; for "all the laboring women . . . who teach in our seminaries, academies and common schools for a miserable pittance; the widows, who are taxed without mercy; the unfortunate ones in our work houses, poor houses and prisons" (605). That list was intended to suggest how widespread were the effects of the laws governing married women.

Finally, she asked, "who are they that we do not now represent?" Her answer was a vivid, dramatic metaphor:

> But a small class of the fashionable butterflies, who, through the short summer days, seek the sunshine and the flowers; but the cool breezes of autumn and the hoary frosts of winter will soon chase all these away; then, they too, will need and seek protection, and through other lips demand, in their turn, justice and equity at your hands. (605)

This was indeed high style, incorporating the apt metaphor of young women as butterflies — beautiful, fragile, and ephemeral. She transformed that metaphor from a compliment into a dire prediction about the fate of those who dismissed the demands of the movement as irrelevant to them. Soon they would be older, they would become wives and mothers and widows, and in their current legal status they would be as capable of dealing with the vicissitudes of their lives as are butterflies in surviving the frosts of winter. It was a striking, dramatic conclusion that exemplified the rhetorical genius of the entire speech.

Despite extensive adaptation to the attitudes of the audience, this speech was also highly confrontational. The analogy between men and slaveowners, previously cited, was a powerful attack on sexism. While Cady Stanton used traditional concepts of woman as the basis of her appeals, she called such concepts into question, as when she contrasted man's logical nature "to the moral and affectional nature which predominates, *as is said*, in woman" (598; emphasis added). Women's anger shone through her words. She said, for example, "Would to God you could know the burning indignation that fills woman's soul when she turns over the pages of your statute books, and sees there how like feudal barons you freemen hold your women" (604). In her conclusion, she asked sarcastically: "Do you suppose that any woman is such a pattern of devotion and submission that she willingly stitches all day for the small sum of fifty cents, that she may enjoy the unspeakable privilege, in obedience to your laws, of paying for her husband's tobacco and rum?" (605).

When discussing the position of woman as widow, Cady Stanton made the most extreme statements of the speech. She said:

> Man has ever manifested a wish that the world should indeed be a blank to the companion whom he leaves behind him. The Hindoo makes that wish a law, and burns the widow on the funeral pile of her husband; but the civilized man, impressed with a different view of the sacredness of life, takes a less summary mode of drawing his beloved partner after him; he does it by the deprivation and starvation of the flesh, and the humiliation and mortification of the spirit. (603)

The sentiments were elegantly stated, but this was a biting, even vicious attack on males. She might have called the tyrant Custom in her introduction, but here he emerges as the implacably misogynist husband, whose laws reflect his desire to dominate his wife even after death.

Even Cady Stanton's supporters recognized that her speech was highly confrontational.[4] She adapted to audience norms in developing logical arguments based on legal evidence and in appealing to men in their traditional male roles to assist women in their traditional female roles. At the same time, though, her speech revealed women's deep commitment to change, their intense anger at their legal condition, and their belief that the motives of males who had made these laws were open to question. Given attitudes at that time, especially among such conservative auditors, it is not surprising that the legislature rejected Cady Stanton's pleas for woman's rights. At least her speech may have succeeded in convincing them that some highly influential women were deeply committed to basic changes in women's legal status.

The proposed legislation was referred to a select committee of the legislature. A key paragraph in its report to the assembly on March 27 reads as follows:

> A higher power than that from which emanates legislative enactment has given forth the mandate that man and woman shall not be equal; that there shall be inequalities by which each in their own appropriate sphere shall have precedence to the other; and each alike shall be superior or inferior as they well or ill act the part assigned them. Both alike are the subjects of Government, equally entitled to its protection; and civil power must, in its enactments, recognize this inequality. We can not obliterate it if we would, and legal inequalities must follow. (HWS 1:616)

That statement revealed the dimensions of the resistance Cady Stanton encountered in attempting to persuade her audience to change the law. In effect, committee members argued that the legislature could not alter an inequality fixed by nature.[5] What is truly remarkable is that major changes were made just six years later, in 1860. Unquestionably, other factors were at work besides the efforts of woman's rights advocates. However, Cady Stanton also spoke to the legislature on that occasion, both in favor of woman suffrage and on behalf of the woman's rights contained in the bill that ultimately passed.[6]

Like its predecessor, the style of Cady Stanton's 1860 speech was elevated, and metaphors played a key role in it. There were, however, two key shifts. The 1860 speech was grounded in natural rights philosophy; no attempt was made to base appeals on traditional notions of woman's nature or sphere. As a result, the speech made a clear, direct demand for equality, which was a radical stance. However, the speech was somewhat less confrontational than the 1856 address: it made no direct attributions of motive to any group of males, it mitigated its attacks on males, and it appealed positively to legislators to act to make the nation more fully a republic.

The speech's lengthy conclusion told the story of a competition in ancient Athens over which of two statues of the goddess Minerva should grace a temple constructed in her honor. The story became an extended metaphor designed to praise the "new women" of the day:

> brave, courageous, self-reliant and independent . . . who, in the face of adverse winds, have kept one steady course upward and onward in the paths of virtue and peace — they who have taken their gauge of womanhood from their own native strength and dignity . . . who have learned for themselves the will of God concerning them. (*Proceedings* 1860, 45-46)

The conclusion illustrated once again Cady Stanton's ability to use metaphor as the basis of argument and to produce a peroration worthy of the most skilled orator of her time. In contrast to the 1854 conclusion, substantively this conclusion was a positive affirmation rather than a grim warning, for it urged legislators to raise this new woman to her rightful place.

The 1860 speech began not with a dramatic tableau but with a rather straightforward exposition of the concept of natural rights, followed by the argument that no one's rights need be abridged in order to extend civil rights to women. None of her appeals was grounded in traditional views of woman's nature, although she caustically commented:

> you are not yet prepared for any thing more than a partial legislation, believing, as you do, that womanhood is such a subtle essence of frivolities and contradictions that it needs some special code of laws to meet its exigencies, on the low ground of expediency and precedent must we plead our cause. (36)

She continued, in a move similar to that of her 1854 speech, to suggest that men found it hard to identify with women's wrongs. Here, however, she drew an analogy not between men and slaveowners but between women and slaves. In one memorable paragraph, she combined a legal argument with a description that amplified and underscored her point. She said:

> Allow me just here to call the attention of that party so much interested in the slave of the Carolinas, to the similarity in his condition and that of the mothers, wives, and daughters of the Empire State. The negro has no name. He is Cuffy Douglas or Cuffy Brooks, just whose Cuffy he may chance to be. The woman has no name. She is Mrs. Richard Roe or Mrs. John Doe, just whose Mrs. she may chance to be. Cuffy has no right to his earnings; he cannot buy or sell, or lay up anything that he can call his own. Mrs. Roe has no right to her earnings; she can neither buy nor sell, make contracts, nor lay up anything that she can call her own. (37)

Although these comparisons forcefully asserted legal similarities between white women and Afro-American male slaves, they constituted a somewhat less direct attack on her male auditors.

Cady Stanton responded to the argument that women would be contaminated by exposure to the polls by lifting the veil on family life in ways that might well have offended notions of Victorian modesty.

> Now, gentlemen, do you talk to woman of a rude jest or jostle at the polls, where noble, virtuous men stand ready to protect her person and her rights, when, alone in the darkness and solitude and gloom of night, they have [sic] trembled on their own thresholds, awaiting the return of husbands from their midnight

revels? — when, stepping from her chamber, she has beheld her royal monarch, her lord and master, — her legal representative, — the protector of her property, her home, her children and her person, down on his hands and knees slowly crawling up the stairs? Behold him in her chamber — *in her bed*! (41)

This was traditional womanhood with a vengeance, and as in the earlier speech, her satiric tone is evident.

Near the end of the 1860 speech, Cady Stanton added material refuting arguments made in the legislative committee reports of 1854 and 1856, which alleged the impotence of legislators to repeal the laws of God and nature. In a series of clever rhetorical devices, she stated the opposing position ("But, say you, God has appointed woman's sphere; it is His will that she is as she is" [41]), and then stated an opposing claim ("Well, if that be so, then woman will be kept in her sphere by God's laws" [41]). She then supported her position with an allusion to a popular authority ("It is folly, said Daniel Webster, to rënact [sic] God's laws" [41]), and an example ("You might as well pass laws to keep Venus, the beautiful morning star, from refreshing herself by an occasional promenade on the broad belt of Saturn" [41]). She concluded with a series of comparisons, reminding her audience of the varied conditions of women in Turkey ("enervated and voluptuous by confinement . . . in the Turkish harem"); Switzerland and Germany ("exhausted by toil and out-door labor"); China ("her feet compressed in iron boots"); Christian America ("standing all day in the intense heat of a summer's sun in the cotton field and rice plantation"); England ("with the crown and scepter ruling the mightiest nation on the globe"); and India ("burning on the funeral pile of her husband" [42]).

Sarcastic comments provided the most confrontational moments in the speech. For example, as part of the natural rights argument, she commented: "We may safely trust the shrewd selfishness of the white man, and consent to life under the same broad code where he has so comfortably ensconced himself" (39). A little later, she stated:

In pity for man, we would no longer hang like a millstone round his neck. Undo what man did for us in the dark ages, and strike out all special legislation for us; strike the name, *woman*, from all your constitutions, and then, with fair sailing, let us sink or swim, live or die, survive or perish together. (44)

Such moments hint at less than admirable motives, and drip with irony; yet a distinction of sorts can be made between such statements and the blazing attacks of the earlier speech.

CONCLUSION

In her speech before the Vermont legislature, Clarina Howard Nichols used stories as her only vehicle for confronting the audience. In other ways, she feminized the role of rhetor and appealed to the traditional values underlying "true womanhood." By contrast, Elizabeth Cady Stanton was highly confrontational, particularly in 1854, and made few efforts to feminize her role or adapt to audience beliefs about women. Where such adaptations existed, the overall tone of the speeches mocked them. The two Cady Stanton speeches discussed in this chapter were also stronger in tone than those she delivered at Seneca Falls or in the 1860 convention debate. It is as if she was kinder to movement sympathizers than to outsiders, no matter how powerful or important they were. Finally, despite great differences in tone, in these speeches Cady Stanton shared with Lucretia Coffin Mott a commitment to the scholarly use of evidence, as in the 1849 speech explored in chapter 3. In Coffin Mott's case, that evidence was predominantly scriptural; in Cady Stanton's case, it was predominantly legal.

Clarina Howard Nichols played a small but significant role in the early movement. She began her work for woman's rights in 1847 by writing a series of articles for the Windham County *Democrat*, in which she deplored the legal and economic disabilities of married women, and applauded a recent bill granting married women the right to inherit, own, and bequeath property. Subsequent to her speech to the Vermont legislature in 1852, she began a career as a lecturer in New England, and between 1850 and 1854 she spoke at eight different woman's rights and temperance conventions. She met Susan B. Anthony at the national woman's rights convention at Syracuse, New York, in 1852, developing a close friendship that lasted until Howard Nichols's death in 1885. In 1854 she moved to the far West as part of the effort to make Kansas a free state. As Kansas approached statehood, she campaigned for the inclusion of woman's rights clauses in its constitution, and when the constitutional convention met in 1859, she lobbied tirelessly, ultimately addressing the convention by invitation at a special session. As a result of her influence, Kansas entered the Union with the most liberal laws relating to women of any state, including property rights, equal guardianship of children, and the right to vote in school district elections. In 1867, Howard Nichols joined Anthony and others in the unsuccessful Kansas referendum campaign for woman suffrage, which ended her participation in movement activities. In ill health, she moved to California and remained a correspondent for a number of Kansas and New England newspapers, writing on activities related to woman's rights until her death.

NOTES

1. In addition to the speeches indicated in the text, HWS indicates that Mary Upton Ferrin addressed the judiciary committee of the Massachusetts legislature in 1850 (HWS 1:213); Cady Stanton addressed the legislature in January of 1853 advocating divorce for drunkenness; Lucy Stone spoke that year in Boston to the Massachusetts constitutional convention calling for revisions that would eliminate the word "male" wherever it appeared; Amelia Jenks Bloomer was invited to appear before the Nebraska house of representatives in 1856; and Stone and Wendell Phillips appeared before the Massachusetts legislature in 1857 to present petitions for woman suffrage (HWS 1:258-59).

2. Some textual material remains from women's abolitionist efforts before state legislatures. Angelina Grimké spoke on slavery to a committee of the Massachusetts legislature in 1838; as noted in chapter 1, a partial text survives. Prior to 1840, Lucretia Coffin Mott also spoke on slavery to the legislatures of Delaware, New Jersey, and Pennsylvania; no texts survive.

3. Frederick Douglass praised the speech but criticized "the seeming assumption for woman, which it contains, of superiority over negroes" in her protest against classifying women "with idiots, lunatics, and negroes" (Foner 1976, 73-74).

4. Those attending the woman's rights convention in Albany recognized this mixture of adaptation and confrontation. The convention adopted the address by only a slim majority (*New York Tribune*, 29 March 1854), and in a letter of 29 March 1854 to Cady Stanton, Sarah Grimké said the speech was "too caustic" (Wagner 1978, 320).

5. A similar bill was rejected in 1856. On that occasion, the report of the judiciary committee concluded "that, if there is any inequality in the case, the gentlemen are the sufferers." Also, noting instances in which both the husband and the wife had signed petitions in support of the bill, the report recommended that the parties "apply for a law authorizing them to change dresses, so that the husband may wear petticoats, and the wife the breeches, and thus indicate to their neighbors and the public the true relation in which they stand to each other" (HWS 1:629-30).

6. HWS is inaccurate about the date on which the speech was given. According to the *New York Times* of March 21, 1860, p. 5, column 2, she spoke on March 20. No copy of this text exists in Cady Stanton's papers in the Library of Congress; no part of the text was printed in New York newspapers or as part of the records of the New York legislature. The text in HWS 1:679-85 is incomplete. A complete text of the speech as delivered in May at the tenth national woman's rights convention is found in the convention proceedings (*Proceedings* 1860, 34-46). According to one biography of Cady Stanton, she entitled this speech "A Slave's Appeal" (Griffith 1984, 101).

7

Seeking a Judicial Route to Suffrage: Anthony in Behalf of Herself

The speech that is the focus of this chapter constitutes a special kind of appeal to males. The speech itself, delivered many times, is so important as a rhetorical act and in relation to the movement that it merits a separate chapter, but the rhetorical concerns it highlights are related to those featured in the last chapter. Quite simply, how did this famous woman activist, barred from speaking in court, defend herself against the criminal charge of voting illegally?

By 1872 Susan B. Anthony had emerged as a major force in efforts for woman's rights and woman suffrage. From the time that she met Elizabeth Cady Stanton in 1852, she devoted her energies to woman's rights, temperance, and the abolition of slavery. She toured with Cady Stanton in Kansas in 1867 in support of the state referenda on black male and woman suffrage; together they brought the *Revolution* into being in 1868 and they formed the National Woman Suffrage Association in 1869. By the time of these speeches of self-defense, she was a prominent speaker who lectured all over the country. She was a prime mover in the merger of the two rival woman suffrage organizations into the National American Woman Suffrage Association (NAWSA), and she assumed leadership of NAWSA from 1892-1901. Although more conservative in her views than Cady Stanton, her decision to vote in 1872, her defense of her action, and her trial made her a hero to the young radicals of the National Woman's Party of the 1910s and 20s.

Because of their extraordinary contributions to abolitionism and to the Union's cause in the Civil War (Flexner 1959, 105-12, 142-55), woman's rights advocates expected to be given the vote as a reward. Instead, they were told that it was "the Negro's hour," and when in 1868 the Fourteenth Amendment was ratified, for the first time, the word "male" appeared in the United States Constitution. An effort to insert the word "sex" into the Fifteenth Amendment failed. As a result, unless women could gain the franchise through the courts or through a declaratory act of Congress, their only route to suffrage would be the difficult one of a federal amendment. Thus, as an act of desperation, Susan B. Anthony registered and voted in the election of 1872 and thereafter was compelled to defend herself rhetorically.

Anthony voted in Rochester, New York, on November 5; on November 18 she was arrested and pled not guilty. Immediately after her arrest, Anthony began a speaking tour of Monroe County, the county in which she would be tried and from which the panel of jurors would be drawn. The prosecuting attorney requested and gained a change of venue, and the trial was delayed and moved to Canandaigua in neighboring Ontario county. During the twenty-two days between the change of venue and her trial on June 17, 1873, Anthony spoke twenty-one times to potential jurors, and, with the help of Matilda Joslyn Gage, her case was made to audiences in every postal district in the county. She had no opportunity to speak in her own defense at the trial — the judge ruled that she was not competent to bear witness. When she did attempt to speak, prior to sentencing, and began the arguments she had made to the public, she was silenced by the judge (HWS 2:629-90).

Susan Anthony was not the first woman to register or to vote, nor was she the first to argue that citizenship, now clearly defined for the first time in the Fourteenth Amendment, entailed the franchise. Efforts along these lines began in England in 1867 and continued in the United States until the issue was finally decided by the Supreme Court in 1875. The *Revolution*, for which Anthony was business manager, published reports of these activities and of the arguments made in their support; therefore, Anthony was in an ideal position to adapt these ideas to her specific case in order to persuade those who would render a verdict on it. Three of the earlier attempts to enfranchise women are of particular significance in evaluating Anthony's speech: (1) the resolutions, with supporting arguments, developed by Francis Minor and adopted by the Missouri Woman Suffrage Association; (2) the Victoria Claflin Woodhull memorial*; and (3) the case brought

---

*Memorials are statements of fact or petitions addressed to a legislative body or an executive, usually justified by speeches in their support.

by women in the District of Columbia and argued by attorneys Albert G. Riddle and Francis Miller.

A Missouri lawyer, Francis Minor, first saw the significance of the Fourteenth Amendment for woman suffrage and developed arguments that played a central role in Anthony's speech. At the Missouri Woman Suffrage Convention in St. Louis in October, 1869, Minor presented six resolutions that were adopted by the convention. These resolutions, together with a speech by his wife Virginia Minor, president of the Missouri association, were forwarded to the *Revolution*, printed, and "ten thousand extra copies . . . were . . . sent to friends throughout the country, laid on every member's desk in Congress, and circulated at the Washington [NWSA] Convention of 1870" (HWS 2:411).

Minor's resolutions were simple. They claimed that citizenship was national in character; that while states might set qualifications for voting, they had no power to deprive any group of the franchise; that laws depriving women of the vote were unconstitutional because states were prohibited from making or enforcing laws abridging the privileges and immunities of citizenship; and that because naturalization was expressly withheld from the states, the right to deprive any person of the franchise must also be withheld. All were derived directly from the language of the Fourteenth Amendment, and "on this interpretation the officers of the National Association began soon after to base their speeches, resolutions and hearings before Congress, and to make divers attempts to vote in different parts of the country" (HWS 2:407). Anthony's decision to vote and her speech of self-defense were part of this larger effort.

On December 19, just prior to the 1871 convention of the National Woman Suffrage Association, Victoria Claflin Woodhull presented a memorial to the Congress, which was referred to the congressional judiciary committees. On January 12, Claflin Woodhull appeared before the House Judiciary Committee to present the arguments on which she based her plea that Congress pass "such laws as in the wisdom of Congress shall be necessary and proper for carrying into execution the right vested by the Constitution in the citizens of the United States to vote, without regard to sex" (HWS 2:444-48; Woodhull 1871). Anthony was present for the speech and took part in the committee discussion that followed. Anthony also heard the speech that attorney Albert G. Riddle made in support of Claflin Woodhull's memorial. The Committee on the Judiciary rejected Claflin Woodhull's memorial, but William Loughridge and Benjamin F. Buter produced a detailed, carefully argued minority report, and it, too, provided Anthony with arguments and evidence that she would incorporate into her defense of her right to vote.

A third significant set of events occurred later in 1871, when seventy women in the District of Columbia attempted first to register and then to vote. Their suit against the Board of Inspectors was brought in the Supreme Court of the District in October 1871. Albert G. Riddle and Francis Miller, distinguished lawyers and advocates of woman suffrage, were retained by the plaintiffs. Riddle and Miller argued that the franchise was a natural right, that women had always had the right to vote under English common law, and that the definition of citizenship in the Fourteenth Amendment, together with the prohibition against denial of a pre-existing right in the Fifteenth Amendment, demonstrated the right of women to vote. The case was lost; Chief Justice Cartter delivered the opinion of the court. An appeal was made to the United States Supreme Court, which refused to hear the case, thereby affirming Cartter's decision (HWS 2:599-600). Anthony referred to this case and to Judge Cartter in her speech.

ANTHONY'S SPEECH

Susan B. Anthony's speech defending her vote in the 1872 election is a curiosity because it is a forensic speech that was never given in a courtroom (Anthony 1874, 151-78; Harper 1898; 2:977-92; HWS 2:630-47)[1]. Yet to understand what kind of rhetorical act it was, how it worked to achieve its ends, and why it stands as a persuasive masterpiece, it must be viewed as an example of forensic rhetoric (Arnold 1958; Black 1943; Brigance 1943; Howell and Hudson 1943; Maloney 1947, 1955; Mills 1942, 1943; Sanbonmatsu 1971). Such a speech characteristically is addressed to an audience of jurors, concerns past events, develops via accusation and defense, involves refutation, and pivots on the issue of justice. Because arguments in such a speech are based on law, they tend to be deductive and are usually cast in a middle style.

From the outset, Anthony made it clear that she was speaking as a defendant to peers who had to decide whether or not she had committed a crime. She began:

> *Friends and Fellow-citizens*: I stand before you to-night, under indictment for the alleged crime of having voted at the last Presidential election, without having a lawful right to vote. It shall be my work this evening to prove to you that in thus voting, I not only committed no crime, but, instead, simply exercised my

citizen's right, guaranteed to me and all United States citizens by the National
Constitution, beyond the power of any State to deny. (Anthony 1874, 151)

Anthony admitted that she had voted, but insisted the issue was whether
or not that action was criminal. She developed her case deductively, and
her plea for justice was based on three principles fundamental to what she
referred to, again and again, as "our democratic republican government."
These were natural rights principles: (1) that persons have rights as
persons, rights are not conferred on them by governments; (2) that
government is a compact to protect citizens' rights; and (3) that all
government rests on the consent of the governed, expressed through the
franchise. Each of these principles was supported from the written law or
its equivalent: the Declaration of Independence, the U.S. Constitution,
the Articles of Confederation, writings of the framers of the Constitution,
opinions of Supreme Court justices and New York state judges, and the
New York constitution and New York state statutes. These sources affirmed the premises from which she argued, and they were the major
forms of evidence used in the speech. They were also the kind of evidence
most appropriate for forensic decision making.

Four kinds of argument recurred in the speech, all of which were
insistently deductive: (1) arguments from legal priority, for example,
that laws granting women citizenship and its privileges took
precedence over laws limiting the vote to males; (2) arguments from
consistency or noncontradiction, that is, laws which required women
to assume the obligations of citizenship ought to extend them the
privileges as well; (3) arguments from authority or legal precedent, for
example a Supreme Court decision which treated male pronouns as
generic and inclusive of women; and (4) arguments from logical entailment, namely that given natural rights principles, the franchise is
entailed in the very concept of citizenship.

The argument from legal priority addressed the question of which
part of the written law should be deemed applicable to Anthony's case.
Early in the speech, Anthony considered the section of the New York
state constitution that stated: "Every male citizen of the age of twenty-one years, & c., shall be entitled to vote" (156). The statement would
appear to be grounds for prohibiting women from voting. But Anthony
turned to other sections of the New York constitution to reach a
different conclusion. She began by citing Article 1, a direct prohibition
against disfranchisement: "No member of this State shall be dis-
franchised or deprived of the rights or privileges secured to any citizen
thereof, unless by the law of the land or the judgment of his peers." In

addition, the New York constitution specified who might not vote (those "convicted of bribery, larceny or any infamous crime"), but it stated that neither "being kept at any alms house, or other asylum, at public expense, nor being confined at any public prison, shall deprive a person of his residence, and hence his vote" (156).

Because of these other provisions, Anthony argued that the omission of the adjective "female" in the constitutional description of voters was of no consequence. She concluded:

> "The law of the land," is the United States Constitution: and there is no provision in that document that can be fairly construed into a permission to the States to deprive any class of their citizens of their right to vote. Hence New York can get no power from that source to disfranchise one entire half of her members. Nor has "the judgment of their peers" been pronounced against women exercising their right to vote; no disfranchised person is allowed to be judge or juror—and none but disfranchised persons can be women's peers; nor has the legislature passed laws excluding them on account of idiocy or lunacy; nor yet the courts convicted them of bribery, larceny, or any infamous crime. Clearly, then, there is no constitutional ground for the exclusion of women from the ballot-box in the State of New York. (157)

The question was whether or not the statement about male voters should be taken at face value. Anthony rejected that view by placing the statement in the context of legal principles with greater force and wider compass. The conflict between the narrow provision for male suffrage and the more encompassing principles defining the rights of citizenship had to be resolved in favor of the larger principles, which, she argued, supported her position.

A second form of argument, more common but closely related, was argument from inconsistency or contradiction. The most noteworthy example concerned the issue of the generic pronoun. Anthony said:

> But, it is urged, the use of the masculine pronouns *he*, *his*, and *him*, in all the constitution and laws, is proof that only men were meant to be included in their provisions. If you insist on this version of the letter of the law, we shall insist that you be consistent, and accept the other horn of the dilemma, which would compel you to exempt women from taxation for the support of the government, and from penalties for the violation of laws. (160)

Anthony dramatized this inconsistency in one of the few moments of emotional appeal in her speech—the pathetic story of the "Pixley Sisters," who formed a theatrical company to support themselves but who, of course, could not vote: "Yet every night a United States officer stretched out his long fingers, and clutched six dollars of the proceeds of those orphan girls, who, but a few years before, were half starvelings in the streets of Olympia [Washington]" (160).

Anthony cited examples of women who had protested such taxation without representation by refusing to pay taxes. Finally, she applied the argument to herself:

> The same with the law of May 31st, 1870, the 19th section of which I am charged with having violated; not only are all the pronouns masculine, but everybody knows that the particular section was intended expressly to hinder the rebels from voting. It reads: "If any person shall knowingly vote without *his* having a lawful right," &c. (161)

She reported that, in her case, the Clerk of Court had changed all the pronouns, and commented: "I insist if government officials may thus manipulate the pronouns to tax, fine, imprison and hang women, women may take the same liberty with them to secure to themselves their right to a voice in the government" (162). The argument from consistency turned the tables on the opposition with this calm but deadly move.

Arguments from authority were common, but Anthony's most interesting was the extension of the argument on male and female pronouns. She used the Supreme Court opinion in *Silver v. Ladd*, December 1868, to demonstrate the generic character of male pronouns. She quoted the Court as saying:

> "In construing a benevolent statute of the government, made for the benefit of its own citizens, inviting and encouraging them to settle on its distant public lands, the words 'single man,' and 'unmarried man' may, especially if aided by the context and other parts of the statute, be taken in a generic sense. Held, accordingly, that the fourth section of the Act of Congress, of September 27th, 1850 . . . embraced within the term *single man* an *unmarried woman*." (163)

This was, of course, also an appeal to treat such pronouns consistently.

Finally, arguments from logical entailment were fundamental to Anthony's stance, because her entire defense was based on the position that citizenship entailed the franchise. The transition she made from discussion of the Fourteenth Amendment to discussion of the Fifteenth Amendment revealed that the address was not only organized deductively, but structured like a legal brief to explore all possible grounds for justifying her act of voting. The approach she followed is called a "method of residues," in which a series of justifications is presented, such that if the audience rejects the first, a second follows, and if that is rejected, a third emerges, and so forth. Anthony said:

> But, however much the doctors of the law may disagree, as to whether people
> and citizens, in the original constitution, were one and the same, or whether the
> privileges and immunities in the fourteenth amendment include the right of
> suffrage, the question of the citizen's right to vote is settled forever by the
> fifteenth amendment. "The citizen's right to vote shall not be denied by the
> United States, nor any State thereof; on account of race, color, or previous
> condition of servitude." How can the State deny or abridge the right of the
> citizen, if the citizen does not possess it? There is no escape from the conclusion,
> that to vote is the citizen's right, and the specifications of race, color, or previous
> condition of servitude can, in no way, impair the force of the emphatic assertion,
> that the citizen's right shall not be denied or abridged. (169)

This final argument of the speech, concerning the Fifteenth Amendment,
included the most daring claims in the speech.

Anthony began making these daring claims by saying:

> But if you will insist that the fifteenth amendment's emphatic interdiction
> against robbing United States citizens of the right to vote "on account of race,
> color or previous condition of servitude," is a recognition of the right, either of
> the United States, or any State, to rob citizens of that right, for any or all other
> reasons, I will prove to you that the class of citizens for which I now plead, and
> to which I belong, may be, and are, by all the principles of our government, and
> many laws of the States, included under the term "previous condition of
> servitude." (170-71)

The argument that followed was severely logical. Slavery was defined by
laws that governed slaves in the states of the South. Then, for each facet
of the definition, Anthony showed that women were or had been in a
similar position. The married woman, like the slave, had (or had had) no
right to control of her person, her earnings, the custody of her children,
and no ability to sue or be sued. To demonstrate that all women, not just
married women, were included, she returned to her opening natural rights
arguments, that all women were "taxed without representation, governed
without their consent, tried, convicted and punished without a jury of their
peers" (174). This was no analogy: it was a claim of the *legal* identity of
slaves and women.

Not only were her arguments deductively derived from fundamental
political principles, but these principles were tied to vivid historical
allusions and evocations of patriotic values. Anthony connected the
current struggles of women with past struggles against oppression in
the American Revolutionary War, the Civil War, the Protestant Reformation, and even the struggle of British lords against the king as
codified in Magna Charta. For example, immediately after the argument cited above, that women were taxed without representation and
governed without their consent, she said:

And is all this tyranny any less humiliating and degrading to women under our democratic-republican government to-day than it was to men under their aristocratic, monarchical government one hundred years ago? ... What was the three-penny tax on tea, or the paltry tax on paper and sugar to which our revolutionary fathers were subjected, when compared with the taxation of the women of this republic? (174)

Similarly, she concluded her argument about the inability of states to disfranchise citizens with this appeal to Union and abolitionist values:

I admit that prior to the rebellion, by common consent, the right to enslave, as well as to disfranchise both native and foreign born citizens, was conceded to the States. But the one grand principle, settled by the war and the reconstruction legislation, is the supremacy of national power to protect the citizens of the United States in their right to freedom and the elective franchise, against any and every interference on the part of the several States. (176)

Earlier, when discussing basic principles, she referred to them as

declarations of the framers of this government, every one of which was based on the immutable principle of equal rights to all. By those declarations, kings, priests, popes, aristocrats, were all alike dethroned, and placed on a common level, politically, with the lowliest born subject or serf. By them, too, men, as such, were deprived of their divine right to rule, and placed on a political level with women. (153)

Listeners were urged, in this appeal, to associate the alleged prerogatives of males with the discredited claims to special prerogatives of kings, popes, and aristocrats and, hence, to view them as equally illegitimate.

Even a brief survey of Anthony's arguments, evidence, and appeals demonstrates how fully the speech exemplified the qualities of the forensic genre. It was a legal brief developed through deductive arguments based on appeals to fundamental, shared values. It accused those who had arrested her and those who denied women citizens the right to vote, and it defended her act of voting as just and right. Most fundamentally, it argued that justice could be done only if she were acquitted and if it were recognized that female citizens had the same rights as their male counterparts.

Like other great forensic addresses in the Anglo-American tradition, Anthony appealed to her audiences to transcend their role as jurors, at least as narrowly defined, to reach a verdict that would make new law.[2] Like Antigone, Anthony was in a situation in which the law as written made her a criminal. She had to appeal to a higher law, in this case to the principle that citizenship entailed the franchise, which was based on the natural rights philosophy underlying democratic-republican government. She asked her audiences of potential jurors, in effect, to make law, to act as legislators and to give women the vote because that would be consistent with true justice. Her speech probed the intent of the written law and contrasted intention with application.

As in so many great forensic addresses, structure was a primary factor. Anthony's speech was structured deductively to show that citizenship entailed the franchise. It was also structured so that if the audience rejected one reason, another would follow: if one rejected natural rights, one had to confront the principles of the United States Constitution; if one clung to the section referring to male voters, one had to confront the contradictions posed by other sections of the New York state constitution; if one rejected these, one had to deal with the definition of citizenship in the Fourteenth Amendment and the limitations on state action against voting citizens in the Fifteenth. Finally, if all these were dismissed, one was confronted with the astonishing notion that because women had been or were in a legal position identical to that of slaves, they were enfranchised by the Fifteenth Amendment. These diverse arguments were linked together because all were based on the three fundamental principles of natural rights philosophy. Moreover, in order to reject Anthony's arguments, one had to be prepared to reject almost the whole of Western political history.

Anthony's speech was not only a legal brief that exhausted the arguments for woman suffrage, it was also structured to rise to a climax. The speech moved from legal definitions to their impact on real women and, finally, to the argument that the legal condition of women in the United States had been or was equivalent to that of slaves, the lowliest of all humans. This dramatic climax linked the narrow issue of woman suffrage to the wide range of issues encompassed under the phrase "woman's rights." The final argument, based on the Fifteenth Amendment and the structure into which it was fitted, was Anthony's major claim to originality. All the other arguments she developed had been rehearsed in the earlier events noted above; this argument alone was new. In addition, as she developed it, it was a unique instance in which the broad range of woman's rights concerns that characterized the movement from 1835 to 1861 was shown to be integrally related to the narrower issue of woman suffrage that became the movement's focus after the war.

Like other great forensic orators, Anthony fused the logic of her arguments, her appeals to cultural values and principles, and the force of her own character. She integrated logic and feeling both in rational arguments developed from historically powerful premises and in dramatic instances illustrating the inconsistency between the principles of democracy and their application to women. Since the defendant spoke on her own behalf, acting, in effect, as her own advocate, her character (*ethos*) or credibility was inseparable from her arguments and her appeals. She was the proof of the claims she made, and male voters were compelled to ask themselves, should anyone who could give such a speech be barred from voting because of her sex?

In contrast to those whose efforts had preceded her, Anthony was in a uniquely favorable position in this case. Unlike other women who attempted to gain the franchise through the courts, Anthony had three significant advantages: first, she was a well-known, public person; second, she was a defendant rather than a plaintiff; and third, she was speaking in her own behalf. Each of these circumstances contributed to Anthony's ability to influence potential jurors in the upstate New York counties of Monroe and Ontario.

Anthony was a well-known lecturer who had spoken throughout the United States. In fact, between the time of her indictment by the federal grand jury and her trial in Canandaigua, she traveled extensively, as one biographer explains:

[although she] was technically in the custody of the United States Marshal, who objected to her leaving Rochester, she managed to carry out a full schedule of lectures in Ohio, Indiana, and Illinois, and also the usual annual Washington and New York woman suffrage conventions at which she told the story of her voting, her arrest, and her pending trial, and where she received enthusiastic support. (Lutz 1959, 204)

In mid-1871 she made a lecture tour that included most states in the West and Midwest. She wrote in her diary on January 1, 1872: "6 months of constant travel, full 8,000 miles, 180 lectures. The year's work full 13,000 miles travel—170 meetings" (Lutz 1959, 191). She also lectured for the Republican party in the East during the 1872 presidential campaign, and she was a well-known speaker throughout New York state (Harper 1898, 1:264, 272, 381, 401; 2:993).

Anthony was known as a committed reformer, a temperance worker and abolitionist, as well as a worker for woman's rights and woman suffrage. Her family had been a force in the Rochester community for many years, and two of her brothers had become important citizens of Kansas; Daniel owned a newspaper and was mayor of Leavenworth (Lutz 1959, 108). As a result of the prominence of her family and of her national reputation, her words had a special authority and credibility: she was heard and listened to as other women were not. In addition, her case received attention and commentary from all over the nation.

In all other cases in which women sought the franchise through the courts, women were the plaintiffs, and Anthony expected to be placed in that position. However, her wise planning altered the situation. Because she promised to pay any court costs or fines incurred by the registrars, she was permitted to register and vote. Other women had to sue for the right to vote; Anthony was arrested for exercising the franchise. As she said in her speech: "But, friends, when . . . I went to the ballot-box, last November, and exercised my citizen's right to vote, the courts did not wait for me to appeal to them—they appealed to me, and indicted me on the charge of having voted illegally" (159). As a result, she was able to capitalize on her position and on that of the other women who voted with her. Indeed, the press reported: "The majority of these law-breakers were elderly, matronly-looking women with thoughtful faces, just the sort one would like to see in charge of one's sick-room, considerate, patient, kindly" (Harper 1898, 1:428).

Those who sued for the franchise acted aggressively and publicly in violation of the norms of femininity; by contrast, Anthony appeared to be the victim of federal power, a position altogether consistent with the traditional female role. Although public speaking itself was a violation of feminine norms, speaking in one's own defense was more acceptable.

CONCLUSION

Anthony was tried, found guilty, and fined one hundred dollars. Yet given the obstacles she faced, her persuasive success remains noteworthy. The prosecutor's request for a change of venue demonstrated her effect on potential jurors in Monroe County. The judge's refusal to allow her to testify in her own behalf was further evidence of the power of her arguments. Moreover, the judge's refusal to allow the jury to deliberate or vote, and his decision to direct a guilty verdict, implied his fear of her persuasive impact on jurors in Ontario County; the statements of some jurors appear to justify his fear (HWS 2:689). The fine was puny, and no attempt was ever made to collect it, despite Anthony's defiant statement in court that she would never pay it. Ultimately, the registrars who allowed her to vote received a presidential pardon. The chivalry of Anthony's lawyer in paying her bail and the refusal of the court to confine her until the fine was paid deprived her of the opportunity to appeal her case to the Supreme Court on a writ of habeas corpus. Instead, the suit by Virginia Minor against the Missouri registrars went forward and was rejected by the Supreme Court in 1875. While it is dubious that Anthony would have been successful in gaining woman suffrage through the courts, her case would have been a more difficult one for the Supreme Court to adjudicate.

Anthony's speech illustrated the rhetorical power of a combination of character, circumstance, and argument. Anthony was uniquely suited to make this case; the situation in which she found herself was such that she could make the best possible case; and she was able, because of her position and her abilities, to bring all the arguments of others to bear on her defense. When viewed this way, it is easy to see possible analogies: the unique opportunity offered Dr. Martin Luther King, Jr., when he found himself in Birmingham jail, in receipt of a letter from white clergymen criticizing his form of protest (Fulkerson 1979; Snow 1985); the unique opportunity offered Abraham Lincoln when at Cooper Union he addressed the issue of whether or not the framers of the Constitution approved of slavery (Leff and Mohrmann 1974; Mohrmann and Leff 1974). In each instance, a historical process, a specific event, and the unusual abilities of an individual came together. Forensic addresses are always linked to specific events; forensic masterpieces emerge when great issues find great speakers to articulate them at propitious moments.

Although this speech is an extreme example unlike any other speech thus far examined, there were elements of forensic rhetoric in those other speeches. For example, Elizabeth Cady Stanton's 1854 and 1860 speeches to the New York legislature relied on legal evidence in a similar way. Lucretia Coffin Mott relied on scriptural and legal evidence in a speech designed to respond to accusations by the lecturer Richard Henry Dana. Finally, of course, legal issues pervaded the rhetoric of the early woman's rights movement.

Susan B. Anthony was one of the major figures in the early movement, a position she shared with only two others — Lucretia Coffin Mott and Elizabeth Cady Stanton. Anthony came to the movement through her friendship with Cady Stanton, which began in 1852, as well as through her outrage at being refused permission to speak at an Albany Temperance Society rally in 1852. Her role in the movement began that year at the national woman's rights convention in Syracuse and continued undiminished until her death. She was a woman of exceptional organizational ability and political acumen who worked behind the scenes prior to the Civil War. During the war, she and Cady Stanton organized the Women's National Loyal League, which secured thousands of signatures on petitions in support of an amendment ending slavery. After the war she joined with Cady Stanton in publishing the *Revolution* (1868-1870) and in forming the National Woman Suffrage Association (1869). From 1870 to 1876 she lectured on the lyceum circuit on topics related to woman's rights and temperance. She and two colleagues dramatically presented a "Woman's Declaration of 1876" at the Fourth of July ceremonies in Philadelphia celebrating the centennial of the nation.

With the help of Cady Stanton and Matilda Joslyn Gage, she financed and published the first volume of the *History of Woman Suffrage* in 1881, followed by two more volumes in 1882 and 1886. A fourth volume was issued by Anthony with the assistance of Ida Husted Harper in 1902. In 1890, after years of negotiations, Anthony arranged the merger of the two suffrage organizations into the National American Woman Suffrage Association. Anthony was its president from 1892 to 1900, when she chose Carrie Chapman Catt to succeed her. In 1888 she founded the International Council of Women, and in 1904 in Berlin, with Catt's assistance, she founded the International Woman Suffrage Alliance and became its honorary president. In February 1906, she attended her last woman suffrage convention in Baltimore and left her message for the future: "Failure is impossible" (Lutz 1971, 57).

NOTES

1. All citations are from the 1874 publication. Joslyn Gage's speech is found on pp. 179-205.
2. The characteristics of forensic excellence are described in a number of critical essays. Arnold (1958), for example, wrote that Thomas Erskine "joined fact, reason, and feeling to central principles of justice" (19), and added that the principles that formed the premises of Erskine's arguments "were not usually rules of law. They were propositions about justice or the way to justice, about truth or the way to truth.... Characteristically they suggested strongly but indirectly that judge and juror ought to *make* law, ought to refashion social patterns by *creating* precedents" (20). He concluded: "Almost without exception, Thomas Erskine's speeches at the bar illustrate that the best persuasion is unitary, that forensic rhetoric is neither reason on a work detail nor parade-ground polish on review. His rhetoric was an integration of reason, suggestion, and functional symbols organized to form a complete and dynamic economy" (29). Sanbonmatsu (1971) noted Clarence Darrow's emphasis on the broader significance of the case at hand (36) and cited the prosecutor in the Gitlow case who recognized and resented Darrow's appeal to the jury to set aside the law

and create a precedent (46). Black (1943) cited a letter by Chauncey Goodrich to Rufus Choate describing Daniel Webster's forensic skill in presenting "a chain of reasoning so easy to be understood and yet approaching so nearly to absolute demonstration, that he seemed to carry with him every man of his audience without the slightest effort or weariness on either side." (638) Mills (1943) noted that when Webster addressed juries, "his style was characterized by simple words, vivid imagery, emotional appeals, and less involved sentences" (425). Mills (1942) also cited Webster's precepts on rhetorical arrangement, that, in general, speeches should be "systematic and coherent. . . . If a speaker wants to make an immediate, favorable impression upon his [sic] audience, he must set forth his issues, principles, and laws early in the speech." (135) Howell & Hudson develop similar principles (1943, 669). Black (1943) commented that Rufus Choate "thought that juries were popular assemblies and demanded special treatment" (454).

8

Social Feminism: Frances Willard, "Feminine Feminist"

This chapter continues to explore the nature of rhetorical adaptation to specific audiences and situations, as well as the relationship between movement ideology and arguments from expediency or benefits (Kraditor 1965, 43-74). As noted in previous chapters, the argument from benefits surfaced very early in woman's rights rhetoric, for example, in Clarina Howard Nichols's 1851 speech, *The Responsibilities of Woman.* However, arguments from benefits reached their zenith in the work of the Woman's Christian Temperance Union (WCTU) and in the rhetoric of Frances Willard, "the womanly rebel, the pious iconoclast, the feminine feminist" (Bordin 1986, 39).

William O'Neill ends his history of feminism in the United States by concluding that the early movement failed; he attributes its failure to the arguments that came to dominate its rhetoric. In his view, after 1875, "social feminism" displaced the more radical views of leaders such as Elizabeth Cady Stanton. Briefly, social feminists accepted traditional views of woman but argued that her distinctive influence should be extended to areas outside the home. O'Neill writes:

> while social feminism had its virtues, it was incapable of coping with those customs and institutions that prevented women from securing the advantages and opportunities enjoyed by men as a matter of course. This was . . . because their entire rationale precluded the attainment of genuine equality. By justifying their activities on the grounds that society was an extension of the home and woman's work in it merely an enlargement of her maternal powers, social feminists froze the domestic status quo. (O'Neill 1971, 352-53)

O'Neill's conclusion, although apt, needs to be refined. With the wisdom of hindsight one can see that the rhetoric of social feminism fixed a view of woman so similar to the tenets of "true womanhood" that it precluded both analysis of the barriers to full equality and reform efforts to remove such obstacles. However, social feminism was a kind of feminism (Blocker 1985, 468); as such, it succeeded in enlarging woman's conception of her sphere, and it enabled "true women" to perceive the ballot as consistent with femininity. And, as O'Neill suggests, both of these effects — the achievements and the failures — were related to its rhetoric.

The WCTU was founded in 1874; five years later, Willard, one of its founders, was elected president. During Willard's tenure the union grew to be the largest women's organization in the United States, with 250,000 adult members, and branches in every state and territory, all cities, and most local communities. By contrast, the membership of the combined NAWSA in 1890 was estimated to be about 13,000, which was also the number of dues-paying members in the WCTU fourteen years earlier, in the fall of 1876 (Bordin 1981, 94; 1986, 99).

The attraction of the WCTU for women was, to a very significant degree, its charismatic president. Willard's leadership met the needs of women who were frustrated in their attempts to effect change by influencing men. Willard first proposed a suffrage resolution at a WCTU convention in 1875, and her election to the presidency in 1879 signaled that the organization would henceforth be committed to the ballot for women (Bordin 1981, 46; Willard 1889, 576-89). Under Willard's leadership, the WCTU became an organization dedicated to using every righteous means to achieve its goals, as the motto "Do Everything" proclaimed. Ultimately, Willard developed a broad program, advocating such diverse reforms as women police officers, kindergartens, the eight-hour day, putting a monetary value on housework, manual and physical training for girls, co-education, raising the age of consent, and laws making men and women legal and economic equals in marriage. Willard attempted to justify these reforms on grounds that made them consistent with "true womanhood" and acceptable to the evangelical Protestant culture from which most WCTU women came.

Frances Willard's power came from her leadership ability which, in turn, was directly related to her skill as a speaker. She traveled almost constantly during her presidency, lecturing to members and to general audiences in all sections of the country (Bordin 1981, 76; 1986, 114-15). She was a direct, personal link between the national organization and its local branches. Analysis of many key speeches would be required to illustrate the development of her concerns and of her rhetorical skills (1883; 1886). Here, however, I shall limit my analysis to a single long speech, "A White Life For Two," that was later printed as a pamphlet (1890). It can serve as a rhetorical touchstone because it was delivered at the height of Willard's influence, and because sections of the speech recurred in her other rhetoric (1888, 88-89, 90-91; 1889, 410, 422, 474, 607, 611-14; 1891; 1895). Above all, it was a summative statement of all the concerns that constituted WCTU feminism in the nineteenth century.

A WHITE LIFE FOR TWO

As a rhetorical act, *A White Life For Two* embodied the paradox of "feminine feminism." On the one hand, it was romantic in tone, idealistic in attitude, and affirmed traditional values. At the same time, it called for woman suffrage, a coalition with labor, legal and economic equality for women (including wives), co-education, name and dress reform, physical and manual training for girls, strengthening laws against rape, and woman's control over procreation; this was a collection of positions ostensibly more suited to Elizabeth Cady Stanton. *A White Life* illustrated Willard's ability to fuse traditional values to proposals for social change, a skill that was demonstrated dramatically in her earlier call for woman suffrage as a means to "Home Protection" (1883; Bordin 1981, 58, 61). Here and elsewhere in her rhetoric, Willard attempted to transmute apparently radical demands into minor reforms by treating them as the means to reaffirm traditional values. She framed her demands for change so that they appeared to reinforce traditional gender roles; she also used euphemisms and abstract terms inviting varied interpretations when discussing sexually charged and controversial topics. Finally, she herself personified and enacted the fusion of traditional values and proposals for change presented in her speeches. But although Willard was able to persuade most WCTU members to support woman suffrage, even at her most appealing she was unable to fix the WCTU on a course pursuing a broad range of reforms, because her rhetoric was ill-equipped to promote such major social change.

The discourse of social feminists, such as Frances Willard, had many of the characteristics of sermons.[1] As rhetorical acts, sermons are distinctive in that they are addressed to the converted, and, as a result, the range of possible persuasion is usually limited to reaffirmation and recommitment. Argument is grounded in the authority of a sacred text whose meaning is interpreted and enriched through amplification by the speaker. In this process, audience members renew their covenant with God and pledge to incorporate these values, now more fully understood, into their lives.

Willard's speeches resembled sermons not because she sometimes relied upon religious authority, a form of evidence frequently used by woman's rights activists, but because she consistently appealed to traditional religious and patriotic values linked to the cult of true womanhood, and because she refused to disturb her listeners' prior beliefs by taking controversial positions. Following Willard's election to the presidency, writings and speeches of WCTU members began to include many references to women of the Bible who served God in the public sphere, such as those listed in Lucretia Coffin Mott's 1849 speech. WCTU speakers also began to juxtapose Galatians 3:28 ("There is neither Jew nor Greek, there is neither bond nor free, there is neither male nor female: for ye are all one in Christ Jesus") against restrictive passages from the Pauline epistles; they argued that Jesus was woman's emancipator, freeing her from the curse of a more limited sphere (Gifford 1986, 113-14).

Religious speech is an outgrowth of conversion. Analyzing the careers of seventeenth-century female prophets in England, Christine Berg and Philippa Berry write:

> prophecy might be described as appearing first of all as a proclamation of one individual's secured salvation and election. This election is subsequently inter-preted as an injunction to the prophetic individual to accept responsibility for the public articulation of the divine *logos*, as part of a missionary or revolution-ary programme. (1981, 41)

Willard herself contended that in her conversion to woman suffrage, she not only received the command to speak for woman's ballot but "a complete line of argument and illustration" (1889, 351). The speech of pious "true women" was a direct expression of profound religious ex-perience; as a result, "if one claimed to receive a changed, re-interpreted image of woman as the content of the conversion experience, the claim would be difficult for another to challenge, particularly if the challenger shared a belief in the possibility of individual conversion" (Gifford 1986, 108). Sermonlike speeches, based on a conversion experience, became the means to convince religious women that woman suffrage was consis-tent with the tenets of true womanhood and with the biblical conception of woman's role. Carolyn Gifford refers to this as a process of "re-conver-sion," through which the evangelical Protestant women of the WCTU came to believe in a concept of true womanhood that included the ballot as a means to "Home Protection" (Gifford 1986, 111-13).

Willard could "re-convert" WCTU women to the ballot because of the extremity of the alcohol abuse problem in the nation at the time, and because temperance women were frustrated by their unsuccessful attempts to effect reform through male agents of change. WCTU women knew the problems of alcohol firsthand, and they had experienced male perfidy in attempting to bring about reform. As a result, they were ready for the revelation Willard offered, particularly when her revelation made the ballot consistent with Scripture and true womanhood. Through this process, the woman's ballot was accepted, not as a right, but as the means to an end — protection of the home, the peculiar sphere of the true woman (Hardesty 1984).

The setting of *A White Life for Two*, for example, was "God's country, a gracious Mother-land," in which a dramatic struggle was taking place, where "women well might live to serve or die to save." The warlike connotations of this phrase were emphasized by affirmations that "Home Protection" was a "battle cry" and that the last presidential election campaign was a "mighty war of words . . . waged . . . in the interest of the home" (Willard 1890, 3). All issues, all concerns, were encompassed by the home; as a result, all issues were "domesticated" — a move that made such issues the rightful concern of women while placing women's concerns center stage. Woman's sphere was altered by absorbing into it whatever concerned the home and its protection. In Willard's words, "the fount from which they [temperance, labor, the woman question] flow . . . is Home itself, and back of Home is the one relationship [marriage] that makes it possible" (3).

As the speech illustrates, the home was the symbol that unified Willard's appeals and linked all of the WCTU's efforts. As an end, protection of the home seemed to legitimize every available means. Calls for the woman's ballot, labor reform, co-education, and the like became acceptable because they were means to create ideal homes. Alcohol-related issues, despite their centrality in WCTU efforts, took on significance only in relation to protecting the home. The other key terms of the speech — marriage and motherhood — derived their importance from their relationship to the home. Willard praised marriage as the height of civilized, Christian development, offering a kind of fusion of religious thought and a Darwinian view of progress: "This gentle age into which we have happily been born, is attuning the twain whom God hath made for such great destiny, to higher harmonies than any other age has known, by a reform in the denaturalizing methods of a civilization largely based on force." (5)

Willard refuted the idea that the home was merely a woman's issue by arguing that marriage was central to the lives of men as well as of women. In her words, "Nay, it is the sum of earthly weal or woe to *both*" (4). Material progress ("a Corliss engine, which she could guide as well as he"), political and moral progress ("rooting out all that remains of the medieval, continental and harem philosophies"), and religious progress ("a more complete humanity upon the Christ-like basis that *'there shall be no more curse'* ") were linked to temperance reform, labor reform, the equal suffrage movement, and the social purity movement (5). Willard thus implied that the changes she was calling for were natural, moral, religiously sanctioned, evolutionary, interdependent, and inevitable.

This new ideal of womanhood, she continued, was depicted by a statue created by Kentucky sculptor Joel Hart, and expressed in William Wordsworth's poem, "She was a phantom of delight" (6). Willard's revised conception seemed to emphasize woman's role as a civilizing agent and to diminish her role as a sexual object. Woman was "the companion and counsellor not the incumbrance and toy of man" (6), and, in response to the changes wrought by this new woman, "how grandly men themselves are growing" (7). Willard called for an elimination of the double moral and sexual standard; she argued that "sweeter manners, purer laws" were "as much in man's interest as our own" (8).

Willard's rhetorical alchemy involved relabeling and reframing proposals in ways that transformed them from demands for social change into reaffirmations of traditional arrangements and values. Demands for physical and manual training for girls were presented as a means to healthier motherhood and more efficient domestic labor. Education was not a means for female self-actualization and entry into the professions, but, echoing both Plato's *Gorgias*, with which Willard was familiar (1889, 160), and Mary Wollstonecraft (1792), it was a means to make women purer — greater virtue would grow out of greater knowledge. Co-education would make relationships between men and women more brotherly and sisterly and, presumably, less lustful. Legal and economic equality for women would produce better wives who, in turn, would contribute to the progress toward ideal marriages. Greater autonomy for young women would make women less vulnerable to seduction and, hence, remove temptation from the path of young men, and so forth. Who could object to such proposals if they were the means to bring us closer to purer women, ideal marriages, better homes? This strategy reached its climax in Willard's description of the utopia that would come into existence following these reforms:

My theory of marriage in its relation to society would give this postulate. Husband and wife are one, and that one is — husband and wife. . . . One undivided half of the world for wife and husband equally; co-education to mate them on the plane of mind; equal property rights to make her God's own free woman . . . left free to go her honored and self-respecting way as a maiden *in perpetuo*, rather than marry a man whose deterioration through the alcohol and nicotine habits is a deadly menace to herself and the descendants that such a marriage has invoked — these are the outlooks of the future that shall make the marriage system, never a failure since it became monogamous, an assured, a permanent, a paradisical [sic] success. (13-14)

Thus would true womanhood be perfected.

Finally, in Willard's hands even such a controversial and sexually charged issue as rape could be rendered conventional and respectable:[2]

Why is the age of protection or consent but ten years in twenty States, and in one, only seven years? Who would have supposed, when man's great physical strength is considered, he would have fixed upon an age so tender, and declared that after a child had reached it, she should be held equally accountable with her doughty assailant for a crime in which he was the aggressor? And who would not suppose that the man who had been false to one woman would be socially ostracized by all the rest of womankind? What will explain the cruelty of men and the heartlessness of women in this overmastering issue of womanhood's protection and manhood's loyalty? (8)

The problem of rape was reduced to the problem of statutory rape, which was legally defined in terms of the age of consent. Raising the age of consent was made more palatable by relabeling it the age of protection. She affirmed traditional notions of the physical superiority of men. She phrased demands as rhetorical questions, to which the audience could only give assent. She held men and women equally culpable for the problem, to avoid any suggestion that males were particularly blameworthy. Willard's success in rendering this reform acceptable to white, Christian, middle-class men and women was demonstrated by the fact that the WCTU was able, through the use of petitions, to have the age of consent raised to sixteen in twenty of the offending states (Bordin 1981, 110).

Willard's success in enlarging the membership of the WCTU demonstrated the power her rhetoric held for women. She was equally skillful in adapting her message to men who had the power to take action. Although the WCTU was made up entirely of women, Willard's lectures and speeches, including *A White Life*, both as delivered and in pamphlet form, were intended for general audiences. As illustrated by her treatment of the crime of rape in this speech, no blame was attached to males; even when discussing legislators, she presented their intentions in the most positive light. For example, referring to the laws that had lowered the age of consent, Willard said: "The very laws which good men in the past had meant for her [woman's] protection, became to her a snare and danger" (8).

Willard created grounds for identification between men and women by emphasizing the importance of the home and the values it symbolized for men. She introduced illustrious examples, such as Dante, Petrarch, and Washington Irving, among others, in order to demonstrate the importance of love and marriage to men. Others who lived "uncompanioned lives" were incorporated under "the principle that underlies those memorable words applied to [George] Washington: 'Heaven left him childless that a Nation might call him Father' " (5). Willard also attempted to create her audience, that is, she described men in terms designed to transform those exposed to her message into an ideal audience. As she characterized them, the men in her audience were chaste and committed to marriage; they were individuals for whom the family and the values it represented were central. She not only selected as her target audience those most likely to be sympathetic to her views, she also invited male audience members to see themselves as she described them.

Finally, she appealed to men in terms of their traditional role as protectors of women. The reforms she proposed were all part of an effort to protect women from evil forces. In responding to Willard's pleas, men did not need to alter their conceptions of their role or sphere; they merely acted as true men to create conditions in which true women might play their roles more fully and safely. Presumably, with these changes, men would have better wives, more loving marriages, and happier homes. As Willard presented her case, no social costs would accrue to men if the reforms she proposed were enacted.

Willard faced the same obstacles that confronted all other women who spoke publicly. In her biography, Ruth Bordin reports that as late as 1866 Willard had a man read a speech she had written in order to avoid violating social conventions (1986, 76). Willard chose certain strategies to deal with these obstacles, but in so doing she paid a terrible price. Her real achievement was in making suffrage acceptable to more conservative women, but she did so at the cost of making other reforms — reforms that would have attacked the tenets of true womanhood — far more difficult, if not impossible.

Willard's strategies can be juxtaposed against those of other women speakers. The women who spoke at Pennsylvania Hall in 1838 had the temerity to give advice to males, even as they presented themselves as prophets or appealed to Scripture. Lucretia Coffin Mott asserted her moral authority; Elizabeth Cady Stanton was defiant and confrontational, even as she phrased her analysis of oppressive marriage laws in terms of woman's traditional roles. Susan B. Anthony made no adaptations to traditional norms, or only minimal ones. In other words, whatever the extent of their adaptation to social expectations, woman's rights speakers were persuaders first and ladies second; the conflict between their attempts to adapt and the principles they espoused is apparent in their discourse. They wanted to be heard and to be persuasive, but they had to make their case, and in so doing they confronted their audiences with the intensity of their commitment and with the gap between the nation's espoused values and its treatment of women.

Willard stands in sharp contrast to the other great speakers of the woman's rights movement. Both in content and in style, Willard was wholly feminine, utterly ladylike. In her extraordinary efforts to be persuasive and to adapt to her audiences, she ended up generating discourse which was suited only to reinforce existing beliefs. By entirely avoiding confrontation, by refusing to challenge, much less to blame men, even for the rape of children, she chose rhetorical strategies at odds with the major reforms she herself espoused.

However, Willard's rhetoric does not demonstrate that the feminization of style equals rhetorical failure. In contrast to Lucretia Coffin Mott and Clarina Howard Nichols, Willard addressed her audiences not as her peers but as her superiors, inviting approval rather than participation. Unlike them, too, she avoided extended examples, preferring vague, undetailed references whose content would be determined by her audiences rather than herself. Unlike those speakers, she proceeded deductively, concealing the generalizations that were the premises for her arguments under flowery statements. As noted, the presuppositions from which she argued were those of "true womanhood," and in that respect, her views most resemble those of Howard Nichols's 1851 speech; however, unlike Howard Nichols, she did not offer examples that might have challenged the audience. Similarly, while Coffin Mott feminized her role, her arguments grew out of natural rights premises. In other words, both in style and in content, Willard was an extreme case. Her arguments were grounded in woman's special and distinct nature, precluding any fundamental alteration in woman's sphere; stylistically, every choice she made closed down opportunities for any form of persuasion other than reinforcement of existing beliefs.

CONCLUSION

Frances Willard was herself a major element in her rhetorical appeal. She embodied the paradox of "feminine feminism" and "womanly rebellion" that seems to have been the essence of her discourse. On the one hand, Willard used every available means to enhance her femininity and to increase her personal appeal. Her professional clothes were usually made for her by a dressmaker, and her dresses were ladylike and fashionable, usually "black or brown velvet or silk" with "a blue ribbon or a touch of white or ivory lace at the throat, and a tasteful bonnet that she removed when she spoke." Reputedly, she would have made a superb actress; her voice was described as orotund, "yet so flexible as to be full of varying intonations. . . . She gesticulated frequently with the forefinger of her left hand, and the gesture had almost a coquettish quality" (Bordin 1981, 67-68). In her biography, Bordin incorporates an 1881 letter to the editor of *Our Union* into her description of Willard as " 'a graceful beautiful woman, simply yet tastefully dressed,' speaking in 'soft sweet tones,' a womanly woman" (1986, 114). In short, Willard was charming, feminine, dramatic. Bordin summed up her personal appeal this way: "She was loved, she was adored. Her intense, almost sexual attractiveness to members of her own sex was a major factor in her success" (1981, 68-69).[3]

Part of her appeal may have been the paradoxes she embodied. She extolled marriage and the home, yet she was unwed. She was the skillful and powerful leader of a major organization, yet she played the role of the traditional lady. She discussed the most controversial sexual issues in public, but in a language of delicacy and circumlocution. She was the ideal of womanhood she described in the speech, "tender [and] sweet," but with "strength and individuality, a gentle seriousness; there is more of the sisterly, less of the syren [sic] — more of the duchess and less of the doll" (Willard 1890, 6). Seeing and hearing Willard, her audiences — male and female — must have believed they could have it all: femininity and reform, successful female leadership which affirmed true womanhood and separate spheres.

By the 1890s, WCTU women, led by Willard, had gained noteworthy legislative successes. Dozens of local option laws had passed, and, as noted above, the age of consent had been raised in twenty states where it had been disturbingly low. As a result of WCTU lobbying, scientific temperance education had been mandated for the public schools in all states except Georgia, and a number of states had passed laws requiring special institutions for the treatment of handicapped and delinquent females, again with WCTU support (Bordin 1981, 110, 138; 1986, 175).

The WCTU had also been active in the numerous campaigns that extended various forms of suffrage to women: full suffrage in four states, municipal suffrage in Kansas, and limited school suffrage in twenty-three states. How much credit they deserved for these achievements, though, is difficult to determine. On the one hand, the WCTU made woman suffrage acceptable to large numbers of more conservative women who were alienated by what they perceived as the radicalism of the suffrage associations. On the other hand, the most significant resistance to woman suffrage came from liquor interests, who were alarmed by the connection between woman suffrage and prohibition that was popularized by the WCTU (Catt and Shuler 1923). These successes testify to the power of Willard's rhetoric and to the force of the social feminism it embodied.

Willard died in 1898. The aftermath of her death demonstrated how transient her impact was, even on the women in her own organization. Between 1897 and 1910 no gains of any sort were made for woman suffrage; anti-suffrage activism was at its height. Moreover, the WCTU underwent a startling transformation. "The change in emphasis was immediate, abrupt, and dramatic," writes Ruth Bordin; WCTU women went from being "the best, most respected, most forward looking women in town to narrow-minded antilibertarians riding a hobbyhorse" (1981, 154-55). Other factors contributed to this narrowing of concerns, but Willard's rhetoric played a key role. Willard had not converted the WCTU membership to the broad range of reforms that she had espoused.

As this analysis demonstrates, Frances Willard's career, although significant for early feminism, was independent of that movement. Most fundamentally, involvement in WCTU activities widened the horizons of its many members, easing the reform efforts of other groups. Willard herself was a member of the more conservative American Woman Suffrage Association, but she boldly introduced Susan B. Anthony of the more radical National Woman Suffrage Association to a WCTU convention in 1881, prompting a walkout of some conservative members. In 1888, she was a leader in the International Council of Women, called to commemorate the Seneca Falls convention. But it was the WCTU that dominated Willard's life, and her involvement in woman's rights and woman suffrage stemmed from her perception of their relationship to the goals of that organization.

NOTES

1. Clark's content analytic study (1977) identifies sermons as functioning to interpret the Scriptures, as formal and abstract in tone, involving moral issues, relying heavily on authority evidence while eschewing personal testimony, treating the Scriptures, particularly the life of Jesus, as the source of moral models, presupposing a shared world view that leads to reinforcement as their primary purpose. He also suggests that sermons may be unusually coherent organizationally and that, given their positions, ministers need not work to develop ethos. Only the last two traits do not fit the rhetoric of Frances Willard.

2. For a discussion of the WCTU's concern to protect abused wives and children and the limitations placed on such concerns, see Blocker 1985, 462-64.

3. As Carroll Smith-Rosenberg has argued (1975), it is extremely difficult to determine which nineteenth-century women were sexually active lesbians. There are hints that Frances Willard had sexual relationships with other women, but the evidence is not clear. Willard's autobiography (1889) provides evidence on both sides of this issue.

9

The Humanistic Underpinnings of Feminism: "The Solitude of Self"

As social movements grow and age, new rhetorical obstacles emerge. The arguments developed in the crucible of debate become familiar, and no longer retain their original force; movement advocates are taxed to invent means to render their appeals fresh and compelling. The speech that is the subject of this chapter is an outstanding example of meeting that challenge. Indeed, the challenge was met so well that the speech still has the power to reinvigorate the premises underlying feminist demands.

In 1892, near the end of her long career as a leader in the woman's rights and woman suffrage movement, Elizabeth Cady Stanton made her farewell address to the National American Woman Suffrage Association. That speech, "The Solitude of Self," was unlike the usual rhetoric of social activists in any period, and it was a startling departure from the typical speeches and arguments of nineteenth-century feminists. The address was extraordinary because it was a philosophical statement of the principles and values underlying the struggle for woman's rights in the United States. It was also extraordinary because it was a social reformer's defense of humanistic individualism, and because it was a rhetorical statement of the limits of what could be achieved through words or social action. Cady Stanton's address illustrates how a speech delivered in the nineteenth century can still speak to a contemporary audience.

Cady Stanton delivered "The Solitude of Self" three times near the close of a speaking career stretching over forty years. It was first presented to the House Committee on the Judiciary on the morning of January 18, 1892 (Stanton 1892b, 1-5). That afternoon Stanton delivered it at the twenty-fourth national convention of the National American Woman Suffrage Association, as the group's retiring president. Two days later she repeated the speech at a hearing before the Senate Committee on Woman Suffrage.[1] The text was published subsequently in the *Woman's Journal* (Stanton 1892a), thus reaching a wider audience of suffragists (Mäsel-Walters 1980). As presented to the congressional committees, the speech was part of the yearly lobbying effort of the NAWSA, carried out in conjunction with its national convention in Washington, D.C., to persuade Congress to pass a federal woman suffrage amendment.

In 1892 Elizabeth Cady Stanton was seventy-six years old, and the contemporary reader may wonder whether the qualities of the speech reflect her rhetorical skill or her recognition of approaching death. Cady Stanton lived for ten more years, however, and, in the period between this speech and her death, she published, with others, the two volumes of the *Woman's Bible* (1892, 1895), a work that is strong evidence of her energy, mental acuity, and continued commitment to social change. In other words, "The Solitude of Self" was delivered before policy makers in the United States Congress and fellow activists at the NAWSA national convention by a highly skilled persuader who, despite advanced age, was fully alert and actively engaged in efforts for reform.

Indeed, this speech could only have been given late in the development of the movement by a leader who had been associated with the movement from the beginning, one who was thoroughly familiar with its stock of arguments and with the resistance these familiar arguments faced. More than twenty years earlier, addressing the 1870 convention of the National Woman Suffrage Association, Cady Stanton had described the rhetorical barriers that woman's rights advocates confronted:

> Knowing that we hold the Gibraltar rock of reason on this question, they resort to ridicule and petty objections. Compelled to follow our assailants, wherever they go, and fight them with their own weapons; when cornered with wit and sarcasm, some cry out, you have no logic on your platform, forgetting that we have no use for logic until they give us logicians at whom to hurl it, and if, for the pure love of it, we now and then rehearse the logic that is like a, b, c, to all of us, others cry out — the same old speeches we have heard these twenty years. (HWS 2:349)

She had made the familiar arguments in her presidential addresses and speeches to congressional committees throughout the years preceding the 1892 address.[2] She had treated the problem of holding the attention of male members of Congress in a description of what she and other suffragists had experienced before a Senate committee in 1878:

> The peculiarly aggravating feature of the present occasion was the studied inattention and contempt of the chairman. . . . He alternatively looked over some manuscripts and newspapers before him, then jumped up to open or close a door or window. He stretched, yawned, gazed at the ceiling, cut his nails, sharpened his pencil, changing his occupation and his position every two minutes, effectually preventing the establishment of the faintest magnetic current between the speakers and the committee. (HWS 3:93n; Forster 1985, 232)

Now, after all these years and all these speeches, Cady Stanton assumed her audience's familiarity with the oft-repeated arguments in order to make a fresh, even startling appeal.

Although "The Solitude of Self" is unlike her other rhetorical efforts, it was highly praised by her contemporaries. Susan B. Anthony, her close friend and co-worker, thought it was "the speech of Mrs. Stanton's life" (Kraditor 1965, 46n.4). The Rev. Dr. Anna Howard Shaw, an outstanding speaker in the early movement, called it "an English classic" (Lutz 1940, 290); Frederick Douglass, the great abolitionist orator and writer, remarked, "After her—silence" (HWS 4:205). These opinions were shared by many others; as Anthony and Harper wrote later, "it . . . is considered by many to be her masterpiece" (HWS 4:186). Yet editors have only recently included the address in anthologies, and it remains little known.[3] This treatment may be explained, at least in part, by the fact that it was delivered by a woman, by Cady Stanton's radicalism, and by the unusual character of the speech.

Rhetorically, the address violated nearly all traditional rules. It lacked the cogent refutation of Cady Stanton's first speech at Seneca Falls, the dramatic confrontation of the audience of Angelina Grimké [Weld]'s speech in 1838, and the systematic use of evidence apparent in Lucretia Coffin Mott's "Discourse on Woman." It made only the simplest of arguments, and it presented no evidence. The thesis, if it can be called that, was the following:

> The strongest reason for giving woman all the opportunities for higher education, for the full development of her faculties, forces of mind and body; for giving her the most enlarged freedom of thought and action; a complete emancipation from all forms of bondage, of custom, dependence, superstition; from all the crippling influences of fear—is the solitude and personal responsibility of her own individual life. (Stanton 1892a, 1)

The speech consisted of the simple repetition of this one idea in many forms. It referred briefly at the outset to the shared values of republicanism and Protestantism, but it made no appeal to them. It had no proper introduction, and it ended abruptly with a pointed but poignant question.[4] Yet its power persists.

STRUCTURE

The speech was unusual, first, because its structure and tone resemble those of the lyric, a form that is associative and develops through enumeration. Typically, a lyric poem attempts to explore and express all facets of a feeling or attitude in a series of statements referring to a single idea or theme. The parts are related to each other as the spokes of a wheel are related to the axle. A paradigmatic lyric is Elizabeth Barrett Browning's "How do I love thee? Let me count the ways." The lyric is intimate in tone, relies on personal experience, and uses sensual or aesthetic materials, including metaphor, to induce a response in the audience. The tone of the lyric is so subjective that it seems rhetorically inappropriate, as if the speaker were washing emotional linen in public. For this reason, the lyric is usually described as a kind of indirect address that is "overheard" by the audience.

Cady Stanton's speech exhibited many of the qualities of a lyric. It explored a single concept — the solitude of the human self, the idea that each person is unique, responsible, and alone. It began with a string of powerful associations: "The point I wish plainly to bring before you on this occasion is the individuality of each human soul; our Protestant idea, the right of individual conscience and judgment, our republican idea, individual citizenship" (1). Cady Stanton ignored the powerful appeal of the concept of a priesthood of believers, as well as the forceful yet familiar arguments for woman's rights and woman suffrage based on the concepts underlying democratic-republican government. Instead, she concerned herself exclusively with still more fundamental rights, the rights of women as persons. The speech developed by presenting a hierarchy of the rights of woman. Most basic was what belonged to her as an individual; next came her rights as a citizen; third were the rights that arise from the "incidental relations of life such as mother, wife, sister, daughter" (1).

Natural rights philosophy asserts that individuals have rights because they are human beings. If asked why individuals should have inalienable rights as persons, most find it difficult to respond. Cady Stanton's speech answers the question by saying that individuals have rights because as persons they are unique, individually responsible, and separate — alone. The conceptual significance of the speech is that it unearthed the values underlying natural rights philosophy, that it demonstrated why the personhood of each individual is of such ultimate significance.

Structurally, the speech was an exhaustive enumeration of all the dimensions of human solitude — through the stages of life from childhood to old age; in the varied roles of wife, mother, and widow; and in the extremities of poverty, childbirth, triumph, catastrophe, and death. To encounter the speech was to experience the enormity of human solitude.

Cady Stanton's audience confronted a distinguished old woman, who a year earlier had been described in the press as "looking as if she should be the Lord Chief Justice with her white hair puffed all over her head, and her amiable and intellectual face marked with lines of wisdom" (Hersh 1978, 103). She became a guide who showed them the existential reality of their lonely lives through imagery: life is a solitary voyage each makes alone; each of us is a soldier requiring provisions from society, a soldier who must fight alone. The human condition, Cady Stanton said, is like the terrible solitude of Jesus — fasting and tempted on the mountain top, praying alone in Gethsemane, betrayed by a trusted intimate, and, in the agonies of death, abandoned even by God. In a concluding series of figurative comparisons, Cady Stanton said:

> And yet, there is a solitude which each and every one of us has always carried with him, more inaccessible than the ice-cold mountains, more profound than the midnight sea; the solitude of self. Our inner being which we call our self, no eye nor touch of man or angel has ever pierced. It is more hidden than the caves of the gnome; the sacred adytum of the oracle; the hidden chamber of Eleusinian mystery, for to it only Omniscience is permitted to enter. (Stanton 1892a, 32)

One paragraph from the speech illustrated dramatically its lyric tone and style, its appeal to personal experience and to the emotions called forth by extreme situations. Cady Stanton said:

> Alike amid the greatest triumphs and darkest tragedies of life, we walk alone. On the divine heights of human attainment, eulogized and worshipped as a hero or saint, we stand alone. In ignorance, poverty and vice, as a pauper or criminal, alone we starve or steal; alone we suffer the sneers and rebuffs of our fellows; alone we are hunted and hounded through dark courts and alleys, in by-ways and highways; alone we stand in the judgment seat; alone in the prison cell we lament our crimes and misfortunes; alone we expiate them on the gallows. In hours like these we realize the awful solitude of individual life, its pains, its penalties, its responsibilities. (32)

Consistent with other lyrical elements in the speech, Cady Stanton's relationship to the audience was unusually indirect. Only the opening and closing sentences betrayed an unambiguous awareness of an immediate audience. The audience implied by the address was not merely composed of the delegates to the convention or the members of the congressional committees; it included all persons. Cady Stanton appeared to have been musing aloud about what it means to be a human being, and the audience was permitted to eavesdrop.

How did her lyric expression become a work of rhetoric? How did the speech move from the evocation of personal experience to become a basis for justifying woman's rights? Completely by indirection, "The Solitude of Self" breathed new life into the religious concept of the priesthood of all believers and into the political concepts expressed in natural rights philosophy. That individuals are unique, responsible, and alone is the philosophical basis for the Protestant attack on priestly intercession and the republican notion that rights are not granted by governments but are inherent in persons. Members of Cady Stanton's audience affirmed these values more intensely because she evoked the experience of human solitude that underlies them.

Although the appeal of such ideas was universal, Cady Stanton created a sharp contrast between the condition of all humans and the special nature of woman's place. At one point, she expressed the discrepancy in a vivid allusion:

> Shakespeare's play of "Titus Andronicus" contains a terrible satire on woman's position in the 19th century. Rude men (the play tells us) seized the king's daughter, cut out her tongue, cut off her hands, and then bade her to go call for water and wash her hands. What a picture of woman's position! Robbed of her natural rights, handicapped by law and custom at every turn, yet compelled to fight her own battles, and in the emergencies of life to fall back on herself for protection. (32)[5]

Cady Stanton told the audience that women, at all stages and in all conditions of life, were handicapped and yet responsible for their lives. Woman's solitude of self became a dramatic refutation of the argument that women were dependent on men or that a woman could be protected by a man:

> Whatever the theories may be of woman's dependence on man, in the supreme moments of her life, he cannot bear her burdens. Alone she goes to the gates of death to give life to every man that is born into the world; no one can share her fears, no one can mitigate her pangs; and if her sorrow is greater than she can bear, alone she passes beyond the gates into the vast unknown. (32)

Similarly, the uniqueness of each individual was a refutation of the inferiority of woman. Moreover, individual solitude and responsibility entailed the right to education, as well as other opportunities for personal development and the exercise of choice. Cady Stanton commented: "The talk of sheltering woman from the fierce storms of life is the sheerest mockery, for they beat on her from every point of the compass, just as they do on man, and with more fatal results, for he has been trained to protect himself, to resist, and to conquer" (32).

The concept of self-sovereignty refuted the view that man could act for woman at the ballot box, in legislatures, or on juries. Cady Stanton's conclusion was a pointed question: "Who, I ask you, can take, dare take on himself the rights, the responsibilities of another human soul?" (32). The principle that each person is unique, responsible, and alone denied the view of woman as property; it also implied her right to keep her wages, to own property, to sue and make contracts, and to have custody of her children. In other words, in spite of its associative structure, subjective tone, figurative language, and indirect address, Cady Stanton's speech was a forceful rationale for the specific rights claimed by nineteenth-century feminists.

PERSPECTIVE

The form of the speech and its modes of expression were similar to those of the lyric, but its perspective was tragic, a perspective rare in rhetoric (Burke 1961, 4-5; Frye 1957, 64; Langer 1953, 333-34). Most speeches take a comic perspective because they affirm that groups can act successfully to produce change, whereas tragedy focuses on destiny or fate as it affects the individual. Like a tragedy, this speech focused on the life of the individual. It emphasized beginnings and endings; in fact, it reminded audience members vividly that suffering and death are the inevitable lot of humans. It isolated the individual from the community, focused on fate as an element in human affairs, and emphasized the crises of human experience.

In Cady Stanton's tragic view, feminism could not change the human condition. If all the necessary laws were passed and all the changes made, humans, both male and female, would still be unique, responsible, solitary individuals, forced to confront their inevitable trials alone. In her words,

> when all artificial trammels are removed, and women are recognized as individuals, responsible for their own environments, thoroughly educated for all positions in life they may be called to fill; with all the resources in themselves that liberal thought and broad culture can give; guided by their own conscience and judgment, trained to self-protection, by a healthy development of the muscular system, and skill in the use of weapons of defense; and stimulated to self-support by a knowledge of the business world and the pleasure that

> pecuniary independence must ever give: when women are trained in this way,
> they will in a measure be fitted for those hours of solitude *that come alike to all,
> whether prepared or otherwise*. (32; emphasis added)

This tragic view of life might dampen enthusiasm and lessen motivation
for social reform as it reminded women of the limits of what could be
achieved through the movement for woman's rights and woman suffrage.
As depicted in the speech, human life is a pain-filled struggle, a condition
no reform can alter. Philosophically, Cady Stanton denied the traditional
American view of progress, but her perspective had an important ad-
vantage. If one accepted the view of human beings articulated in the
speech, woman's rights were not a matter for justification or argument;
rather, they were entailed by the nature of the human condition.

For legislators and the public, this point of view had special force
because it was fresh and unexpected. In addition, the speech indicated
that women did not expect legislators to enact laws to usher in a golden
age; as redefined by Cady Stanton, legislation extending woman's
rights simply provided an opportunity for individual effort, a perspective consistent with American views of individualism and self-reliance.
To deny her claims was to reject the concept of humanity affirmed by
the culture's dominant political and religious systems of belief. One
who disagreed was compelled to argue that women were not persons
who could rightfully claim their rights as citizens or as children of God.

Cady Stanton's apparent choice of individualism as a philosophical
posture could have been rhetorically as well as ethically problematic.
Individualism can take the form of a malign social Darwinism used to
blame individuals, including women, for their own oppression, a point
of view hostile to all reform efforts. That kind of individualism is
illustrated, for example, in Antoinette Brown [Blackwell]'s speech in
the 1860 convention debate, analyzed in chapter 5. Political individualism can become an anarchism that precludes social movements (Solomon 1988). Religious individualism, at its extreme,
produces what Kierkegaard called the "tragic hero," who acts on the
dictates of conscience to transcend the ethical rules of the community
and whose reasons for action are incommunicable to others (1941,
64-77, 91-129).

Cady Stanton avoided these extremes because she opted, not for an
extreme individualism, but for a humanistic concern for the experience of the living person in the here and now. The changes she
sought would alter the individual lives of real persons in the present,
but there was in the speech no dream of progress toward a utopia. In

fact, as Cady Stanton described it, there was an element of absurdity in all reform efforts. No matter what was done to alter the circumstances of women and men, each person would continue to be unique, responsible, and alone; reforms could ease the struggles of individuals, but they could not change the givens of human life.[6] As she expressed it: "Rich and poor, intelligent and ignorant, wise and foolish, virtuous and vicious, man and woman; it is ever the same, each soul must depend wholly on itself" (32). Cady Stanton's tragic perspective was modified by a humanistic emphasis on the living individual and by an absurdist recognition of the limits of social change.

As is evident in the speech, Cady Stanton was concerned with the conditions of all humans, not just women. Her inclusion of, and appeals to, males were both strategically desirable and philosophically consistent. After all, those who had the power to effect the changes she sought were men, who held virtually all political and economic power. Under such conditions, there was no conflict between expediency and principle. Early in the speech, for example, as Cady Stanton dismissed "social roles" as a basis for woman's rights, she used the male as the standard from which her conclusion was drawn:

> In discussing the sphere of man, we do not decide his rights as an individual, as a citizen, as a man, by his duties as a father, a husband, a brother or a son, relations he may never fill. Moreover, he would be better fitted for those very relations, and whatever special work he might choose to do to earn his bread, by the complete development of all his faculties as an individual. Just so with woman. (Stanton 1892a, 1).

Similarly, when she referred to the uniqueness of individuals, she said: "There can never again be just such . . . environments as make up the infancy, youth and manhood of this one"; and she illustrated the need to rely on one's own resources with Prince Peter Kropotkin's experiences in a Russian prison.

Although nearly all the examples in the speech were particularly applicable to females, one passage was noteworthy for its appreciation of the constraints of the male role:

> When suddenly roused at midnight, with the startling cry of "Fire! Fire!" to find the house over their heads in flames, do women wait for men to point the way to safety? And are the men, equally bewildered, and half suffocated with smoke, in a position to do more than try to save themselves? (32)

In other words, not only were men incapable of protecting women from the vicissitudes of life, but it was unjust to demand that they should attempt to do so. Clearly, the philosophical grounds for woman's rights were goals for all persons as human beings. As she said:

> We see reason sufficient in the outer conditions of human beings for individual
> liberty and development, but when we consider the self-dependence of every
> human soul we see the need of courage, judgment and the exercise of every
> faculty of mind and body, strengthened and developed by use, *in woman as well
> as man*. (32; emphasis added)

Thus, as Cady Stanton addressed male legislators and her co-workers in
the National American Woman Suffrage Association, she reminded them
of the wider meaning of woman's rights principles, that this was a movement not solely aimed at votes for women but at equality of opportunity
in all areas of life for all persons. This was a speech for woman's rights
broadly conceived; more properly, it was a speech for human rights.

In her first public speech at the first woman's rights convention held
in 1848 at Seneca Falls, Cady Stanton said:

> Woman herself must do this work; for woman alone can understand the height,
> the depth, the length, and the breadth of her own degradation. Man cannot
> speak for her, because he has been educated to believe that she differs from him
> so materially, that he cannot judge of her thoughts, feelings, and opinions by his
> own. Moral beings can only judge of others by themselves. (*Proceedings* 1870, 3)

Now, near the end of her long speaking career, Cady Stanton
demonstrated her moral pre-eminence as one who could judge the
conditions of others by her own experience. As a result, she spoke for all
women, of all ages, in all roles, and in all conditions of life; indeed, she
spoke for all persons, rich and poor, male and female, educated and
uneducated. What she expressed and evoked was the nature of the human
condition, and what her audience experienced was the lonely and troubled
solitude of the individual, a condition requiring that each person have all
the opportunities that can be provided by society.

Cady Stanton's speech was a rare moment in the protest rhetoric of
the woman's rights movement. The address hardly mentioned, and
quickly abandoned, demands to grant women the vote, and to provide
them with educational, economic, and legal equality. Instead, the
speech set forth a newer and deeper purpose. No matter what else was
true of the oppression of women, whenever the right to vote and the
right to legal, educational, and economic equality of opportunity was
denied them, men were presuming, out of motives malign or benign,
to take responsibility for women. And it is just here that Cady Stanton's
speech, lyric and tragic though it was, attained its full power. Men
cannot take responsibility for women, as her examples demonstrated;
men can take responsibility only for themselves. The speech presented

the rights of women as a natural and inevitable part of the human birthright.

Cady Stanton's speech succeeded in its time: "the Senate Committee made a favorable majority report. The House Committee were so impressed by her speech that they had 10,000 copies reprinted from the Congressional Record and sent throughout the country" (Lutz 1940, 290). Today it has the power to speak to us, precisely because it transcends its time and place to talk of what it is to be human and of how our common humanity is the basis of all rights.

CONCLUSION

"The Solitude of Self," Cady Stanton's final presidential address, was a rhetorical act that achieved its ends through poetic means. In contrast to more familiar forms of logical argumentation found in her other speeches, this address is nondiscursive and nonpropositional. However, as Cady Stanton's audience encountered the solitude of human life as evoked through her imagery, descriptions, and examples, they recalled and reaffirmed the bases for their most fundamental beliefs.

Two women came to dominate the woman's rights movement of the nineteenth century: Elizabeth Cady Stanton and Susan B. Anthony. Of the two, Cady Stanton was the pre-eminent thinker and publicist, while Anthony was the greater administrator and organizer (Campbell 1987). In addition to being the moving force behind the first woman's rights convention at Seneca Falls, Cady Stanton was a founder and president of the New York Woman's Temperance Society (1851–1853), a founder and president of the American Equal Rights Association (1866–1869), a founder and president of the National Woman Suffrage Association (1869–1890), and president of the merged National American Woman Suffrage Association (1890–1892).

From 1848 until her death in 1902, Cady Stanton's voice and pen were dedicated to woman's rights. She wrote countless newspaper articles and letters to the editor; many of her numerous speeches were published in newspapers and as pamphlets. For eight months of each year between 1869 and 1882 she lectured, usually twice a day, on the lyceum circuit. With Susan B. Anthony as publisher, she and Parker Pillsbury edited the *Revolution* (1868–1870); with Anthony and Matilda Joslyn Gage, she compiled and edited the first three volumes of the *History of Woman Suffrage*. As her speeches and writings attest, she was the early movement's chief theorist; she was also one of its chief publicists, and she was one of those who preserved its history. Above all, consistent with her role as movement philosopher, she was author of the two clearest statements of early movement ideology, the Declaration of Sentiments of the Seneca Falls convention and "The Solitude of Self."

NOTES

1. Sources differ about whether the speech was read for Cady Stanton before the House Judiciary Committee. According to her diary, however, she delivered it herself all three times (Stanton and Blatch 1922, 2:280).

2. Speech to the U.S. Senate Special Committee on Woman Suffrage, Washington, D.C., 8 February 1890; speech to the House Judiciary Committee, 12 February 1890. Reprinted in *Woman's Tribune*, 15 February 1890, 50-53.

3. The address appeared in no major anthology published between 1896 and 1981 (Campbell 1985). An excerpt appears in DuBois 1981, 246-54. It was reprinted in its entirety in 1983 (Kennedy and O'Shields).

4. The single sentence used to introduce the speech to the congressional committees announced that she would not rehearse the arguments suffragists had made before such committees in the past.

5. Cady Stanton failed to mention that Shakespeare's Lavinia was also raped.

6. The philosophy of individualism places the interests of the individual above those of the society or the social group, as illustrated in the political philosophy of Thomas Hobbes or Ayn Rand. In contrast, humanism is a philosophy or attitude concerned with the achievements, interests, and welfare of human beings rather than with abstract beings or theoretical concepts. Cady Stanton's humanism is quite similar to the existential and absurdist humanism of Jean-Paul Sartre in "Existentialism is a Humanism" (1956, 287-311) and in his introduction to *Les Temps Moderne* (1962, 432-41). In the latter work, Sartre wrote that human life is limited by certain givens, "the necessity of being born and dying, of being *finite*, and existing in a world among other men [sic]" (438).

10

The Heavy Burdens of Afro-American Women: Sex, Race, and Class

Historically, in addition to the terrible burdens arising out of slavery, racism, and the poverty they engendered, Afro-American women faced all the problems other women faced. When married, they were civilly dead; unmarried, they were dependents with few possibilities for self-support; and regardless of marital and socioeconomic status, they were oppressed by the cult of true womanhood (Coleman 1981; Guy-Sheftall 1984, 18-19). As a result, as Maria W. Miller Stewart's career illustrates, even free Afro-Americans in the North prior to the Civil War confronted all the proscriptions against speaking in public that their middle-class white counterparts faced, and when they spoke, they were censured. Sojourner Truth's 1851 speech dramatically illustrated the burdens of race, sex, and class that encumbered Afro-American women, most of whom were former slaves.

Given commonalities as well as differences arising from the special conditions confronting Afro-American women, their rhetoric requires special treatment. This chapter examines the ways in which, if at all, it resembled the rhetoric of other women activists, and the degree to which the activities of Afro-American women were related to the woman's rights and woman suffrage movement (Davis 1981; Fitzgerald 1985; Giddings 1984; Hooks 1981; Terborg-Penn 1977). Similarities and differences are explored here through speeches by Ida B. Wells and Mary Church Terrell who, along with Miller Stewart and Truth, were pre-eminent Afro-American speakers of the early period.

IDA B. WELLS

Many Afro-American women were involved in efforts for woman suffrage, because they saw the vote as a means to fight for their own causes, particularly against segregationist legislation that denied Afro-Americans continued participation in or entry into American life. Ida B. Wells and Mary Church Terrell were part of this group. Wells, for example, founded the first Afro-American woman suffrage club, and Church Terrell spoke at National American Woman Suffrage Association Conventions (1898), at the International Council of Women in Berlin (1904), and at the International Congress of Women in 1918 in Switzerland. However, their primary concerns were Afro-American problems: segregation, lynching, the share-cropping system that kept former slaves in peonage, and abuses arising from the convict-lease system—often with special emphasis on their impact upon women.

Ida B. Wells's speech, "Southern Horrors: Lynch Law in All Its Phases," delivered October 5, 1892 (Wells 1892, 4-24), stands as a counterpoint to two more frequently studied rhetorical events. On December 22, 1886, Henry Grady, a prominent white Southern journalist, delivered a speech on "The New South" to the New England Society of New York City at its annual banquet (1886). Wells referred to this speech, and stated explicitly that what she said was intended to be a dramatic refutation of the picture of a changed South that Grady had painted. Three years after Wells began her anti-lynching campaign, Booker T. Washington was invited to address the opening of the Cotton States' Exposition at Atlanta, Georgia, on September 18, 1895 (Washington 1901). Washington addressed a mixed audience of whites and Afro-Americans and articulated the view that Southerners of both races could cooperate in all things economic while remaining socially separate. His gradualist views were in contrast to those of W. E. B. Du Bois, who demanded full legal equality and economic opportunity. Wells's speech makes it clear that she sided with Du Bois; indeed, with him, she was one of the founders of the National Association for the Advancement of Colored People (NAACP). In fact, Wells's calls for economic boycotts and armed self-defense would have been congenial to black power advocates of the 1960s.

Wells's speech is important as a historical document and as the initiating event in what became an organized effort to end lynching; as a rhetorical work, it is noteworthy in three respects. First, as in her writings, she used evidence and argument in highly sophisticated ways, ways that prevented members of the audience from dismissing her claims as biased or untrue. Second, the speech was an insightful and sophisticated analysis of the interrelationship of sex, race, and class. Third, in contrast to the rhetorical acts of some other women, this speech contained no apparent indications of attempts by a woman

speaker to appear "womanly" in what was perceived as a male role —
that of speaker.

Wells's use of evidence and argument had to overcome severe
obstacles. She had to refute the cultural history of sexism and racism
that made a white woman's cry of rape adequate justification for
violence against Afro-Americans (Aptheker 1901; Grant 1975). She
had to show that lynchings were frequent and that rape was not even
alleged in a majority of cases. She had to draw this evidence from
unimpeachable sources, and she had to use the statements of whites
to reveal the real motives behind these acts.

The evidence Wells presented was part of a carefully constructed
case. Initially, she argued: "White men lynch the offending Afro-
American, not because he is a despoiler of virtue, but because he
succumbs to the smiles of white women" (6). Some seventeen detailed
examples were presented in support of this claim. This was the final,
relatively brief instance in the series:

> Ebenzer [sic] Fowler, the wealthiest colored man in Issaquena County, Miss.,
> was shot down on the street in Mayersville, January 30, 1885, just before dark
> by an armed body of white men who filled his body with bullets. They charged
> him with writing a note to a white woman of the place, which they intercepted
> and which proved there was an intimacy existing between them. (Wells 1892,
> 10-11)

The detailed examples created a very unusual rhetorical structure, and
they allowed her audience to weigh the evidence and consider its
plausibility. Also, the fact that much of the information came from the
public press, in some cases from white Southern newspapers, added to the
credibility of her accounts. She left her audience in no doubt that real
human beings were caught in lethal dilemmas again and again throughout
the South, and she aroused an emotional response by the number of
examples and the details she provided rather than by exhortation. The
long list of crimes became a litany that gathered force as it continued. At
the same time, the details never induced the kind of revulsion that would
make it difficult for an audience to continue listening (Janis 1972).

Wells's argument also revealed the terrible double standard: "The
utterances of the leading white men show that with them it is not the
crime but the *class*" (11), she said, referring to the fact that when the
victims were Afro-American women, no protection was afforded, no
vengeance was needed. Once again, her proof was a series of six
dramatic examples intended to show that no one attempted to protect
Afro-American women or female children or to punish those who

assaulted them. This was the first in the series:

> Last winter in Baltimore, Maryland, three white ruffians assaulted a Miss
> Camphor, a young Afro-American girl, while out walking with a young man of
> her own race. They held her escort and outraged the girl. It was a deed dastardly
> enough to arouse Southern blood, which gives its horror of rape as an excuse
> for lawlessness, but she was an Afro-American. The case went to the courts, an
> Afro-American lawyer defended the men, and they were acquitted. (11)

If the reason for lynching was not the protection of Afro-American
or white womanhood, some other motive was at work. Wells argued
that lynching was done to control Afro-Americans — lynching was
political, with the allegation of rape used as justification. She first
pointed to the other forms of control that were then widespread
throughout the South, particularly the so-called Jim Crow laws, which
were passed after the 1875 Civil Rights Act was declared unconstitutional in 1883 (Motley 1966). Wells noted that despite these other
forms of control, lynching had increased. Here she used evidence
gathered by a Northern white newspaper, the *Chicago Tribune*, to
document with statistics the extent of the problem and the fact that in
only one-third of the cases was rape even alleged.

She then cited editorials from white Memphis newspapers. The first
quotation embodied the myth of the bestial Afro-American rapist,
despite the fact that no incidents supporting that myth had occurred
in Memphis. The second editorial made explicit the intent to coerce
submission through violence. It was a classic statement of the view that
"uppity Negroes" should be punished severely. Wells quoted the
editorial:

> "the chief cause of trouble between the races in the South is the Negro's lack of
> manners. In the state of slavery he learned politeness from association with
> white people, who took pains to teach him. Since the emancipation came . . .
> there are many Negroes who use every opportunity to make themselves offen-
> sive, particularly when they think it can be done with impunity. . . . *The white
> people won't stand this sort of thing, and whether they be insulted as individuals
> or as a race, the response will be prompt and effectual.*" (17; emphasis in original)

Wells went on to describe the 1892 lynching in Memphis about
which she had written, an act that had put her life in jeopardy. This
particular lynching, occasioned by economic competition, became a
paradigmatic case of lynching throughout the South. Wells concluded
by stating that all who disapproved of lynching and remained silent
became accessories, because lynch mobs would not persist if their
members knew that the forces of law and order would be used against

them. Throughout this argument there was a strong appeal to fundamental values of fairness, to the right to trial by jury, and to the right to full and careful investigation of crimes. These appeals added weight to her accusation that silent bystanders were guilty of complicity.

Wells concluded that, given the absence of legal protection or redress, Afro-Americans had to turn to self-help. They had to learn the facts of such cases for themselves in order to judge what the truth was. The cases she cited called for more investigative reporting like her own. In addition, Afro-Americans had to use economic boycotts to demand appropriate legal action against lynchers, and they had to arm themselves to act in self-defense to prevent mob violence. Here, too, she used examples, including one from Memphis, where a boycott in response to the 1892 lynching had had some effect, although not enough to force action against the lynchers, all of whose names were known. Two examples where lynchings were prevented by armed self-defense were noted, but without details. Wells ended by proposing that these three solutions in concert could solve the problem, that is, stamp out lynch law.

Wells made a carefully constructed case that rested on kinds of evidence that made the problem vivid, demonstrated its scope, supported the speaker's analysis of its causes, and suggested the futility of alternative solutions. Wells understood the kind of problem she faced. Given the general acceptance of the myth that lynching was caused by sexual assaults on white women, Wells recognized that her audience would find it hard to believe her. She carefully selected her evidence in order to prevent such a response. Hearers and readers encountered case after case that challenged their casual assumptions. They learned the statistical facts from a white Northern newspaper. They heard the myth and the political coercion from the mouths of the editors of newspapers in the very town from which Wells had been driven. Wells was calling into question her audience's prior beliefs and opening their minds to future evidence. The soundness, indeed, the power of Wells's analysis of the relationship of sex, race, and class in the phenomenon of lynching is attested to by the fact that her conclusions recurred in the resolutions, declarations, and speeches of the white women of the Association of Southern Women for the Prevention of Lynching, founded in 1930 under the leadership of Jessie Daniel Ames (Hall 1978, 1979).

Wells's speech was a well-made case. It was also a cogent analysis of the interrelationship of sex, race, and class. The language of the speech was blunt, as, for example, when she said: "Nobody in this section of the country believes the old threadbare lie that Negro men rape white women" (4). The speech's structure was deductive. Its tone was authoritative, at times, even sarcastic. Wells stated her claims clearly, and although the Memphis example came from her personal experience, she did not present it as her personal experience — it was a model instance to be examined objectively. The analogies were literal; metaphors were not used, with a single exception that cast Afro-American men as Samsons tempted by white Delilahs. Wells spoke as an authority and as a leader who could determine the right courses of action, as illustrated by her conclusion. She spoke impersonally; the pronoun "I" appeared only when she asserted her claims. She used white male newspaper editors as authorities, but only in ways that were damaging to them. She was willing to speak the accusations, to make the indictments, in her own voice. The speech was replete with bold assertions such as, "To the Afro-American the South says, 'the white man must and will rule.' There is little difference between the Ante-bellum and the New South" (20).

The address was lengthy. On one level, it was little more than a list of examples, but these examples were chosen in such a way that they amplified and intensified the briefly developed arguments that linked the major sections of the speech. The sources, the careful use of detail, and the cumulative weight of the examples made them a particularly powerful force in the speech.

Like other women activists in this period, Wells was defiant, intensely committed, and highly assertive. These qualities created difficulties for her (Sterling 1979, 116). Paula Giddings comments: "By 1924 Ida Wells-Barnett had managed to run afoul of almost everyone with her strident independence and refusal to compromise her principles" (1984, 180). What is noteworthy here, however, is that Wells made no attempt to diminish the impact of her egregious violations of taboos against women speaking and of audience expectations about how women should make such violations less disturbing. The use of examples, often one of the characteristics of "feminine" style, was quite the opposite here — a quiet but fierce recitation of horror piled upon horror.

MARY CHURCH TERRELL

Much later, in the 1930s, white women organized to fight against lynching, and their analyses recognized the interrelationship between racism and sexism. However, the next speech considered here is a sharp reminder of the gulf between Afro-American and white women.

"What It Means to Be Colored in the Capital of the United States" was delivered by Mary Church Terrell in 1906 as an attempt to make whites understand just what it was to be Afro-American, particularly an Afro-American woman, in the nation's capital, that symbol of national values (Terrell 1907).[1]

Mary Church was born in 1863 into a wealthy Afro-American family in Memphis, Tennessee. She was well-educated and well-traveled, served on the District of Columbia School Board for eleven years, and in 1896 became the first president of the National Association of Colored Women, a federation of Afro-American women's clubs. She toured the country speaking against lynching and for the civil rights of Afro-Americans, and she spent her life working for the rights of all Afro-Americans and all women.[2] Her commitment to such causes is reflected in the many texts of her speeches which remain in her papers. In fact, she was linked to Ida B. Wells's anti-lynching effort; she introduced Wells when, in February of 1893, Wells addressed a large meeting at the Metropolitan African Methodist Episcopal Church in Washington, D.C. (Giddings 1984, 89; Sterling 1979, 85; Terrell, 1893). In her autobiography, Church Terrell wrote: "I was not on the lecture platform to make money, but to create sentiment in behalf of my race and to acquaint the public with facts which it did not know then and does not know today" (1940, 185). Like other women, when she began her career as a speaker in the 1890s, she encountered resistance:

> For years I had been wishing that the opportunity of creating sentiment in favor of our group would be presented to me in some way, and it seemed that going on the lecture platform would give the longed-for chance. . . . When, however, my husband consented . . . some of his friends were so shocked and horrified that words simply failed them as they attempted to express their disapprobation. (1940, 158)

Her 1906 speech was a deeply moving statement of what Afro-Americans faced at the turn of the century as segregation became enshrined in law in the United States. What she revealed about the experiences of Afro-Americans was proof of the gap between America's proclaimed principles and their application to those with "a fatal drop of African blood . . . percolating somewhere through [their] veins" (Terrell 1907, 183). The speech was a long series of examples intended to evoke identification with the plight of Afro-Americans. Because Church Terrell was a well-educated, middle-class woman, she was able to function as a mediator between Afro-Americans and her white, middle-class audience. Given the nature of racism, the fact that she could have passed for white might have enhanced her ability to induce identification (Terrell 1940, passim).

Church Terrell was well aware of the kinds of rhetorical problems she faced. In a speech on "The Effects of Disfranchisement Upon the Colored Women of the South," she discussed the obstacles that arose from the attitudes of her white audiences:

> It is a dangerous thing to tell the truth about the injustice and barbarism inflicted upon colored people in the U.S. at the present time. . . . No matter how tactfully one discusses the painful and revolting conditions under which thousands of my race live, the individual who discusses the subject is accused even by those who say they want to know the facts of exaggerating them and of being so bitter and biased himself [sic] as to be incapable of telling the truth. This is particularly true when a colored person refers to the hardships and humiliations to which his race is subjected and urges redress of wrongs. (Terrell c.1913, 2-3)

She also recognized difficulties involved in describing the problems of Afro-American women: "If I tell the plain unvarnished truth about certain conditions which affect colored women in the South, I shall be accused by some of casting foul aspersions upon the women of my race" (3-4). This speech is subtly crafted to avoid both of these pitfalls.

The speech began as refutation of what whites might have imagined was the situation of Afro-Americans in the nation's capital, and was designed to give her white audience a glimpse of the world as Afro-Americans experienced it. She started with her own experiences. What the audience saw was an attractive woman, dressed like any other middle-class woman of her time. What they heard was that her life was vastly different from their own. An Afro-American could not sleep or eat in most areas of the capital, had to travel in a segregated trolley to visit the Washington Monument, and would be thrown in jail and fined if she protested. She could not worship in a church like others; she could not earn her living unless she were willing to work at the most menial occupations.

Church Terrell moved from her own experiences to those of others. The examples she chose were almost entirely of talented and aspiring Afro-Americans, those most like her audience, people with artistic gifts to develop, people with intellectual abilities who wished to pursue higher education, people who sought decent work as stenographers and sales clerks, people who taught in the public schools, and, finally, people who sought admission to trade unions or were skilled workmen who sought to ply their trades. Her choices were appropriate for her audience. They would have found it difficult to identify with those most unlike themselves, poor, unskilled, uneducated Afro-Americans. Her cases depicted scenes in which her white auditors might easily have imagined themselves.

Church Terrell's examples not only demonstrated the discrepancy between American principles and practices, they refuted the claims that the poor conditions of Afro-Americans were a result of their own inadequacies. In each case, able, eager, hard-working Afro-Americans were prevented from self-improvement and self-support for no reason other than their "color." They were ambitious, demonstrably talented, and polite. As she indicated in her conclusion, "To the lack of incentive to effort, which is the awful shadow under which we live, may be traced the wreck and ruin of scores of colored youth" (Terrell 1907, 186).

The examples were an ideal vehicle for evoking empathy. Each was presented in sufficient detail to allow listeners to imagine themselves in such circumstances, forced to spend "the entire night wandering about"; or "ravenously hungry and abundantly supplied with money with which to purchase a meal, without finding a single restaurant in which . . . [they were] permitted to take a morsel of food" (181); or humiliated by segregation; or rejected and discharged because of prejudice. She linked each example to her personal experience, mentioning, for instance, "Another young friend" (183) and "one of my little daughter's bosom friends" (184). She believed her audience did not know what her life and the lives of other Afro-Americans were really like, and she sought to arouse their sense of fair play by the stories she told. The speech was also intended to show how racism caused the conditions for which Afro-Americans were blamed and to prevent passage of a bill mandating segregated street cars in the District of Columbia.

The speeches of Wells and Church Terrell differed significantly, but both were in simple, straightforward language, especially when compared with that of Frances Willard, and both relied on a long series of examples as their major form of proof. Unlike Wells, in her speech Church Terrell adapted to audience expectations.[3] She spoke from personal experience, which she linked to the personal experience of others, whereas Wells presented her examples impersonally. Church Terrell's speech developed inductively; it relied on appeals to the feelings of the audience. The conclusions were implied rather than bluntly stated. It was a speech by a woman that conformed to traditional expectations for women speakers, and it used forms of appeal and support that were highly appropriate for a white, middle-class, largely female audience. In addition, it carefully avoided offending Afro-Americans or feeding into the racism that would blame the victims for their problems. However, although Church Terrell feminized her rhetorical role, her speech was significantly different from that of Frances Willard. Unlike Willard, she used detailed examples, and those examples confronted the audience by refuting stereotypical notions of Afro-Americans. Church Terrell also worked inductively, inviting identification and participation from her audience, and addressed them as peers. However, in contrast to the 1854 and 1860 speeches of Elizabeth Cady Stanton to the New York Legislature, there was no biting sarcasm, no uncontrolled anger.

In her resolute refusal to adapt to audience expectations, Wells was Church Terrell's antithesis. Wells argued deductively; as a well-made case, her speech most resembled that of Susan B. Anthony in defense of her vote. As with the examples presented by Clarina Howard Nichols, the cases Wells detailed persuaded her audience through a steady process of accretion; but unlike Howard Nichols and Church Terrell, who linked each example to themselves, Wells's instances were presented impersonally, as the product of the research of an investigative journalist. And although she was less overtly sarcastic than Cady Stanton, the tone of Wells's speech was ironic, at times even bitter.

CONCLUSION

Ida B. Wells was a significant figure in the struggle for Afro-American woman's rights. She is rightly famous for spearheading an anti-lynching crusade and for her role in stimulating the organization of Afro-American women into clubs aimed at self-improvement and social reform. In addition to forming the first Afro-American woman suffrage club, she marched in suffrage parades in Washington, D.C., in 1913, and in Chicago, when 5,000 suffragists converged in torrential rain on the 1916 Republican National Convention to demand a suffrage plank in the party platform. Her militancy led to conflicts and personal disappointments in both the National Association of Colored Women and the NAACP, but she was a major figure in organized efforts by Afro-Americans to secure their rights.

Mary Church Terrell was deeply involved in reform activities throughout her life. However, her most significant contributions to the advancement of Afro-Americans in general and Afro-American women in particular were as a lecturer and writer. She was deeply committed to woman suffrage; she picketed the White House with the National Woman's Party, and following passage of the Nineteenth

Amendment, she directed work among colored women for the Republican National Committee and urged passage of an equal rights amendment. She remained active in reform activities to the very end of her life. In 1948, at age 85, she was instrumental in breaking down the color bar of the American Association of University Women; in 1950, she was part of a group that desegregated restaurants in Washington, D.C. In 1949 she led a delegation to the United Nations and spoke in support of Rosa Ingram, who, with her teenage son, was sentenced to life imprisonment when her son defended her from attack by a white man and, in so doing, caused the white man's death. As late as 1954, she traveled to Georgia to seek a pardon for Ingram from the governor (Sterling 1979, 154-55).

As these women's careers demonstrate, leading Afro-American women reformers felt that the problems of race were more compelling than the grievances of women, but they recognized the relationship between the civil rights of all Afro-Americans and the civil rights of all women. Most particularly, they recognized and struggled against the multiple burdens borne by Afro-American women.

NOTES

1. No text of this speech, other than the published version, exists in the Mary Church Terrell papers in the Library of Congress or in the Moorland-Spingarn Collection at Howard University. The language of its title reflects the speaker's strong preference for the word "colored" rather than "Negro" in describing herself and those of her race (Terrell 1948). In 1943 she wrote:

> I never use the word Negro when I can avoid it. If a man is a Negro, it follows as the night the day that I am a Negress. I will not allow anybody to call me a 'Negress' if I can prevent it. 'Negress' is a term of reproach which the colored women of this country cannot live down for thousands of years. . . . Our group will never receive the respect and considera- tion to which we are entitled as long as we allow ourselves to be designated as Negroes (Terrell 1943, 57).

2. In a sketch, "Women on the Platform," by Col. William French for *Talent* magazine, her concerns as a speaker were described this way: "The theme which has most attracted her rare abilities are the rights of women and the wrongs of the colored race" (Mary Church Terrell Papers, Moorland-Spingarn Collection, Howard Univer- sity, Box 102-9, folder 201). In 1943 she wrote: "I have been trying to present the colored man's case clearly, strongly, and tactfully to the people of the dominant race" (57). She linked these causes in a "Talk to Young Men" at Howard University, March 2, 1925, when she said:

> The colored woman has a double burden to carry—the burden of race in addition to sex. White women all over the civilized world showed how heavy they thought was the burden of sex by the desperate efforts they made to secure suffrage. . . . The colored woman has

two such heavy loads to carry (Moorland-Spingarn Collection, Box 102-3, folder 120, p. 7).

3. Church Terrell could also be confrontational and defiant. See, especially, the 1905 "A Plea for the White South by a Colored Woman" (Library of Congress, Reel 21, container 29, 137-152).

11

The Coming of Woman Suffrage: The Orator, the Organizer, and the Agitator

After the Fourteenth Amendment inserted the word "male" into the Constitution in 1868, and after the Supreme Court in *Minor v. Happersett* (1875) closed the judicial route to suffrage (Hoff-Wilson 1987, 8; Hodes 1970), women were forced to seek a federal suffrage amendment, and had to take their case directly to male voters. In the words of movement leader Carrie Chapman Catt:

> To get the world "male" in effect out of the Constitution cost the women of the country 52 years of pauseless campaign thereafter. During that time they were forced to conduct 56 campaigns of referenda to male voters; 480 campaigns to get Legislatures to submit suffrage amendments to voters; 47 campaigns to get State Constitutional Conventions to write woman suffrage into State Constitutions; 277 campaigns to get state party conventions to include woman suffrage planks; 30 campaigns to get presidential party conventions to adopt woman suffrage planks in party platforms; and 19 campaigns with 19 successive Congresses. . . . It was a continuous, seemingly endless, chain of activity. (Walker 1951, 229)

Despite this effort, the period between 1890 and 1915 was known as the "doldrums" because the movement made little progress (Lerner 1971, 159-161). By 1912, for example, after sixty-four years of organized effort, only nine Western states with forty-five electoral votes allowed women to vote.

Several explanations are possible. During this period the movement's original leaders died: Lucy Stone (1893), Elizabeth Cady Stanton (1902), and Susan B. Anthony (1906); there was a major transition and upheaval in leadership. The years 1896 to 1907 were a time of anti-suffrage ascendancy: in the twelve years from 1898 to 1909, the suffragists suffered a total of 164 defeats, an average of one every twenty-seven days (Camhi 1973, 97, 349). Hostility to woman suffrage did not diminish until progressivism grew in power and influence. The successful state referendum campaigns ending the doldrums occurred in states that had passed one or more of the progressive reforms of initiative, referendum, and recall, for example, Washington in 1910; California in 1911; Oregon, Kansas, and Arizona in 1912. After 1910, in other words, the tide began to change. This chapter is about the role of rhetoric in that process.

Suffrage advocates were engaged in a persuasive campaign. They had to persuade ordinary voters to approve referenda, they had to persuade politicians to support a federal amendment and to ratify it on the state level, and they had to agitate in order to attract attention to an effort that had gone on for over fifty years. They also had to maintain the morale of suffrage workers, enabling women to continue their extended struggle for the ballot. Three major leaders met the needs of the movement during this period: a great orator, the Rev. Dr. Anna Howard Shaw (Shaw 1915; Flexner 1971); a great organizer, Carrie Chapman Catt (Peck 1944; Fowler 1986; Van Voris 1987); and a wily and dedicated agitator, Alice Paul (Gornick 1978; Irwin 1964).

In this final stage of their long effort, woman suffrage advocates confronted the special problems that arise in any sustained persuasive effort—how to keep arguments fresh and attention-getting, how to respond to changing conditions, how to explain defeats, and how to refute the charges of an increasingly articulate and organized opposition. Like most who had preceded them, these three leaders continued to ground their arguments in natural rights principles. In the case of Anna Howard Shaw, these principles were combined with refutation and a style of humor that delighted audiences. In the case of Carrie Chapman Catt, they were an integral part of her argument that woman suffrage was inevitable. Most dramatically, these values underlay the confrontational strategies used by Alice Paul and her co-workers in the Congressional Union, which became the National Woman's Party.

THE ORATOR

Following their defeats in the courts and in Congress, woman suffrage advocates turned to state referenda as a means to enfranchisement. Between 1870 and 1910, only two, in Colorado and Idaho, out of eleven succeeded. Between 1910 through 1917, the record was:

Year	Won	Lost
1910	WA	OR
1911	CA	
1912	OR, KS, AZ	WI, MI, OH
1914	MT, NV	ND, SD, NE, MO, OH
1915		NY, NJ, MA, PA
1917	NY	ME

Clearly, suffragists were struggling to persuade ordinary male voters of the justice of their cause.

The leading speaker of this period was the Rev. Dr. Anna Howard Shaw (Linkugel 1960; 1963; 1987). Catt herself recognized this when she said that Shaw "stood unchallenged as the greatest orator among women the world has ever known" (Catt and Shuler 1923, 268). Anna Howard Shaw began lecturing for the Massachusetts Woman Suffrage Association, became a temperance lecturer for the WCTU, then a paid lecturer for the American Woman Suffrage Association in 1888; she continued in that role after 1890 for the National American Woman Suffrage Association. During the last forty years of her life, Shaw proclaimed woman's right to suffrage in every state; from 1881 to 1919, Shaw regularly delivered several hundred speeches a year, often speaking as frequently as eight times a day. In 1915, for example, she made 204 speeches in New York state alone (Linkugel 1963, 166). In the movement's own history of the suffrage campaign, it was claimed that Shaw won more people for equal suffrage than any other advocate (Catt and Shuler 1923, 268-69). Given her prominence and her success, Shaw's speeches are an ideal source of information about how women tailored their speeches for male voters.

Shaw's speeches are noteworthy for techniques of adaptation and refutation. She adapted to ordinary audiences by inducing auditors to laugh at their fears and at her opponents, by transmuting familiar arguments into dramatic narratives, and by providing detailed examples. She was particularly skilled in refuting opposing arguments, frequently reducing them to absurdity and exploiting their mutually contradictory character. In addition, as a speaker Shaw herself reassured male voters that the "new woman" was sensible and pleasant, not the frightening monster described by her opponents. Of the extant texts of her speeches, "The Fundamental Principle of a Republic" is her masterpiece, a paradigmatic example of her skills and her strategies (Shaw 1915).

"Fundamental Principle" was another speech in colloquial style, and thus akin to the rhetoric of Sojourner Truth, including humor, broken grammar, and the associative structure of extemporaneous delivery. "Fundamental Principles" had three relatively distinct parts. In the first Shaw argued for enfranchisement based on natural rights; in the second she refuted opponents' arguments; and in the third she considered whether women would fight if they could vote.

Humor, particularly noteworthy in her speaking, was most prominent in the second section, although it appeared throughout the speech. Shaw's humor was often devastating to her opponents and to men, but as she presented it, it became a means to confront male voters without alienating them. She induced listeners to laugh with her—sometimes at themselves. She was particularly skilled at using humor to refute arguments, often by highlighting their internal contradictions. She began the second section of her speech, for instance, by telling the audience that the anti-suffragists "never make an argument but they answer it." She remarked that they argue that if women had the ballot, they would not use it, but that they then point to the awful results which happen when women do use the ballot. They argue that woman suffrage is a useless expense because wives will vote just as their husbands do, but then turn around and argue that wives will not vote as their husbands do, which will produce discord and divorce. Shaw's summary of their arguments is a humorous reductio ad absurdum:

> We will either vote as our husbands vote or we will not vote as our husbands vote. We either have time to vote or we don't have time to vote. We will either not vote at all or we will vote all the time. It reminds me of the story of the old Irish woman who had twin boys, and they were so much alike that the neighbors could not tell them apart, and the mother always seemed to be able to tell them apart so one of the neighbors said, "Now Mrs. Mahoney, you have two of the finest twin boys I ever saw in all my life, but how do you know them apart?" "Oh," she says, "that's easy enough, anyone could tell them apart. When I want to know which is which, I just put my finger in Patsey's mouth and if he bites it is Mikey." (Shaw 1915, 3)

Her refutation linked humor and examples, many drawn from personal experience. Opponents argued enfranchised women would neglect their duties as mothers, so Shaw went to a place where women had the vote to find out what happened to babies on election day:

> I went to Denver and I found that they took care of their babies just the same on election day as they did on every other day; they took their baby along with them, when they went to put a letter in a box they took their baby along, and when they went to put their ballot in the box they took their baby along. If the

mother had to stand in line and the baby got restless she would joggle the go-cart, most everyone had a go-cart, and when she went in to vote a neighbor would joggle the go-cart, and if there was no neighbor there was the candidate and he would joggle the cart. That is one day in the year when you could get a hundred people to take care of any number of babies. I have never worried about the babies on election day since that time. (3)

In what is perhaps the climax of Shaw's humor, she used her personal experience both to refute an opposition claim and to cast her male auditors in an image supportive of suffrage:

A gentleman . . . in California . . . said he and his wife had lived together for twenty years and never had a difference of opinion in the whole twenty years and he was afraid if women began to vote that his wife would vote differently from him and then that beautiful harmony which they had had for twenty years would be broken, and all the time he was talking I could not help wondering which was the idiot, — because I know that no intelligent human beings could live together for twenty years and not have differences of opinion. All the time he was talking I looked at that splendid type of manhood and thought, how would a man feel being tagged up by a little woman for twenty years saying "me too, me too." . . . What a reflection is that on men. If we should say that about men we would never hear the last of it. . . . Great big overgrown babies! Cannot be disputed without having a row! While we do not believe that men are saints, by any means, we do believe that the average American man is a fairly good sort of fellow. (2)

Shaw made an important transition into a restatement of the natural rights argument that ends this section of the speech. The transition distinguished between topics for which humor was suitable and those for which it was not. She said:

Now what does it matter whether the women will vote as their husbands do or will not vote; whether they have time or have not; or whether they will vote for prohibition or not. What has that to do with the fundamental question of democracy, no one has yet discovered. But they cannot argue on . . . the fundamental basis of our existence, so that they have to get off all these side tracks to get anything approaching an argument. (3)

She then contended that democracy

is more than a form of government; it is a great spiritual force emanating from the heart of the Infinite, transforming human character until some day, some day in the distant future, man by the power of the spirit of democracy, will be able to look back into the face of the Infinite and answer, as man cannot answer today, "One is our Father, even God, and all we people are the children of one family." (3)

The fundamental principles of a republic were matters of great spiritual import and seriousness; by contrast, the trivial and self-contradictory arguments of anti-suffragists could be treated with levity.

Consistent with her encomium to democracy, the natural rights argument Shaw had offered in the first section of the speech resembled those made by others, but with some distinctive features. Shaw made her position clear at the outset:

> Now one of two things is true: either a Republic is a desirable form of govern-
> ment, or else it is not. If it is, then we should have it, if it is not then we ought
> not to pretend that we have it. We ought, at least to be true to our ideals, and
> the men of New York have, for the first time in their lives the rare opportunity,
> on the second day of next November, of making the state truly part of a Republic.
> (2)

In what follows, two strategic adaptations are apparent. Shaw transformed logical arguments into historical narratives, and she provided detailed enumeration of her claims to ensure that listeners would understand precisely what she was arguing. The historical narrative explaining the nature of a republic began: "If we trace our history back we will find that from the very dawn of our existence as a people, men have been imbued with a spirit and a vision more lofty than they have been able to live" (2). She told the story of the Puritans: they were "men of profound conviction and yet these men who gave up everything in behalf of an ideal, hardly established their communities in this new country before they began to practice exactly the same sort of persecutions on other men which had been practiced upon them" (2).

Shaw reaffirmed the commitment of the nation's founders to republican ideals, but noted that after the Revolution, they were unable to put their ideals fully into practice: "Before the word 'male' in the local compacts they wrote the word 'church-member'; after that they rubbed out 'church-member' and they wrote in the word 'tax-payer.'" Then "there arose a great Democrat, Thomas Jefferson," who saw the dangers of accumulated wealth "and so the Democratic party took another step in the evolution of a Republic out of a monarchy and they rubbed out the word 'taxpayer' and wrote in the word 'white.' . . . And then the Republican party took out that progressive evolutionary eraser and rubbed out the word 'white' from before the word 'male.'" The conclusion of this story reflected the humor that pervaded the speech: "They were all in, black and white, rich and poor, wise and otherwise, drunk and sober; not a man left out to be put in" (2).

As is typical of speeches to ordinary audiences, there was much repetition, designed to insure that points are made, clarified, and hammered home. To make her points vividly, Shaw incorporated metaphors, as for example when she referred to a typical Fourth of July speaker who proclaims: "the voice of the people is the voice of God," but "forgets that in the people's voice there is a soprano as well as a bass." (2) More important, she spelled out in great detail just what she meant. Here, for instance, is how she explained the difference between proper and improper voting qualifications as established by the states:

> Whenever a Republic prescribes the qualifications as applies equally to all the citizens of the Republic, so that when the Republic says in order to vote, a citizen must be twenty-one years of age, it applies to all alike, there is no discrimination against any race or sex. When the government says that a citizen must be a native born citizen or a naturalized citizen, that applies to all; we are either born or naturalized; somehow or other we are here. Whenever the government says that a citizen, in order to vote, must be a resident of a community a certain length of time . . . that applies to all equally. There is no discrimination. (2)

No one in the audience could have mistaken what Shaw was claiming.

The final section of the speech addressed the difficult issue raised by the war that had begun in Europe: "If women vote, will they go to war?" Shaw's responses mirrored the ambivalence of woman suffrage advocates. She claimed that women preferred talk, based on the example of the International Suffrage Association meeting in Rome, at which women from nations that would shortly go to war had been able to cooperate. She then shifted the issue and made a highly sentimental appeal to motherhood. She recalled a question from a man in North Dakota, "Well, what does a woman know about war anyway?" She asked another man to hold up a paper with the headline "250,000 Men Killed Since the War Began," and she responded:

> No woman knows the significance of 250,000 dead men, but you tell me that one man lay dead and I might be able to tell you something of its awful meaning to one woman. I would know that years before a woman whose heart beat in unison with her love and her desire for motherhood walked day by day with her face to an open grave, with courage, which no man has ever surpassed . . . and if there was laid in her arms a tiny little bit of helpless humanity, I would know that there went out from her soul such a cry of thankfulness as none save a mother could know. . . . That mother looking into the dark years to come knows that when her son died her life's hope died with him, and in the face of that wretched motherhood, what man dare ask what a woman knows of war. (3)

This was a sharp departure from the tone and argument of the rest of the speech. Her claim was highly emotional, and the tone was intense, perhaps reflecting the weakness of logic grounded in traditional concepts of motherhood. Shaw concluded by saying that women do not want the ballot in order to fight but in order to help keep men from fighting, thus narrowly avoiding a claim that women are by nature more peace-loving than men. The complexity of responding to this issue was increased by the link made between the ballot and the capacity to enforce voting decisions in anti-suffrage rhetoric (Camhi 1973, ch. 9).

Shaw's speech was an appeal to popular audiences that combined logical argument, including refutation, with a humor that encouraged a detached examination of opposition arguments and a more sensible view of political action by women. Further, her style of argument—commonsensical and good-humored—suggested that the "new woman," at least as personified by Shaw, was someone whose entry into the public sphere would not spell catastrophe for morals or government. At one point, for example, she said: "There are some women who want to hold office and I may as well own up, I am one of them" (Shaw 1915, 3). She confessed that she had always wanted to be a police officer and explained that she saw the function of the police as the prevention of crime. She claimed that women on the police force were needed "at every moving picture show, every dance house, every restaurant, every hotel . . . and every park, every resort where the vampires who fatten on the crimes and vices of men and women gather" (3).

More generally, however, this was a "new woman" who was deeply patriotic and spiritual, knew how to tell a joke, make an argument, answer a challenge, and, in the process, maintain her equilibrium. She was, herself, a strong argument for woman's entry into all facets of the public sphere. Shaw made a good case for her cause, she put her audience in a frame of mind to consider that case in good humor, and she presented herself as a prime example of what it would be like if women voted. Shaw stands alone among early speakers in using so much humor so effectively. Her efforts and those of women speakers like her made woman suffrage increasingly acceptable to ordinary voters.

THE LEADER

As the movement's "doldrums" demonstrated, persuasion by in-dividual speakers was not enough. The movement needed organiza-tion and leadership, and it found them in the special talents of Carrie Lane Chapman Catt. Catt was a skilled organizer, an effective leader, and an able speaker (Walker 1951; Clevenger 1955; Katz 1973). She began her political work on the NAWSA Organization Committee and demonstrated her skills early on, in the successful Idaho referendum campaign of 1896. In 1897, for example, organizers from her committee held over one thousand meetings; they formed two state branches, 113 county branches, and 110 local societies. She was president of the NAWSA from 1900 until 1904, and returned to that position in 1915 to lead the membership through the final campaigns until suffrage was achieved. The "Winning Plan" that she announced in 1916 was an administrative and tactical masterpiece designed to put maximum political pressure on Congress to pass a suffrage amendment, based on a hard-nosed analysis of what realistically could be achieved.[1]

Catt was also a realist about suffrage rhetoric.[2] In 1899, for example, she wrote a ruthless analysis of the unsuccessful South Dakota referendum campaign that included this statement: "We are appealing to justice for success, when it is selfishness that governs mankind" (Peck 1944, 65; Catt 1899). As a result of this pragmatism, her speeches included arguments addressed to the self-interest of political decision makers as well as arguments based on principle. Catt's speeches also illustrate how suffrage arguments could be framed to raise the morale of suffrage workers.

Addresses Catt delivered in 1902, 1916, and 1917 exemplify her leadership and political skills. The first was delivered during a time of great frustration; the second prepared for the introduction of her "Winning Plan"; the third was a triumphal statement following the successful referendum campaign in New York, which all recognized as clear evidence that victory was in sight.

When compared to Shaw or Cady Stanton, Catt was a competent but not a great speaker. Published and unpublished accounts of her speaking emphasized that she was "seldom dramatic," that "she spoke with impersonality and a certain detachment" although "her delivery was commanding," or, more generally, that she was "a fluent talker, eloquent, witty, well informed, and logical" (Walker 1951, 145, 4, 6). Many accounts refer to her presence or authority and to the clarity of her diction.

Catt's 1902 speech was cast in moderate to high style, and it reflected her lifelong belief in progress through evolution. According to her unsigned autobiography, Catt thought Darwin's *Origin of Species* the single greatest influence on nineteenth-century thought (Walker 1951, 18). David H. Katz concludes: "Mrs. Catt's public life was, on the most basic level, the acting out of a single conviction: that humanity was, despite periodic setbacks, destined to follow an upward curve towards ever greater enlightenment and achievement" (1973, 3). Her 1902 speech illustrated how such beliefs could be instruments for persuading male agents of change while raising the morale of suffragists. Catt did not rehearse arguments for natural rights, she simply described self-government as an idea that, once articulated in the Declaration of Independence, spread around the world: "Wherever self-government for men exists, it will stay; and where it does not exist, it will come" (Catt 1902, 2). Moreover, "Hard upon the track of the man-suffrage movement presses the movement for woman suffrage, a logical step onward" (3).

Although Catt called the plea for woman suffrage "dignified, calm and logical" (5), she recognized that sex-prejudice was a formidable obstacle. This is noteworthy because, although her analysis was sketchy, it was one of the earliest attempts to analyze what is now called sexism.

> What *is* prejudice? An opinion, which is not based upon reason; a judgment, without having heard the argument; a feeling, without being able to trace from whence it came. And sex-prejudice is a pre-judgment against the rights, liberties and opportunities of women. A belief, without proof, in the incapacity of women to do that which they have never done. (5)

She explained sex-prejudice as "the outgrowth of a theory practically universal" that "men were the units of the human race. . . . Women were auxiliaries, or dependents, with no race responsibilities of their own" (6). The condition created by this theory, what contemporary feminists call patriarchy, was perpetual tutelage, a system that

> permitted her no opinions and then said she did not know how to think. It forbade her to speak in public, and said the sex had no orators. It denied her the schools, and said the sex had no genius. It robbed her of every vestige of responsibility, and then called her weak. It taught her that every pleasure must come as a favor from men, and when to gain it she decked herself in paint and fine feathers, as she had been taught to do, it called her vain. (7)

Catt refuted sexist theories on biological grounds, noting that the German scientist Karl Ernst von Baer, founder of modern embryology, "pricked the bubble of the fallacy that 'man is the race' in 1827 when he demonstrated that father and mother contribute equally to the physical, mental and moral characteristics of their children" (8). Based on that knowledge, she argued that the progress of any group depends on the development of its members, both men and women.

In her conclusion, she summed up the evolution of human rights:

A little more than a century ago men asked, "why are some men born to rule and others to obey?" The world answered by making sovereigns of those who had been subjects, and now we ask, "why are men born to rule and women to obey?" There is but one answer and that is, to lift the subject woman to the throne by the side of the sovereign man. (12)

Once enunciated, natural rights were treated as self-evident, and the proof of their rightness was factual—the actual changes that had occurred over time. That progress logically led to the extension of suffrage to women. That such progress appeared inevitable heartened suffrage workers who could transcend defeats in the belief that suffrage must come. Catt ended her speech on a realistic and politic note: "Yet before the attainment of equal rights for men and women there will be years of struggle and disappointment. . . . God give us wisdom and courage to face the disappointment and the struggle of the contest, and above all, God grant us patience and tolerance for our opponents" (12).

In effect, Catt argued that because self-government was right, its spread was inevitable. Because biological discoveries confirmed that woman played an equal part in the perpetuation and development of the race, self-government inevitably had to extend to her. Moreover, because opposition to woman suffrage was based on ignorance and irrationality, it would fall.

In this speech, Catt's argument stands in sharp contrast to the natural rights argument of Anna Howard Shaw. Shaw argued from definition and principle; Catt defended the natural rights of woman based on her role in biological evolution as well as on observable evidence of her role in political and moral evolution.

Fourteen years later, at the inception of what would be the final, successful suffrage campaign, Catt made the keynote address at the special Atlantic City convention to prepare NAWSA leaders for her "Winning Plan" (Catt 1916). The speech was intended to persuade suffragists that this was a time of crisis. If it was not a crisis, Catt said, it would be "better to *imagine* a crisis where none exists than to fail to recognize one when it comes; for a crisis is a culmination of events which calls for new considerations and new decisions. A failure to answer the call may mean an opportunity lost, a possible victory postponed" (Catt 1916, 1). One would think that such a purpose would call forth high style, but once again Catt spoke primarily in middle style. She applied evolutionary theory to the movement itself, saying that it must "pass through the stages of agitation and education and finally through the stage of realization" (1). Reversing the words of

those who betrayed the movement following the Civil War, she urged
her listeners to adopt as their own and to repeat endlessly this slogan:
"The Woman's Hour has struck" (2).

She demonstrated that a crisis existed by remarking upon the impact
of World War I: by involving women deeply in the war effort, it had
eroded sex prejudice in men and in women. Catt declared:

> She may not realize it yet, but the woman "door-mat" in every land has
> unconsciously become a "door-jamb"! . . . The men returning may find the new
> order a bit queer but everything else will be strangely unfamiliar, too, and they
> will soon grow accustomed to all the changes together. The "jamb" will never
> descend into a "door-mat" again. (7)

To prove that these changes had affected America, she recalled the history
of the movement to contrast past conditions with those of today. Earlier
activists had built well, she argued; she then asked: "What is our duty?
Shall we spend time in admiring the cap-stones and cornice? . . . Or, shall
we, like the builders of old, chant, 'Ho, all hands, all hands, heave to!' "
(15).

Catt urged her listeners to recognize those whom they would never win
over — the reactionaries, the ignorant and illiterate, and the forces of
evil — but also to measure their own strength. She pointed to party and
church endorsements, to the support of other reform movements and of
great men and women, and, most important, to suffragists "everywhere
about us . . . but inactive and silent." These, she argued, if combined,

> make so irresistible a driving force that victory might be seized at once. How
> can it be done? By a simple change of mental attitude. If we are to seize the
> victory, that change must take place in this hall, here and now! . . . Does it not
> give you a thrill of exaltation; does the blood not course more quickly through
> your veins; does it not bring a new sense of freedom, of joy and of determination?
> Is it not true that you who wanted a little time ago to lay down the work because
> you were weary with long service, now, under the compelling influence of a
> changed mental attitude, are ready to go on until the vote is won? The change
> is one of spirit! (18-19)

The speech was crafted to raise the morale of the membership, to urge
them to continue the work of their predecessors, and to fuel them with a
sense that, if they worked hard enough, victory would come. It was a classic
example of reinterpreting the past as a foundation for future victory in
order to energize workers in the present. The change in attitude created
by this speech prepared Catt's audience to see themselves as part of a
historical process on whose achievements they could build by accepting
her "Winning Plan."

The following year Catt made another presidential address, a speech that she designated one of the most important of her career (Clevenger 1955, 77-78). This "Address to the Congress of the United States" (1917) was delivered at the forty-ninth annual NAWSA Convention in Washington, D.C., to initiate the drive targeted to the Congress to pass a suffrage amendment. An eyewitness described the speech as follows:

> In delivering it the speaker . . . seemed to withdraw her personality utterly, so that there was left only the mental and spiritual content of her message. To hear her was like listening to abstract thought, warmed by the fire of abstract conviction. . . . Hers the crowning achievement to sway an audience to emotion by the symmetry and force of her appeal to its mind. (*Woman Citizen* 1, 69 [22 December 1917]; in Walker 1951, 346-47)

As this commentary indicates, the speech was in the middle style; it was severely logical, its structure was evident.

Catt argued that woman suffrage was inevitable given our theory (natural rights philosophy), our practice (women already voted in several states), and our leadership (the role of the United States in the world). Using an analogy comparing the successful New York state referendum to the battle of Gettysburg, she contended that now was the time for action: "Historians tell us that the battle of Gettysburg brought our Civil War to an end, although the fighting went on a year longer, because the people who directed it did not see that the end had come" (Catt 1917, 7). She presented three reasons for enfranchisement through a federal amendment, and three reasons against the state method. She also responded to three major objections: that wartime is not the time to consider this question, that this change should only come about through popular referenda, that a federal amendment violates states' rights. She concluded with appeals addressed to members of Congress as politicians, suggesting that women voters would be hard on legislators and political parties that stood in the path of their progress. Her final words were a thinly veiled threat: "Woman suffrage is coming—you know it. Will you, Honorable Senators and Members of the House of Representatives, help or hinder it?" (21).

As a pamphlet, the speech was part of the standard literature of NAWSA, and thousands of copies were circulated. It was regarded by suffragists as an absolutely conclusive document (HWS 5:522). It may have had an effect on legislators. On January 10, 1918, the House of Representatives passed the amendment 274 to 136, the first time it was voted on. In the Senate, however, the amendment failed by a vote of sixty-two to thirty-four, on October 1, 1918 (Walker 1951, 347).

The power of the address is logical and evidentiary. The logic was based on premises drawn from natural rights philosophy enunciating shared, traditional values. Those values were established through the authority of revered national figures, such as Thomas Jefferson and Abraham Lincoln, and buttressed by references to such contemporary figures as Secretary of State Elihu Root, Speaker of the House Champ Clark, and President Woodrow Wilson. Catt also linked these values to the United States role in World War I, to invidious comparisons to the enfranchisement of women in Canada, France, Great Britain, and Russia, and to the passage of the Sixteenth Amendment, which by taxing women's income violated the principle of taxation without representation.

The tone was direct and occasionally rather intense. In discussing natural rights philosophy, Catt said: "However stupidly our country may have evaded the logical applications at times, it has never swerved from its devotion to the theory of democracy" (1-2). Following her comments on the injustice of the income tax for women, Catt asked: "Is there a single man who can justify such inequality of treatment, such outrageous discriminations? Not one" (3). Referring to uncomplimentary comparisons to other nations, she said:

> Any man who has red American blood in his veins, any man who has gloried in our history and has rejoiced that our land was the leader of world democracy, will share with us the humbled national pride that our country has so long delayed action upon this question that another country has beaten us in what we thought was our especial world mission. (Catt 1917, 5-6)

She used rhetorical questions to highlight the discrepancy between traditional values and actual behavior, and to indicate the resentment U.S. women felt at the position in which they were placed. For example, in her conclusion she asked:

> Do you realize that in no other country in the world with democratic tendencies is suffrage so completely denied as in a considerable number of our own States? . . .
>
> Do you realize that no class of men in our own or in any other land have been compelled to ask their inferiors for the ballot?
>
> Do you realize that when you ask women to take their cause to State referendum you compel them to do this; that you drive women of education, refinement, achievement, to beg men who cannot read for their political freedom? (19)

The emotional appeal was an integral part of the premises underlying the argument and inherent in the evidence—statements from revered authorities, comparisons tarnishing America's self-image, and an implicit bandwagon appeal implied by in facts about the progress of woman suffrage. Similarly, Catt became a mouthpiece for basic values, acquainting her audience with the logic behind the action she sought, and answering the questions that remained about the soundness of the policy to be enacted.

Although this speech resembled Susan B. Anthony's "Is It a Crime for a U.S. Citizen to Vote?" it was not a legal brief exploring all arguments for woman suffrage but a well-made case that presented only the strongest arguments in its favor and refuted only the major alternatives and key opposition claims. Like her approach to deploying her troops, Catt's 1917 "Address to the Congress" was a triumph of structure, logic, and realistic assessment rather than a rhetorical masterpiece.

THE AGITATOR

But a great popular speaker and a great administrator, while absolutely vital to the movement, were not enough. The issue of woman suffrage had to come alive, public attention had to be focused on it, and the intensity of women's desire for enfranchisement had to be made evident, and this was to be Alice Paul's contribution.

Alice Paul was a highly educated Quaker whose interest in social work took her to England in 1907, where for three years she worked with the radical members of the Women's Social and Political Union. She returned to the United States in 1910 a dedicated, militant suffragist, ready to put her talents and experience to work at home.

She asked NAWSA to send her to Washington to work for passage of a federal amendment, and with the help of Jane Addams, in 1912 she persuaded a reluctant organization to do so, on condition that she not rely on it for money or support of any kind. Activists Lucy Burns, Crystal Eastman, Mary Ritter Beard, the socialite Dora Lewis, and Alice Paul became the Congressional Committee of the NAWSA. In 1913, the group became the independent Congressional Union, then, in 1916 the Woman's Party, and later that year the National Woman's Party (NWP).

Paul brought to the suffrage movement the radical tactics she had learned in England, an abiding commitment to a federal amendment as the means to suffrage, and the notion that suffragists should hold the party in power responsible for the failure to pass a federal amendment. Paul's work illustrates the role of agitation and radicalism in a persuasive campaign that is part of a social movement.

Whatever their differences over tactics, both the NWP and the NAWSA sought to convince the public and the Congress that, contrary to the claims of the anti-suffragists, women wanted the vote passionately, that woman suffrage should be enacted now, that a federal suffrage amendment was the correct means, and that, as a consequence, the United States Congress was responsible for taking action.[3] Moreover, despite their militancy, the NWP consistently combined agitation with traditional means of political persuasion, including lobbying, petitioning, letter writing, speaking, and testifying at hearings.

The more militant tactics of the NWP were of three types: (1) parades, marches, and processions; (2) picketing—chiefly the White House, but also Congress, and the Republican National Convention; and (3) lighting a watchfire and using it to burn the speeches of President Woodrow Wilson and of senators who voted against the suffrage amendment. Each of these tactics was carefully timed and targeted, and each was enhanced by publicity. Tactics were escalated in response to specific events; and cultural conditions, including concepts of woman, police violence, jail conditions, and legal ambiguity, made these tactics more effective.

Together, these tactics were aimed at three main goals. First, they were intended to demonstrate in the most vivid fashion possible the intensity of women's desire for the ballot and the strength of their commitment to their cause. Second, they were used to capture and keep the attention of the public, the President, and the Congress—to place woman suffrage at the top of the political agenda. Finally, they were designed to function as rhetorical confrontation (Scott and Smith 1969). Because confrontation compels audience members to consider an issue, however distasteful that may be, it can be persuasive only if the encounter provokes shame at the discrepancy between shared values and their application, and only if those doing the confronting are willing to pay the price involved.[4]

Initially, the tactics were chosen merely to demonstrate that women really wanted the ballot and to make the issue of woman suffrage salient for the public and for members of Congress—in the words of their official chronicle, "to attract the eye of the country to the Suffragists . . . [and] to keep the people watching the Suffragists" (Irwin 1964, 32). Their first effort occurred on March 4, 1913, the day before Wilson's first inauguration. Some 8,000 women marched from the Capitol down Pennsylvania Avenue to the hall of the Daughters of the American Revolution carrying a banner that read: "WE DEMAND AN AMENDMENT TO THE CONSTITUTION OF THE UNITED STATES ENFRANCHISING THE WOMEN OF THE COUNTRY." This peaceful effort was transformed when on-lookers attacked the marchers and District police failed to act. Ul-timately, Secretary of War Stimpson called out troops from Fort Myers to establish order, and an investigation led to the removal of the District's police chief. The attacks caused the demonstration to receive front-page coverage and generated considerable sympathy for the suffragists' cause.

The NWP's tactics remained peaceful and traditional. In March 1913, prior to a special congressional session called by Wilson, they sent three weekly deputations to the President arguing that no subject demanded treatment more urgently than woman suffrage. To buttress such efforts, suffragists from all over the country were urged to and did write their representatives and the President. A second demonstration was held on April 7, 1913, at the start of the special session. Delegates from every congressional district, carrying petitions asking for passage of an amendment, marched behind their state banners to the steps of the Capitol, where they were greeted by members of Congress. On June 13, a favorable report from the Senate Majority Committee on Woman Suffrage was made to the Senate, putting the measure on the Senate calendar for debate for the first time since 1887. A petition drive was initiated in all states, and on July 31, delegations from every state converged in Hyattsville, Maryland, and an automobile procession traveled from there to the Capitol to present the petitions to the Senate.

When the amendment failed, a delegation of seventy-three women from Wilson's home state of New Jersey went to the White House asking the President to support passage by the next Congress of a constitutional amendment enfranchising women. In his December 2 State of the Union message, Wilson failed to mention woman suffrage, and in consequence, a delegation representing each state was ap-pointed to see the President and protest. According to the *Washington Post* of December 9, Wilson told them: "I am not at liberty to urge upon Congress policies which have not had the organic consideration of those for whom I am a spokesman. . . . I have to confine myself to those things which have been embodied as promises to the people at an election." Anna Howard Shaw, a member of the delegation, then asked, "As women are members of no political party, to whom are they to look for a spokesman?" Wilson is supposed to have responded,

"You speak very well for yourself," to which Shaw replied, "But not with authority" (Irwin 1964, 45-46).

In the election of 1914, the NWP took its appeal to the women voters of the country by campaigning in the nine states with woman suffrage against all Democratic candidates for Congress. Their efforts against Democrats reflected their decision to hold the party in power responsible for the defeat of the suffrage amendment. This policy has frequently been criticized as an inappropriate application of the strategies of the British "suffragettes" toward Members of Parliament (Bland 1972), but it reflected a realistic assessment of the power of the Democratic caucus in Congress and its influence on voting on the floor and in committees.[5] However, while Democrats controlled the federal government, Republicans controlled many of the state legislatures to which suffragists would have to appeal for ratification of a federal amendment. Although the NWP recognized prior to the election that most Democrats would win despite them, Paul refused to end the effort. She said, *"If we withdraw our speakers from the campaign, we withdraw the issue from the campaign. We must make this such an important thing in national elections that the Democrats will not want to meet it again"* (Irwin 1964, 183). A similar effort was made in the eleven states with woman suffrage in 1916. In 1918, a few Democrats were excepted from a similar effort.

The first escalation in tactics occurred on December 4, 1916, when five women dropped a huge yellow sateen banner reading "MR. PRESIDENT, WHAT WILL YOU DO FOR WOMAN SUF-FRAGE?" from the gallery of the House during Wilson's State of the Union address (Irwin 1964, 184). The agitation increased when the NWP decided to send the President "a perpetual deputation." On January 10, 1917, twelve women took up positions at the gates of the White House, holding up the purple, white, and gold banners of the NWP alongside two lettered banners: "MR. PRESIDENT, WHAT WILL YOU DO FOR WOMAN SUFFRAGE?" and "HOW LONG MUST WOMEN WAIT FOR LIBERTY?" (Irwin 1964, 202-203).

Picketing went on for a year and a half, and in that time, over one thousand women held lettered banners at the White House gates or in front of the Capitol. Especially when they braved rain and snow, the pickets were treated sympathetically by the police and the public — but only until war was declared. On June 20, 1917, the Russian mission of the new Russian Republic, which had just enfranchised its women, was greeted at the White House gate with what came to be called the "Russian" banner:

PRESIDENT WILSON AND ENVOY ROOT ARE DECEIVING RUSSIA. THEY SAY "WE ARE A DEMOCRACY. HELP US WIN THE WAR SO THAT DEMOCRACIES MAY SURVIVE." WE WOMEN OF AMERICA TELL YOU THAT AMERICA IS NOT A DEMOCRACY. TWENTY MILLION WOMEN ARE DENIED THE RIGHT TO VOTE. PRESIDENT WILSON IS THE CHIEF OPPONENT OF THEIR NATIONAL ENFRANCHISEMENT. HELP US MAKE THIS NATION REALLY FREE. TELL OUR GOVERNMENT THAT IT MUST LIBERATE ITS PEOPLE BEFORE IT CAN CLAIM FREE RUSSIA AS AN ALLY. (Irwin 1964, 215)

As soon as the Russian mission had entered the White House, the sign was torn from its supports by the crowd, and a similar banner was torn down the following day along with other, less confrontational banners, while the police looked on. The women were beginning to pay the price for confrontation.

The protestors were asked to cease their picketing, allegedly because it was feared that the President might be assassinated by someone among the crowds that the pickets collected. Alice Paul refused to comply unless the request was made public, a move the President rejected, and Paul was told that if pickets appeared again, they would be arrested. On June 22, two women eluded the police to hold up a banner reading: "WE SHALL FIGHT FOR THE THINGS WHICH WE HAVE ALWAYS HELD NEAREST OUR HEARTS—FOR DEMOCRACY, FOR THE RIGHT OF THOSE WHO SUBMIT TO AUTHORITY TO HAVE A VOICE IN THEIR OWN GOVERNMENTS.—President Wilson's War Message, April 2, 1917." They became the first of a long list of women to be arrested for picketing the White House (Irwin 1964, 218). When given the alternatives of paying a fine or going to jail, they made a strategic decision to go to jail, and they set a precedent for those who followed. Ultimately, more than 300 women were arrested and detained, or tried and imprisoned, during the second Wilson administration.

Although crowd reaction to the banners reflected hostility generated by United States involvement in the war, the arrests, trials, and sentences backfired for a number of reasons. First, the legal situation was highly ambiguous. Ultimately all of the arrests were thrown out on appeal, and some women sued for damages (Irwin 1964, 267-68; Bland 1972, 131). The women used the trials as suffrage meetings, introducing to their arguments many who would not have been exposed to them. Conditions in the workhouse where most were imprisoned were terrible—the cells were dark, damp, and unhealthful, and the food was moldy and full of maggots (Kettler 1976, 243-45).

Imprisoned women demanded treatment as political prisoners, and when that demand was rejected, refused to eat and were force-fed.

The women who picketed and were punished were almost entirely white, middle-class, well-educated, and well-dressed, and such treatment aroused public sympathy. In a curious way, attitudes toward womanhood probably helped their cause, as many men and women were outraged that women of this sort should be treated in this way. Through their journal the *Suffragist* and through speakers sent throughout the country, the NWP publicized the arrests, trials, force-feeding, and the conditions in the jails. The effect of the picketing on the NWP was an initial drop in membership; it was followed, however, by a surge in membership and a significant jump in contributions (Irwin, 266). But as one historian points out, "Large sums were needed to bring new recruits to Washington, to feed and house them, and to replace the increasing number of banners which were destroyed by the taunting crowds. The Woman's Party assessed damages to their property the week the Kaiser banner was displayed at over $1400 alone" (Bland 1972, 125). The monetary as well as the psychological cost of confrontation had risen dramatically.

On September 16, 1918, after learning that the Senate Rules Committee did not intend to let the suffrage amendment come up for consideration in the next session of Congress, Lucy Branham held aloft the President's speech of that very afternoon addressed to Democratic women from the West and South, saying, "We want action, not words," she burned the speech. The next day, the chairperson of the Senate Suffrage Committee announced that on September 26 he would move to take up the suffrage amendment and keep it before the Senate until a vote was taken. On September 26, President Wilson came to the Senate to speak in support of the amendment. Two days later the amendment failed passage, but because of a motion to reconsider, it was reinserted on the Senate calendar ready to be called up at any time.

On October 7, the NWP began picketing at the Capitol, and shortly thereafter, they began a banner campaign targeted to each of the thirty-four Senators who had opposed the amendment, beginning with a Senator from New York whose wife was an active anti-suffragist:

SENATOR WADSWORTH'S REGIMENT IS FIGHTING FOR DEMOCRACY ABROAD. SENATOR WADSWORTH LEFT HIS REGIMENT AND IS FIGHTING AGAINST DEMOCRACY IN THE SENATE. SENATOR WADSWORTH COULD SERVE HIS COUNTRY BETTER BY FIGHTING WITH HIS REGIMENT ABROAD THAN BY FIGHTING WOMEN. (Irwin 1964, 385)

The confrontational character of the banners is clearest in one that appeared on October 23:

GERMANY HAS ESTABLISHED "EQUAL, UNIVERSAL, SECRET, DIRECT FRANCHISE." THE SENATE HAS DENIED EQUAL UNIVERSAL SUFFRAGE TO AMERICA. WHICH IS MORE OF A DEMOCRACY, GERMANY OR AMERICA? (Irwin 1964, 386)

The police immediately allowed onlookers to destroy it, and more arrests followed.

Systematic burning of the words of the President began on December 16, 1918, when the President departed for the peace negotiations in France without leaving any instructions for the Democrats in Congress regarding suffrage. Alice Paul's idea was to light a watchfire and keep it burning with wood sent from all the states until the suffrage amendment passed, using it to burn the speeches that Woodrow Wilson was making in Europe. Crowds attacked them, overturning the urns and stamping out the fires, sometimes befo.e the eyes of the police. More women were arrested, jailed, and went on hunger strikes. On February 9, 1919, they burned a paper effigy of the President, and there were more arrests. When Wilson returned, he was greeted by pickets and demonstrations. On March 4, Congress adjourned without Senate action on the suffrage amendment. But when the new Congress convened, the House passed the amendment on May 21, 1919, and on June 4, the Senate did likewise; the NWP then returned to conventional politicking to obtain ratification by the states.

It is vital to understand that confrontation, however attention-getting, would have been inadequate if speakers like Anna Howard Shaw had not spent years on the hustings responding to anti-suffrage arguments and enacting a "new woman" that male voters found acceptable, if Carrie Chapman Catt's troops of political realists had not been ready to translate the momentum created by persuasion and confrontation into successful referenda campaigns, pressure on members of Congress, and ratification by state legislatures, and if this had not been the end of a long series of rhetorical acts reaching back through the speeches of Elizabeth Cady Stanton, Ernestine Potowski Rose, Susan B. Anthony, and all the others.

It was through a long, cumulative process that women won the right to vote in 1920. But, of course, the fight for woman's rights was very far from won.

CONCLUSION

Anna Howard Shaw's gift to the women's movement was her skill as a speaker. She was also NAWSA vice president from 1892 to 1904, and president from 1904 to 1915. With the entry of the United States into World War I, she became head of the Woman's Committee of the United States Council of National Defense to coordinate women's contributions to the war effort, and she undertook a speaking tour following the war to rally support for the League of Nations.

Carrie Chapman Catt's gift to the women's movement was her talent for organization. She began her work in state and territorial referenda campaigns and continued it as president of NAWSA, from 1900 to 1904, and from 1915 to 1920. In addition, in 1902 she founded the International Woman Suffrage Alliance, and she organized the League of Women Voters, which took the place of NAWSA after suffrage was won.

Alice Paul's contribution was the agitational tactics of the NWP, but she and the NWP continued their work, discussed in the next chapter.

NOTES

1. In states with suffrage, women voters were to press for passage of a federal amendment; in states where referenda were likely to succeed, passage was to be the focus of efforts; where referenda were likely to fail, the goal was either presidential suffrage or, in the South where primaries in effect were general elections, primary suffrage, which could be achieved by majority vote of state legislatures (Peck 1944, 256-62).

2. Catt is often contrasted to Alice Paul as a moderate or even conservative suffragist. For an example of a radical, combative side rarely shown in public, see Hurwitz 1978.

3. There was brief disagreement when in 1914 a group in the NAWSA supported the Shafroth-Palmer Amendment, which, in effect, made suffrage a state-by-state issue. The amendment read:

> Whenever any number of legal voters of any State to a number exceeding 8% of the number of legal voters voting at the last preceding General Election held in such a State shall petition for the submission to the legal voters of said State of the question whether women shall have equal rights with men in respect to voting at all elections to be held in such State, such question shall be so submitted; and if, upon such submission, a majority of the legal voters of the State voting on the question shall vote in favor of granting to women such equal rights, the same shall thereupon be established, anything in the Constitution or laws of such State to the contrary notwithstanding.

It was renounced by the NAWSA at its December 1915 convention.

4. Martha Vicinus describes radical women's acceptance of the violence involved in militancy, even to the point of viewing militancy as a spiritual exercise (1985,

ch. 7, 247-80). Phyllis Mack suggests a direct relationship between adopting a feminine role and radical action (1986).

5. Prior to 1910, when James Beauchamp "Champ" Clark organized the successful fight against Speaker Joe Cannon and his arbitrary control of legislative procedure, that power had been even greater. Clark served as speaker from 1911 to 1919.

12

After Woman Suffrage

The fight for woman's rights was indeed far from won. Looking back, it can seem bizarre that some activists had believed that the vote would solve all their problems. In fact, in 1920 suffragists faced a new challenge: could their movement survive ratification of the Nineteenth Amendment? More specifically, would the vote prove to be a useful weapon in the struggle for women's emancipation? Would a new cause galvanize women for a continued struggle? The answers were clear in less than a decade. The ballot did little for woman's advancement, no issue unified women reformers, and differing conceptions of emancipation produced the most bitter divisions within the movement since 1869. Just as it is hard to date a movement's beginnings, it is difficult to say just when it ends. However, to all intents and purposes, there was no identifiable women's movement once the child labor amendment failed to gain ratification in 1925.

Woman suffrage had brief, inconsequential impact. A majority of women did not vote, and they received little encouragement from family, friends, or the public to do so (Chafe 1972, 30, 32). Unfortunately, women gained the vote at a time when disillusionment with government and political parties was rife, causing some activists to urge women not to participate in any way in these corrupt institutions (O'Neill 1971, 275).

No overriding, dramatic woman's issue arose to unify and energize former suffragists. Internal disagreements led to the formation of the League of Women Voters (LWV), the successor to NAWSA, formed as a non-partisan organization. The LWV began with about 100,000 members, in contrast to the two million members that NAWSA had at its height (Lemons 1973, 53, 118). The impact of women's votes was lessened still further when it became clear to politicians that women formed no distinctive bloc to be courted (Chafe 1972, 31).

A look at the history of those years discloses various forces that weakened women's electoral power. At the outset, both state and federal legislatures enacted measures of importance for women as a way of appealing to women voters (Chafe 1972, 27-28). In 1921, for example, Congress passed the Sheppard-Towner Act, "the first federally funded health care program to be implemented in the United States . . . [that] made children's health, women's prenatal care, and education in hygiene an explicit function of the state" (Leach 1980, 350). Within a year, however, the American Medical Association attacked the act, and by the end of the 1920s health care had once again returned to the private sector. This was a serious defeat for women medical professionals as well as for women's and children's health. Similarly, the Child Labor Amendment, passed easily by Congress in 1924, fell short of ratification in a process similar to that which sent the Equal Rights Amendment down to defeat in 1982 — it foundered in state legislatures, including those in Massachusetts and New York.[1] The defeat was largely a result of lobbying by the Woman Patriots, a reorganized remnant of the National Association Opposed to Woman Suffrage, who argued that prohibiting child labor would destroy the home (Lemons 1973, 219; Chafe 1972, 29).

Even more important historically was the fact that women's ability to influence political affairs was lessened by severe attacks from their opposition. Women's organizations and women leaders were battered by charges of being agents or dupes of a Bolshevist conspiracy to conquer the United States (Lemons 1973, 209). The climax of the attack came in March 1924 with the publication in the *Dearborn* (Michigan) *Independent* of the so-called Spider Web chart, ostensibly diagraming the communist influence in feminist groups. During the Red Scare of 1919-20, anyone who supported trade unionism or pacifism was suspect, including most women reformers. Jane Addams, for example, founder of Chicago's Hull House, came under fire: she championed the labor movement, was founder and chairperson of the Woman's Peace Party and chairperson of the International Congress of Women (1915), and she remained a pacifist through World War I. Also suspect were Carrie Chapman Catt, another founder of the Woman's Peace Party, who supported U.S. involvement in World War I but was active in peace efforts thereafter; and Florence Kelley, Hull House resident, who was active in the National Consumers' League, and a leading advocate of child labor reform. In fact, "by 1925 *Survey* concluded that red-baiting was the principal reason for the defeat of the child labor amendment" (Lemons 1973, 210). Organizations attacked included the PTA, the YWCA, and the WCTU, and their programs were opposed as threatening the fabric of the nation and its form of government (Lemons 1973, 214-25, 224).

Along with the historical forces that battered the movement went continuing internal conflicts. These conflicts began at least as early as the 1860 national woman's rights convention debate, and they returned with intensity during the 1910s. As their rhetoric demonstrates, suffragists of the WCTU differed from NAWSA suffragists, and women in NAWSA were divided from their counterparts in the NWP over more than tactics. Commitment to suffrage had been the only issue holding these diverse groups together, and after some initial efforts at cooperation, cracks quickly appeared. The issue that finally divided former allies was the equal rights amendment.

As many commentators have recognized, a new era in the movement began on February 18, 1921, when at its convention the NWP voted to reorganize to fight for legal equality through a federal amendment. It was at this meeting that Crystal Eastman, one of the founders of the Congressional Union, proposed a broad feminist program. That program was rejected by Alice Paul and later by a vote of the membership; she claimed it would be unnecessary if an equal rights amendment, which she supported, were passed. As part of that rejection, Paul also refused to address the fact that Afro-American women in the South were being deprived of the vote, on the ground that such discrimination affected men and women equally (Sochen 1973, 117; O'Neill 1971, 274).

Precisely seventy-five years after the Seneca Falls convention, the NWP proposed what was called the Lucretia Mott Amendment. It read: "Men and women shall have equal rights throughout the United States and every place subject to its jurisdiction" (Chafe 1972, 112). The amendment was introduced in Congress by Rep. Daniel Anthony (Susan's brother) and Sen. Charles Curtis. The split among activists recapitulated past conflicts between NAWSA and NWP, but it also reflected profound ideological differences. The LWV and its supporters opted for gradualism; the NWP chose to fight for this one grand, national prohibition of legal inequality.

The NWP saw their goal as creating opportunity for individuals; the LWV saw their goal as protecting women workers, a goal that sometimes tacitly and sometimes explicitly espoused women's inferiority. In the Supreme Court decision *Muller v. Oregon*, which became the legal foundation for protective legislation, the majority wrote that "woman has always been dependent upon man. . . . Her physical structure and a proper discharge of her maternal functions . . . justify legislation to protect her from the greed as well as the passion of man" (Chafe 1972, 289). By contrast, the NWP criticized protective labor legislation as absurd because it made blanket provisions for women whose conditions varied greatly (O'Neill 1971, 279). Finally, while women supporting protective labor legislation could point to those laws as past gains, NWP women saw their efforts to enact specific equal rights measures on the state level go down to defeat, causing them to push for a federal amendment (Becker 1975, 152; Sklar 1986).

During 1921, both sides solicited legal opinions on the effect of such an amendment. The conclusion generally was that it would either nullify or throw open to question all special legislation benefiting women (Lemons 1973, 185). After a heated confrontation in 1926, the Women's Bureau of the Department of Labor became involved in the dispute. Based on evidence it had gathered earlier, and in support of views that it strongly espoused, the Bureau concluded in a report issued in 1928 that "labor legislation was not a handicap to women . . . it did not reduce their opportunities, and . . . it raised standards not only for women but for thousands of men too" (Lemons 1973, 195). The report countered NWP's argument that protective legislation excluded women from important categories of jobs. But another study of the impact of protective laws on women workers was made in 1925 by Dr. Elizabeth Baker, who reached different conclusions. As reported by Marjory Nelson, Baker's research revealed:

> In establishments where women predominate and are an integral and established part of the labor force, restrictive legislation usually results in an improvement in conditions for the women and for the men as well. But in those occupations in which women are just gaining a foothold, where men are in the majority, the positions of the women are jeopardized, if not lost. (Nelson 1976, 231-32)

In other words, depending on the workers' circumstances, both conclusions were accurate.

The feuding groups represented different constituencies. The NWP and those who supported an equal rights amendment represented career-minded single women or women who had families dependent upon them and "would not or could not accept the concept that the male had a superior right to a good job" (Nelson 1976, 233). Those who opposed an equal rights amendment and supported protective labor legislation spoke for women for whom employment was temporary, or an adjunct to family income, whose employment was in lower-paid jobs in factories or in job categories dominated by women.

The NWP continued its fight for an equal rights amendment (Fry 1986), but the Women's Bureau report eroded their public credibility and for many reduced their case to an argument based on symbolism, that "such laws promoted a sense of inferiority among women" (Lemons 1973, 196). However, the NWP argued the necessity of a federal amendment based on the continued legal disabilities of married women: "in 1940 eleven states still provided that a wife could not retain her earnings without her husband's consent; sixteen denied a married women the right to make contracts; seven gave the father superior guardianship rights; and over twenty prohibited women from serving on juries" (Chafe 1972, 121-22). But in the face of the economic problems created by the Depression, such arguments had steadily diminishing force.

Movement rhetoric of this period was also diffuse. Except for early disputes over the equal rights amendment, few addressed general issues relating to women. Some, such as Carrie Chapman Catt, devoted their energies to efforts to achieve world peace. Jane Addams continued her efforts for peace and in settlement work, but she also helped to found the American Civil Liberties Union. Some, like Florence Kelley, continued their efforts in labor unions and consumer rights; some, such as Margaret Higgins Sanger, continued the fight for birth control (Anderson 1984, 143-50). There were two important exceptions — Charlotte Perkins Gilman and Crystal Eastman — though the feminist rhetoric of both went largely unheeded, as might be expected in a dying movement.

Throughout her life (1860-1935), Charlotte Perkins Gilman's primary source of income was lecture fees. She spoke to women's clubs, labor unions, suffrage groups, Unitarian congregations, and others on themes relating to women, labor, and social organization. Her speaking was not in direct support of movement goals, and her advocacy of socialism and radical alterations in domestic life made her controversial and set her off from most other early activists. Despite the importance of her ideas, Perkins Gilman distanced herself from the early movement. She reported that Anthony "wanted me as a suffrage worker," but that she declined (Gilman 1935, 174). In addition, from 1888 to 1900 she lived in California, some 3,000 miles from the centers of activity in the East.

In the 1920s, with the demise of the movement, she lost much of her audience, although she maintained ties with the NWP. Her ideas were expressed in *Woman and Economics* (1898); *The Home: Its Work and Influence* (1903); and in the *Forerunner*, a journal she wrote, edited, and published, that reached only 1,400 subscribers (1909-1916; rpt. 1968, Stern intro., n.p.). Perkins Gilman was an iconoclast whose talents as a feminist philosopher and ideologist rivaled those of Cady Stanton and whose contributions to feminism have continuing relevance (Hayden 1981). Of special note is her short story, "The Yellow Wall-paper" (1892), which describes a woman driven mad by a "rest cure" similar to that developed by Dr. S. Weir Mitchell—a regimen of complete bedrest without any mental stimulation designed to treat women who were unhappy in their traditional roles.[2]

Crystal Eastman, too, was associated with the NWP, as she had been one of the founders of the Congressional Union from which it grew. She held a virtually unique position as an active socialist who was also a dedicated feminist—few socialists were feminists, and few feminists were socialists. In the months following ratification of the Nineteenth Amendment, she made a speech that illustrates the clear link between the feminism that emerged out of the early movement and the ideological concerns of the contemporary movement. As published in the *Liberator* (Eastman 1920), it was entitled, "Now We Can Begin."

In this speech, Eastman described what freedom meant to women. Her definition was a modern version of the earlier demand for equality of opportunity, for the right to be an individual:

> What, then, is "the matter with women"? What is the problem of women's freedom? It seems to me to be this: how to arrange the world so that women can be human beings, with a chance to exercise their infinitely varied gifts in infinitely varied ways, instead of being destined by the accident of their sex to one field of activity—housework and child-raising. And second, if and when they choose housework and child-raising to have that occupation recognized by the world as work, requiring a definite economic reward and not merely entitling the performer to be dependent on some man. That is not the whole of feminism, of course, but it is enough to begin with. (Cook 1978, 40)

Eastman understood that feminism would fail until women came to desire economic independence (1918; in Cook 1978, 47). She also recognized that emancipation for women involved changes in men. As a result, she called for a revolution in the early training and education of boys, a move required to end women's double jeopardy in the marketplace. As she put it: "Two self-supporting adults decide to make a home together: if both are women it is a pleasant partnership, more fun than work; if one is a man, it is almost never a partnership—the woman simply adds running the home to her regular outside job" (Cook 1978, 41). In Eastman's new world boys would learn to do housework and to expect to share such duties in marriage.

Finally, Eastman understood that motherhood posed special problems for women's emancipation. She envisioned a two-pronged attack. On the one hand, she supported birth control or voluntary motherhood. In an essay published in 1918, she wrote:

> Whether other feminists would agree with me that the economic is the fundamental aspect of feminism, I don't know. But on this we are all surely agreed, that Birth Control is an elementary essential in all aspects of feminism. . . . We must all be followers of Margaret Sanger. Feminists are not nuns. That should be established. (Cook 1978, 47)

What she called a motherhood endowment was the counterpart of birth control, intended to establish "a principle that the occupation of raising children is peculiarly and directly a service to society, and that the mother upon whom the necessity and privilege of performing this service naturally falls is entitled to an adequate economic reward from the political government" (42).

Her program emerged as a synthesis of economic analysis and feminism. She spoke as a leader to other women in a direct, assertive tone, but she appealed to their general knowledge and common sense and used information with which all would be familiar. Despite the radicalism of her proposals, she appealed to women's desire to find ways to fulfill needs for love and motherhood while achieving economic independence.

Eastman was unable to convince even the most radical women's group, of which she was a founding member, to support her proposals. It is doubtful that the NWP, led by the fiery Alice Paul, found them too radical. More probably, Paul was searching for that one issue that would unify and energize women reformers, a single, symbolic gesture that would bring women equality in all areas of life. Ironically, Paul's choice, combined with an unwillingness to compromise on both sides, produced a deep and abiding split among women activists. Eastman remained in the NWP and supported the equal rights amendment, but she had envisioned a broad feminist program that combined economic opportunity with an affirmation of women's right to love and the joys of motherhood.

Eastman's speech is this book's final piece of evidence indicating that contemporary feminism is rooted in the earlier woman's rights movement. Unsolved problems and unexamined issues made a second movement inevitable, and the ideological conflicts that remained unresolved in the 1920s still bedevil contemporary activists.

CONCLUSION

Like many others active in the early movement, Alice Paul was a
Quaker, the daughter of middle-class parents active in reform. She was
one of the best-educated women in the movement, with a B.A. from
Swarthmore, an M.A. and Ph.D. from the University of Pennsylvania,
an L.L.B. from Washington College of Law, and an L.L.M. and D.C.L.
from American University. In 1905, she began working in a New York
settlement house; in 1907 she went to England to study at the
Woodbrooke Settlement for Social Work. Here she came under the
influence of Emmeline and Christabel Pankhurst, founders of the
radical Women's Social and Political Union, with whom she worked
for three years. She returned to the United States in 1910, and began
her work for a federal suffrage amendment in 1912, as described in the
last chapter. From 1923 on, the NWP reintroduced an equal rights
amendment to Congress each year, with a brief interruption during
World War II, until its passage in 1972. In 1977, Alice Paul died; twelve
years later, the amendment failed to gain ratification.

Crystal Eastman was a lawyer who participated in the "Pittsburgh
Survey," the first attempt in the United States to study in detail the
effects of industrialism on urban workers. She published her findings
in *Work Accidents and the Law* (1910), a book that did much to advance
the movement for workmen's compensation laws. As a member of the
New York State Employers' Liability Commission, to which she was
appointed by Gov. Charles Evans Hughes, she helped secure passage
of such a law in that state. She was a founding member of the Congressional Union, which became the National Woman's Party, and was
active in the peace movement. In 1917 she became managing editor
of the *Liberator* and wrote articles on labor problems and feminism.
In March 1919, she was one of the organizers of a Feminist Congress
in New York City where, in the name of women, she demanded not
only the vote but equal employment opportunities, birth control,
economic independence, and a single moral standard (*Liberator*,
May 1919, 37). After moving to England in 1921, she helped found a
London branch of the NWP. She returned to the United States in 1927
but her political radicalism and her radical feminism prevented her
from being employed by any agency concerned with women's
problems, despite her proven abilities as a social investigator; the only
job she could find was a temporary position with the liberal journal the
Nation (O'Neill, 288). She died shortly afterward of nephritis in 1928.

AFTERWORD

The key rhetorical works of early woman's rights and woman suffrage advocates offer an opportunity to discover how a major social movement sustained itself for more than seventy-five years and to appreciate the rhetorical diversity required to respond to the varied problems encountered in addressing varied issues through time. Such efforts challenge the most gifted activists and generate rhetorical works of extraordinary power and appeal.

Rhetorical analysis reveals that the struggle for woman's advancement from 1848 to 1925 never was a single unified movement, and that early activists were unable to resolve conflicts between the demand for personhood and the special roles of women (Campbell 1983b). Their failure was related in part to the absence of a systematic analysis of marriage and the family as key institutions that, at least in their traditional form, are major contributors to women's oppression. Analysis of movement speeches also underscores the racism that made most white women activists incapable of identifying with and understanding the problems of their Afro-American sisters; at the same time it calls attention to the sophisticated understanding of the relationship between sex, race, and class among leading Afro-American women activists.

Analysis of the rhetoric of early feminists heightens our appreciation of their achievement. In struggling to overcome the barriers against women speaking, women displayed great invention and creativity. Some, like Angelina Grimké [Weld], appropriated the gender-free persona of prophet. Many others found ways to assume forbidden roles, as did Susan B. Anthony in defending her civil right to vote. Some, like Maria W. Miller Stewart, Sojourner Truth, and Lucretia Coffin Mott, used theology and biblical evidence to defend themselves; others, like Clarina Howard Nichols, used concepts of true womanhood as premises for their arguments. Like Ernestine Potowski Rose and Anna Howard Shaw, many speakers vividly exposed national hypocrisy by contrasting cherished democratic values to the actual treatment of women.

Early feminist rhetoric also varied greatly in style. Some speakers, like Mary Church Terrell and Elizabeth Cady Stanton, demonstrated phenomenal ability in developing appeals to evoke sympathetic identification; others, like Clarina Howard Nichols and Ida Wells, argued and appealed via a host of detailed examples. Some, like Angelina Grimké [Weld] and Maria Miller Stewart, spoke in high style; others, like Anna Howard Shaw and Sojourner Truth, made their appeals colloquially and used humor with telling skill. Some, like Susan B. Anthony and Carrie Chapman Catt, developed arguments deductively; others, such as Lucretia Coffin Mott and Elizabeth Cady Stanton, on occasion, used an inductive, associative pattern. These works not only exemplify the rhetorical diversity essential to a successful social movement, they also underscore the fact that women used the full range of rhetorical possibilities to respond to the obstacles they encountered.

Moreover, analysis of early movement rhetoric uncovers unusually revealing examples of a style rarely taught and infrequently recognized, a style particularly suited to women speakers and women audiences. The need to justify the right to speak and to empower women demoralized by the cult of true womanhood generated a "feminine" style, which reflected women's experience and invited audiences of women to become active participants in defining social wrongs and finding remedies. However, critical analysis demonstrates that the style had little to do with biology as such, because the rhetoric of early women activists contained equally compelling instances of confrontational, deductively developed, assertive rhetoric. Many women were willing to speak the truth, even when the truth was unspeakable, to confront audiences that mocked, sneered, and threatened, and to propound a program of action. As a result, this body of discourse is unusually fertile ground for asking questions about relationships between style, speaker, and audience.

A survey of the whole range of early feminist rhetoric makes evident how many of the concerns they addressed still remain unresolved today. Contemporary feminists can learn much from early rhetoric, not just about women's history, but about the issues that persist, the dilemmas women have faced through time, and the irreducible elements in a feminist program. In addition to the movement to abolish slavery and to obtain and reclaim the civil rights of Afro-Americans, the struggles of early and contemporary feminists constituted the most significant, sustained effort to make the United States live up to the principles it espouses. Looking back at the rhetoric of the early movement helps us to understand what those principles really mean and why it is so difficult to live up to them. The words of the early feminists call on us to recommit ourselves to those principles and to the struggle to see them become a reality in the lives of all women.

NOTES

1. For a history and analysis of amending the Constitution focused on the defeat of the ERA in 1982, see Berry (1988).

2. Perkins Gilman underwent this cure, and in her autobiography she explained that the story diverged from her own, but she wrote: "I had been as far as one could go [toward insanity] and get back" (1935, 95-96, 118-21; cited material on 121).

References

American Equal Rights Association Convention, 10 May 1866. *Proceedings*. 1866. New York: Robert J. Johnston.

Anderson, Judith. 1984. *Outspoken Women: Speeches by American Women Reformers, 1635-1935*. Dubuque, IA: Kendall/Hunt.

Anthony, Susan B. 1874; rpt. 1974. Address of Susan B. Anthony, Delivered in twenty-nine of the Post Office Districts of Monroe, and twenty-one of Ontario, in her canvass of those Counties, prior to her trial in June, 1873. In *An Account of the Proceedings on the Trial of Susan B. Anthony on the Charge of Illegal Voting, at the Presidential Election in Nov., 1872*, 151-78. New York: Arno Press.

Anti-Slavery Convention of American Women held in the City of New York, May 9, 10, 11, 12, 1837. *Proceedings*. 1837. New York: William S. Dorr.

Anti-Slavery Convention of American Women [Third], held in Philadelphia, May 1, 2, and 3, 1839. *Proceedings*. 1839. Philadelphia: Merrihew and Thompson.

Aptheker, Bettina. Ed. 1901; rpt. 1977. *Lynching and Rape: An Exchange of Views* [between Jane Addams and Ida B. Wells]. New York: American Institute for Marxist Studies.

Aristotle's Politics. 1923. Trans. Benjamin Jowett. Oxford: Clarendon Press.

Armstrong, Richard. 1965. *Grace Darling: Maid and Myth*. London: J.M. Dent.

Arnold, Carroll C. 1958. Lord Thomas Erskine: Modern Advocate. *Quarterly Journal of Speech* 44:17-30.

Bacon, Margaret Hope. 1969. *The Quiet Rebels: The Story of the Quakers in America*. New York: Basic Books.

Bacon, Margaret Hope. 1980. *Valiant Friend: The Life of Lucretia Mott*. New York: Walker and Company.

Bacon, Margaret Hope. 1986. *Mothers of Feminism: The Story of Quaker Women in America*. New York: Harper & Row.

Banner, Lois. 1980. *Elizabeth Cady Stanton: A Radical for Woman's Rights*. Boston: Little, Brown.

Barnes, G. H. and D. W. Dumond., eds. 1934. *Letters of Theodore Dwight Weld, Angelina Grimké Weld and Sarah Grimké, 1822-1844*. 2 vols. New York: Appleton-Century.

Bartlett, Elizabeth Ann. Ed. 1988. *Sarah Grimké: Letters on the Equality of the Sexes and Other Essays*. New Haven, CT: Yale University Press.

Basch, Norma. 1986. The Emerging Legal History of Women in the United States: Property, Divorce, and the Constitution. *Signs* 12:97-117.

Becker, Susan Deubel. 1975. An Intellectual History of the National Woman's Party, 1920-1941. Ph.D. diss., Case Western Reserve University.

Beecher, Catharine. 1829. *Suggestions Respecting Improvements in Education, Presented to the Trustees of the Hartford Female Seminary and Published at Their Request*. Hartford, CT: Packard & Butler.

Beecher, Catharine. 1837. *An Essay on Slavery and Abolition with Reference to the Duty of American Females*. Philadelphia: Henry Perkins.

Berg, Barbara. 1978. *The Remembered Gate: Origins of American Feminism, The Woman and the City, 1800-1860*. New York: Oxford University Press.

Berg, Christine and Philippa Berry. 1981. "Spiritual Whoredom": An Essay on Female Prophets in the Seventeenth Century. In *Literature and Power in the Seventeenth Century: Proceedings of the Essex Conference on the Sociology of Literature, July 1980*, ed. Francis Barker et al., 37-54. Essex, England: University of Essex.

Berry, Mary Frances. 1988. *Why ERA Failed: Politics, Women's Rights, and the Amending Process of the Constitution*. Bloomington: Indiana University Press.

Birney, Catherine. 1885; rpt. 1969. *The Grimké Sisters: Sarah and Angelina Grimké, the First American Women Advocates of Abolition and Woman's Rights*. Westport, CT: Greenwood Press.

Bitzer, Lloyd. 1968. The Rhetorical Situation. *Philosophy & Rhetoric* 1:1-14.

Black, John W. 1943; rpt. 1960. Rufus Choate. In *A History and Criticism of American Public Address*, ed. William Norwood Brigance, 1:434-58. New York: Russell and Russell.

[Blackwell], Antoinette Brown. 1849. Exegesis of I Corinthians, XIV, 34, 35; and II Timothy, 11, 12. *Oberlin Quarterly Review*, July.

Blackwell, Henry B. 1870a. Political Organization. The *Woman's Journal*, 8 January, p. 8.

Blackwell, Henry B. 1870b. Political Exclusiveness. The *Woman's Journal*, 19 March, p. 85.

Blackwell, Henry B. 1870c. "Thou Shalt Not Bear False Witness." The *Woman's Journal*, 16 April, p. 113.

Blackwell, Henry B. 1870d. "Why Demand Suffrage Alone?" The *Woman's Journal*, 16 July, p. 220.

Blackwell, Henry B. 1871. Simply to Equalize. The *Woman's Journal*, 24 June, p. 197.

Blackwell, Henry B. 1873. Why the Delay. The *Woman's Journal*, 9 August, p. 252.

Blackwell, Henry B. 1875. Another Dissatisfied Friend. The *Woman's Journal*, 4 December, p. 388.

Blake, Nelson Manfred. 1962. *The Road to Reno: A History of Divorce in the United States*. New York: Macmillan.

Bland, Sidney Roderick. 1972. Techniques of Persuasion: The National Woman's Party and Woman Suffrage, 1913-1919. Ph.D. diss., George Washington University.

Blocker, Jack S., Jr. 1985. Separate Paths: Suffragists and the Women's Temperance Crusade. *Signs* 10:460-75.

Booth, Wayne C. 1982. Freedom of Interpretation: Bakhtin and the Challenge of

Feminist Criticism. *Critical Inquiry* 9:45-76.

Bordin, Ruth. 1981. *Woman and Temperance: The Quest for Power and Liberty, 1873-1900*. Philadelphia, PA: Temple University Press.

Bordin, Ruth. 1986. *Frances Willard: A Biography*. Chapel Hill: University of North Carolina Press.

Brigance, William Norwood. 1943; rpt. 1960. Jeremiah S. Black. In *A History and Criticism of American Public Address*, ed. William Norwood Brigance, 1:459-82. New York: Russell and Russell.

Bryant, Donald C. 1953. Rhetoric: Its Functions and Its Scope. *Quarterly Journal of Speech* 39:401-24.

Buhle, Mari Jo. 1981. *Women and American Socialism, 1870-1920*. Urbana: University of Illinois Press.

Burke, Kenneth. 1961. *The Rhetoric of Religion: Studies in Logology*. Boston: Beacon.

Camhi, Jane Jerome. 1973. Women Against Women: Antisuffragism, 1880-1920. Ph.D. diss., Tufts University.

Campbell, Karlyn Kohrs. 1980. "The Solitude of Self": A Humanistic Rationale for Feminism. *Quarterly Journal of Speech* 66:304-12.

Campbell, Karlyn Kohrs. 1983a. Contemporary Rhetorical Criticism: Genres, Analogs, and Susan B. Anthony. In *The Jensen Lectures: Contemporary Communication Studies*, ed. John I. Sisco, 117-32. Tampa: University of South Florida.

Campbell, Karlyn Kohrs. 1983b. Femininity and Feminism: To Be or Not to Be a Woman. *Communication Quarterly* 31:101-8.

Campbell, Karlyn Kohrs. 1985. The Communication Classroom: A Chilly Climate for Women? *ACA Bulletin*, no. 51:68-72.

Campbell, Karlyn Kohrs. 1986. Style and Content in the Rhetoric of Early Afro-American Feminists. *Quarterly Journal of Speech* 72:434-45.

Campbell, Karlyn Kohrs. 1987. Elizabeth Cady Stanton. In *American Orators Before 1900: Critical Studies and Sources*, ed. Bernard K. Duffy and Halford R. Ryan, 340-49. Westport, CT: Greenwood Press.

Catt, Carrie Chapman. 4 April 1899. Letter to Contributors to Territorial Funds. In Catherine Waugh McCullough Papers, Schlesinger Library, Radcliffe College, Box 3, Folder 37.

Catt, Carrie Chapman. 1902. *President's Annual Address Delivered by Mrs. Carrie Chapman Catt before the 34th Annual Convention of the National-American Woman-Suffrage Association and the First International Woman-Suffrage Conference, held in Washington, D.C., Feb. 12, 13, 14, 15, 16, 17 and 18, 1902*. Washington, D.C.: Hayworth Publishing.

Catt, Carrie Chapman. 1916. The Crisis. In Carrie Chapman Catt papers, New York Public Library.

Catt, Carrie Chapman. 1917. *An Address to the Congress of the United States by Carrie Chapman Catt*. New York: National Woman Suffrage Publishing Company.

Catt, Carrie Chapman and Nettie Rogers Shuler. 1923; rpt. 1969. *Woman Suffrage and Politics: The Inner Story of the Suffrage Movement*. Bellingham: University of Washington Press.

Cazden, Elizabeth. 1983. *Antoinette Brown Blackwell: A Biography*. Old Westbury, NY: Feminist Press.

Chafe, William H. 1972. *The American Woman: Her Changing Social, Economic, and Political Roles, 1920-1970*. New York: Oxford University Press.

Chester, Ronald. 1984. *Women Lawyers in a Changing America*. MA: Bergin & Garvey.

Christiansen, Adrienne E. 1987. Clarina Howard Nichols: A Rhetorical Criticism of Selected Speeches. M.A. thesis, University of Kansas.

Clark, Thomas D. 1977. An Exploration of Generic Aspects of Contemporary American Christian Sermons. *Quarterly Journal of Speech* 63:384-94.

Clarke, Edward H. 1873. *Sex in Education: A Fair Chance for the Girls*. Boston: James R. Osgood and Co.

Clevenger, Ima Fuchs. 1955. Invention and Arrangement in the Public Address of Carrie Chapman Catt. Ph.D. diss., University of Oklahoma.

Coleman, Willie Mae. 1981. Keeping the Faith and Disturbing the Peace: Black Women from Anti-Slavery to Women's Suffrage. Ph.D. diss., University of California, Irvine.

Conrad, Charles. 1978. Agon and Form: A Dramatistic Analysis of the "Old Feminist" Movement. M.A. thesis, University of Kansas.

Conrad, Charles. 1981. The Transformation of the "Old Feminist" Movement. *Quarterly Journal of Speech* 67:284-97.

Cook, Blanche Wiesen, ed. 1978. *Crystal Eastman on Women and Revolution*. New York: Oxford University Press.

Cott, Nancy F. 1977. *The Bonds of Womanhood: "Woman's Sphere" in New England, 1780-1835*. New Haven: Yale University Press.

Cott, Nancy F. 1987. *The Grounding of Modern Feminism*. New Haven: Yale University Press.

Cowper, William. 1835. *The Task, A Poem in Six Books*. Philadelphia: Joseph M'Dowell.

Cromwell, Otelia. 1958. *Lucretia Mott*. Cambridge, MA: Harvard University Press.

Daly, Mary. 1978. *Gyn/Ecology: The Metaethics of Radical Feminism*. Boston: Beacon Press. chp. 3 "Indian *Suttee*: The Ultimate Consummation of Marriage," pp. 113-33.

Mr. Dana's Lecture on Woman. 9 March 1850. The [New York] *Literary World*, p. 224.

Davis, Angela Y. 1981. *Woman, Race & Class*. New York: Random House.

Davis, Marianna W., ed. 1982. *Contributions of Black Women to America*. 2 vols. Columbia, SC: Kenday Press.

Davis, Paulina Wright. 1871; rpt. 1970. *A History of the National Woman's Rights Movement for Twenty Years*. New York: Source Book Press.

The Declaration of Sentiments and Constitution of the American Anti-Slavery Society of 1833. 1835. New York: American Anti-Slavery Society, Wm. Dorr, Printer.

Dow, Bonnie. 1987. The Reformist Rhetoric of Frances E. Willard: The Romantic Appeal of Mother, God, and Home. M.A. thesis, University of Kansas.

Drescher, Seymour. 1982. Public Opinion and the British Colonial Slavery. In *Slavery and British Society, 1776-1846*, ed. James Walvin, ch. 1. Baton Rouge: Louisiana State University Press.

Drish, Ruth Ellen Williamson. 1985. Susan B. Anthony De-radicalizes, Re-organizes, and Re-unites the American Woman Suffrage Movement, 1880-1890. Ph.D. diss., University of Iowa.

DuBois, Ellen, ed. 1981. *Elizabeth Cady Stanton, Susan B. Anthony: Correspondence, Writings, Speeches*. New York: Schocken.

Duster, Alfreda M., ed. 1970. *Crusade for Justice: The Autobiography of Ida B. Wells*. Chicago: University of Chicago Press.

Eastman, Crystal. 1920. Now We Can Begin. The *Liberator* 3 (December): 23-24.

Engels, Friedrich. 1884; rpt. 1972. *The Origin of the Family, Private Property, and the State*. Trans. Robert Vernon. Intro. by Evelyn Reed. New York: Pathfinder Press.

Farrell, Thomas J. 1979. The Female and Male Modes of Rhetoric. *College English* 40:909-21.

Fauset, Arthur Huff. 1938. *Sojourner Truth: God's Faithful Pilgrim*. Chapel Hill: University of North Carolina Press.

Fell, Margaret. 1667; rpt. 1979. Womens [sic] Speaking Justified. In *Womens Speaking Justified*, intro. David J. Latt, 1-19, Publication no. 194. The Augustan Reprint Society, William Andrew Clark Memorial Library, University of California, Los Angeles.

Fell, Sarah (?). 1975. A Seventeenth-Century Quaker Woman's Declaration. Eds. Milton D. Speizman and Jane C. Kronick. *Signs* 1:231-45.

Fitzgerald, Tracey A. 1985. *The National Council of Negro Women and the Feminist Movement, 1935-1975*. Georgetown Monographs in American Studies. Washington, D.C.: Georgetown University Press.

Flexner, Eleanor. 1959; rpt. 1974. *Century of Struggle: The Woman's Rights Movement in the United States*. New York: Atheneum.

Flexner, Eleanor. 1971. Anna Howard Shaw. In *Notable American Women: A Biographical Dictionary*, ed. Edward T. James, 3:274-77. Cambridge, MA: Belknap Press of Harvard University Press.

Foner, Philip S., ed. 1976. *Frederick Douglass on Women's Rights*. Westport, CT: Greenwood Press.

Ford, Linda G. 1984. American Militants: An Analysis of the National Woman's Party, 1913-1919. Ph.D. diss., Syracuse University.

Forster, Margaret. 1985. *Significant Sisters: The Grassroots of Active Feminism, 1839-1939*. New York: Alfred A. Knopf.

Fowler, Robert Booth. 1986. *Carrie Catt: Feminist Politician*. Boston: Northeastern University Press.

Freeman, Jo. 1971. The Building of the Gilded Cage. *The Second Wave: A Magazine of the New Feminism* 1:7-9, 33-39.

Freeman, Jo. 1975. *The Politics of Women's Liberation*. New York: Longman.

Friedman, Lawrence M. 1985. *A History of American Law*. 2d ed. New York: Simon and Schuster.

Fry, Amelia R. 1986. Alice Paul and the ERA. In *Rights of Passage: The Past and Future of the ERA*, ed. Joan Hoff-Wilson, 8-24. Bloomington: Indiana University Press.

Frye, Northrop. 1957. *Anatomy of Criticism: Four Essays*. Princeton, NJ: Princeton University Press.

Frye, Northrop. 1963. *The Well-Tempered Critic*. Bloomington: Indiana University Press.

Fulkerson, Richard P. 1979. The Public Letter as Rhetorical Form: Structure, Logic, and Style in King's "Letter from Birmingham Jail." *Quarterly Journal of Speech* 65:121-34.

Gage, Matilda Joslyn. 1890. The Dangers of the Hour. Delivered 24 February, Woman's National Liberal Convention. Matilda Joslyn Gage Papers, Schlesinger Library, Radcliffe College, MC 377, folder 45.

Gambone, Joseph G. 1973. The Forgotten Feminist of Kansas: The Papers of Clarina I. H. Nichols, 1854-1885. *Kansas Historical Quarterly* 39:12-28.

Giddings, Paula. 1984. *When and Where I Enter: The Impact of Black Women on Race and Sex in America*. New York: William Morrow.

Giele, Janet Zollinger. 1961. Social Change in the Feminine Role: A Comparison of Woman's Suffrage and Woman's Temperance, 1870-1920. Ph.D. diss., Radcliffe College.

Gifford, Carolyn De Swarte. 1986. Home Protection: The WCTU's Conversion to Woman Suffrage. In *Gender, Ideology, and Action: Historical Perspectives on Women's Public Lives*, ed. Janet Sharistanian, 95-120. Westport, CT: Greenwood Press.

Gilman, Charlotte Perkins. 1898; rpt. 1966. *Woman and Economics: A Study of the Economic Relation Between Men and Women as a Factor in Social Evolution*. New York: Harper and Row.

Gilman, Charlotte Perkins. 1903; rpt. 1972. *The Home: Its Work and Influence*, ed. William L. O'Neill. Urbana: University of Illinois Press.

Gilman, Charlotte Perkins. 1909-1916; rpt. 1968. *The Forerunner, Vols. 1-7*. Intro. Madeleine B. Stern. Westport, CT: Greenwood Press.

Gilman, Charlotte Perkins. 1935; rpt. 1972. *The Living of Charlotte Perkins Gilman: An Autobiography*, eds. Annette K. Baxter and Leon Stein. New York: Arno Press.

Goodman, James E. 1985. The Origins of the "Civil War" in the Reform Community: Elizabeth Cady Stanton on Woman's Rights and Reconstruction. *Critical Matrix: Princeton Working Papers in Women's Studies* 1:1-29.

Gornick, Vivian 1978. Alice Paul. In *Essays in Feminism*, 171-78. New York: Harper & Row.

Grady, Henry W. 1890. The New South. In *Life of Henry W. Grady, Including His Writings and Speeches*, ed. Joel Chandler Harris, 83-93. Cassell Company.

Grant, Donald L. 1975. The Function and Mythology of Lynching, 1–19. In *The Anti-Lynching Movement: 1883–1932*. San Francisco: R & E Associates.

Greeley, Horace and Robert Dale Owen. 1860; rpt. 1972. *Divorce: Being a Correspondence Between Horace Greeley and Robert Dale Owen, Originally Published in the New York Daily Tribune*. New York: Source Book Press.

Greene, Dana, ed. 1980. *Lucretia Mott: Her Complete Speeches and Sermons*. New York: Edwin Mellen Press.

Griffith. Elisabeth. 1984. *In Her Own Right: The Life of Elizabeth Cady Stanton*. New York: Oxford University Press.

Grimké, Angelina E. 1836. *Appeal to the Christian Women of the Southern States*. New York: American Anti-Slavery Society.

Grimké, Angelina E. 1838. *Letters to Catharine E. Beecher, in Reply to an Essay on Slavery and Abolitionism, Addressed to A.E. Grimké, revised by the author*. Boston: Isaac Knapp.

Grimké, Sarah Moore. 1838. *Letters on the Equality of the Sexes and the Condition of Woman, Addressed to Mary Parker, President of the Boston Female Anti-Slavery Society*. Boston: Isaac Knapp.

Grossberg, Michael. 1985. *Governing the Hearth: Law and the Family in Nineteenth-Century America*. Chapel Hill: University of North Carolina Press.

Gurko, Miriam. 1976. *The Ladies of Seneca Falls: The Birth of the Woman's Rights Movement*. New York: Schocken Books.

Guy-Sheftall, Beverly Lynn. 1984. Daughters of Sorrow: Attitudes Toward Black Women, 1880-1920. Ph.D. diss., Emory University.

Hall, Jacqueline Dowd. 1978. "A Truly Subversive Affair": Women Against Lynching in the Twentieth-Century South. In *Women of America: A History*, eds. Carol Ruth Berkin and Mary Beth Norton, 370-88. Boston: Houghton-Mifflin.

Hall, Jacqueline Dowd. 1979. *Revolt Against Chivalry: Jessie Daniel Ames and the Women's Campaign Against Lynching*. New York: Columbia University Press.

Hallowell, Anna Davis, ed. 1884. *James and Lucretia Mott: Life and Letters*. Boston: Houghton-Mifflin.

Hamilton, Tullia Brown. 1978. The National Association of Colored Women, 1896-1970. Ph.D. diss., Emory University.

Hardesty, Nancy A. 1984. *Women Called to Witness: Evangelical Feminism in the 19th Century*. Nashville, TN: Abingdon Press.

Harper, Ida Husted. 1898–1908. *The Life and Work of Anthony*. 3 Vols. Indianapolis: Bowen-Merrill, Hollenbeck Press.

Harrison, Brian. 1978. *Separate Spheres: The Opposition to Women's Suffrage in Britain*. New York: Holmes and Meier.

Hayden, Dolores. 1981. *The Grand Domestic Revolution: A History of Feminist Designs for Contemporary Homes, Neighborhoods and Cities*. Cambridge, MA: Massachusetts Institute of Technology.

Hersh, Blanche Glassman. 1978. *The Slavery of Sex: Feminist Abolitionists in America*. Urbana: University of Illinois Press.

Herttell, Thomas. 1839. *The Right of Married Women to Hold and Contract Property Sustained by the Constitution of the State of New York*. New York: Henry Durrell.

Higginson, Thomas Wentworth. 1870a. Turn Your Guns upon the Enemy. The *Woman's Journal*, 19 November, p. 361.

Higginson, Thomas Wentworth. 1870b. Remarks at the Annual Meeting of the American Woman Suffrage Association. The *Woman's Journal*, 3 December, p. 378.

History of Pennsylvania Hall, Which was Destroyed by a Mob on the 17th of May, 1838. 1838. [Ed. Samuel Webb.] Philadelphia: Merrihew and Gunn.

History of Woman Suffrage, 1848–1861, vol. 1. 1881. Eds. Elizabeth Cady Stanton, Susan B. Anthony, and Matilda Joslyn Gage. New York: Fowler and Wells. Cited as HWS 1.

History of Woman Suffrage, 1861–1876, vol. 2, 1882. Eds. Elizabeth Cady Stanton, Susan B. Anthony, and Matilda Joslyn Gage. New York: Fowler and Wells. Cited as HWS 2.

History of Woman Suffrage, 1876–1885, vol. 3. 1887. Eds. Susan B. Anthony and Ida Husted Harper. Rochester, NY: Susan B. Anthony. Cited as HWS 3.

History of Woman Suffrage, 1883–1900, vol. 4. 1906. Eds. Susan B. Anthony and Ida Husted Harper. Rochester, NY: Susan B. Anthony. Cited as HWS 4.

History of Woman Suffrage, 1900–1913, vol. 5. 1922. Ed. Ida Husted Harper. New York: J. J. Little and Ives. Cited as HWS 5.

History of Woman Suffrage, 1913–1920, vol. 6. 1922. Ed. Ida Husted Harper. New York: J. J. Little and Ives. Cited as HWS 6.

Hodes, W. William. 1970. Women and the Constitution: Some Legal History and a New Approach to the Nineteenth Amendment. *Rutgers Law Review* 25:26-53.

Hoff-Wilson, Joan. 1987. The Unfinished Revolution: The Changing Legal Status of U.S. Women. *Signs* 13:7-36.

Homer. *Odyssey* [*The Authoress of the Odyssey*]. 1897; rpt. 1967. Trans. Samuel Butler.

Chicago: University of Chicago Press.

Homer. *Odyssey*. 1932. Trans. T. Shaw [T. E. Lawrence]. New York: Oxford University Press.

Homer. *Odyssey*. 1935. Trans. S. H. Butcher and Andrew Lang. New York: Modern Library.

Homer. *Odyssey*. 1946. Trans. E.V. Rieu. London: Allen Lane/Penguin.

Homer. *Odyssey*. 1980. Trans. Walter Shewring. New York: Oxford University Press.

Hooks, Bell. 1981. *Ain't I A Woman: Black Women and Feminism*. Boston: South End Press.

Howell, Wilbur S. and Hoyt H. Hudson. 1943; rpt. 1960. Daniel Webster. In *A History and Criticism of American Public Address*, ed. William Norwood Brigance, 2:665-734. New York: Russell and Russell.

Hurwitz, Edith F. 1978. Carrie Chapman Catt's "Suffrage Militancy" [7 April 1913]. *Signs* 3:739-43.

Irwin, Inez Haynes. 1964; rpt. 1977. *The Story of Alice Paul and the National Woman's Party*. Fairfax, VA: Denlinger's Publishers.

James, Henry, et al. 1853; rpt. 1972. *Love, Marriage and Divorce and the Sovereignty of the Individual*. New York: Source Book Press.

Janeway, Elizabeth. 1971. *Man's World; Woman's Place: A Study in Social Mythology*. New York: Dell.

Janis, Irving L. 1972. Effects of Fear Arousal on Attitude Change: Recent Developments in Theory and Experimental Research. In *The Process of Social Influence: Readings in Persuasion*, eds. Thomas D. Beisecker and Donn W. Parson, 277-302. Englewood Cliffs, NJ: Prentice-Hall.

Japp, Phyllis M. 1985. Esther or Isaiah?: The Abolitionist-Feminist Rhetoric of Angelina Grimké. *Quarterly Journal of Speech* 71:335-48.

Jerry, E. Claire. 1986. Clara Bewick Colby and the *Woman's Tribune*: Strategies of a Free Lance Movement Leader. Ph.D. diss., University of Kansas.

Jones, Rufus M. 1921; rpt. 1970. *The Later Periods of Quakerism*. 2 vols. Westport, CT: Greenwood Press.

Katz, David Howard. 1973. Carrie Chapman Catt and the Struggle for Peace. Ph.D. diss., Syracuse University.

Kerber, Linda K. 1980. *Women of the Republic: Intellect and Ideology in the American Revolution*. Chapel Hill: University of North Carolina Press.

Kettler, Ernestine Hara. 1976. In Prison. In *From Parlor to Prison: Five American Suffragists Talk About Their Lives*, ed. Sherna Gluck, 227-70. New York: Vintage.

Kierkegaard, Søren. 1941; rpt. 1954. *Fear and Trembling: A Dialectical Lyric*. Trans. Walter Lowrie. New York: Anchor.

Kraditor, Aileen. 1965; rpt. 1981. *The Ideas of the Woman Suffrage Movement, 1890-1920*. New York: W. W. Norton.

Lane, Margaret. 1972. *Frances Wright and the "Great Experiment."* Manchester, England: Manchester University Press.

Langer, Susanne K. 1953. *Feeling and Form*. NY: Scribner's.

Laws of the State of New York Passed at the Eighty-Third Session of the Legislature. 1860. Albany, NY: William Gould.

Leach, William. 1980. *True Love and Perfect Union: The Feminist Reform of Sex and Society*. New York: Basic Books.

Leff, Michael C. and G. P. Mohrmann. 1974. Lincoln at Cooper Union: A Rhetorical

Analysis of the Text. *Quarterly Journal of Speech* 60:346-58.

Lemons, J. Stanley. 1973. *The Woman Citizen: Social Feminism in the 1920s*. Urbana: University of Illinois Press.

Lender, Mark Edward and James Kirby Martin. 1983. *Drinking in America*. New York: Free Press.

Lerner, Gerda. 1967. *The Grimké Sisters from South Carolina: Pioneers for Woman's Rights and Abolition*. New York: Schocken Books.

Lerner, Gerda. 1969. The Lady and the Mill Girl: Changes in the Status of Women in the Age of Jackson. *Midcontinent American Studies Journal* 10:515.

Lerner, Gerda. 1971. *Women in American History*. Reading, MA: Addison-Wesley.

Linkugel, Wilmer A. 1960. The speeches of Anna Howard Shaw, Collected and Edited with Introduction and Notes. 2 vols. Ph.D. diss., University of Wisconsin.

Linkugel, Wilmer A. 1963. The Woman Suffrage Argument of Anna Howard Shaw. *Quarterly Journal of Speech* 49:165-74.

Linkugel, Wilmer A. 1987. Anna Howard Shaw. In *American Orators of the Twentieth Century: Critical Studies and Sources*, eds. Bernard K. Duffy and Halford R. Ryan. Westport, CT: Greenwood Press.

Lipking, Lawrence. 1983. Aristotle's Sister: A Poetics of Abandonment. *Critical Inquiry* 10:61-81.

Lorant, Stefan. 1953. *The Presidency: A Pictorial History of Presidential Elections from Washington to Truman*. New York: Macmillan.

Lougee, Robert W. 1972. *Midcentury Revolution, 1848: Society and Revolution in France and Germany*. Lexington, MA: D. C. Heath.

Lucas, Stephen. 1988. The Renaissance of American Public Address: Text and Context in Rhetorical Criticism. *Quarterly Journal of Speech* 72:241-60.

Lumpkin, Katharine Du Pre. 1974. *The Emancipation of Angelina Grimké*. Chapel Hill: University of North Carolina Press.

Lunardini, Christine A. 1986. *From Equal Suffrage to Equal Rights: Alice Paul and the National Woman's Party, 1910–1928*. New York: New York University Press.

Lutz, Alma. 1931. *Emma Willard: Pioneer Educator of American Women*. Boston: Beacon Press.

Lutz, Alma. 1940. *Created Equal: A Biography of Elizabeth Cady Stanton*. New York: John Day.

Lutz, Alma. 1959. *Susan B. Anthony: Rebel, Crusader, Humanitarian*. Boston: Beacon Hill.

Lutz, Alma. 1971. Susan Brownell Anthony. In *Notable American Women, 1607–1950*, 1:51-57. 3 vols. Cambridge, MA: Belknap Press of Harvard University.

McClelland, David C. 1964. Wanted: A New Self-Image for Women. In *The Woman in America*, ed. Robert Jay Lifton, 173-92. Boston: Beacon Press.

Mack, Phyllis. 1982. Women as Prophets During the English Civil War. *Feminist Studies* 8:19-47.

Mack, Phyllis. 1986. Feminine Behavior and Radical Action: Franciscans, Quakers, and the Followers of Gandhi. *Signs* 11:457-77.

McMillan, Carol. 1982. *Woman, Reason and Nature: Some Philosophical Problems with Feminism*. Princeton, NJ: Princeton University Press.

McPherson, James M. 1975. *The Abolitionist Legacy: From Reconstruction to the NAACP*. Princeton, NJ: Princeton University Press.

Mäsel-Walters, Lynne. 1980. To Hustle With the Rowdies: the Organization and

Functions of the American Suffrage Press. *Journal of American Culture* 3:167-83.

Maloney, Martin. 1947. The Forensic Speaking of Clarence Darrow. *Speech Monographs* 14:111-26.

Maloney, Martin. 1955. Clarence Darrow. In *A History and Criticism of American Public Address*, ed. Marie Kathryn Hochmuth, 3:262-312. New York: Longmans, Green.

Martineau, Harriet. 1848. *Eastern Life, Past and Present*. Philadelphia: Lea and Blanchard.

Martyn, Henry. 1846. *Deceitfulness of the Heart*. Boston: Tract Committee of the Diocese of Massachusetts.

Martyn, Henry. 1851. *Journals and Letters of the Rev. Henry Martyn, B.D.* New York: M. W. Dodd.

Mills, Glen E. 1942. Webster's Principles of Rhetoric. *Speech Monographs* 9:124-40.

Mills, Glen E. 1943. Misconceptions Concerning Daniel Webster. *Quarterly Journal of Speech* 29:423-38.

Mohrmann, G. P. and Michael C. Leff. 1974. Lincoln at Cooper Union: A Rationale for Neo-Classical Criticism. *Quarterly Journal of Speech* 60:459-67.

Mossell, Mrs. Nathan Francis [Gertrude E. H. Bustill]. 1894; rpt. 1988. *The Work of Afro-American Women*. 2d ed. Intro. Joanne Braxton. New York: Oxford University Press.

Motley, Constance Baker. 1966. The Legal Status of the Negro in the United States. In *The American Negro Reference Book*, ed. John P. Davis, 484-521. Englewood Cliffs, N.J.: Prentice-Hall.

Mott, Lucretia [Coffin]. 1850. *Discourse on Woman*. Delivered at the Assembly Buildings, December 17, 1849. Philadelphia: T. B. Peterson.

National Woman's Rights Convention, held at Worcester, October 15, 16, 1851. *Proceedings*. 1852. New York: Fowler and Wells.

National Woman's Rights Convention, held at the Broadway Tabernacle, New York, on Tuesday, Sept. 6th and 7th, 1853. *Proceedings*. 1853. New York: Fowler and Wells.

National Woman's Rights Convention, held at Cleveland, Ohio, on Wednesday, Thursday, and Friday, October 5th, 6th, and 7th, 1853. *Proceedings*. 1854. Cleveland, OH: Beardsley, Spear and Co., Printers, Plain Dealer Office.

National Woman's Rights Convention [Seventh], held at the Broadway Tabernacle, New York, on Tuesday and Wednesday, November 25th and 26th, 1856. *Proceedings*. 1856. New York: Edward O. Jenkins, Printer.

National Woman's Rights Convention, 1859. *Proceedings*. 1859. Rochester, NY: Steam Press.

Nelson, Marjory. 1976. Ladies in the Streets: A Sociological Analysis of the National Woman's Party, 1910–1930. Ph.D. diss., State University of New York at Buffalo.

Nichols, Clarina Howard. 3 December 1852. Woman's Property Rights [Synopsis of Speech to Vermont Legislature]. In Woman's Rights and Wrongs. *New York Daily Tribune*, p. 4.

Nichols, Clarina Howard. 1853. *The Responsibilities of Woman* [1851]. Series of Woman's Rights Tracts. Rochester, NY: Steam Press of Curtis, Butts, and Co.

Nies, Judith. 1977. *Seven Women: Portraits from the American Radical Tradition*. New

York: Viking Press.

O'Neill, William L. 1967. *Divorce in the Progressive Era*. New Haven: Yale University Press.

O'Neill, William L. 1971. *Everyone Was Brave: A History of Feminism in America*. New York: Quadrangle/New York Times.

Peck, Mary Gray. 1944. *Carrie Chapman Catt: A Biography*. New York: H. W. Wilson.

Phillips, Brenda D. 1985. The Decade of Origin: Resource Mobilization and Women's Rights in the 1850s. Ph.D. diss., Ohio State University.

Pleck, Elizabeth. 1983. Feminist Responses to "Crimes Against Women," 1868-1896. *Signs* 8:451-70.

Pryor, Elizabeth Brown. 1987. *Clara Barton: Professional Angel*. Philadelphia: University of Pennsylvania Press.

Quarles, Benjamin. 1969. *Black Abolitionists*. New York: Oxford University Press.

Rabkin, Peggy A. 1975. The Silent Feminist Revolution: Women and the Law in New York State from Blackstone to the Beginnings of the American Women's Rights Movement. Ph.D. diss., State University of New York at Buffalo.

Rabkin, Peggy A. 1980. *Fathers to Daughters. The Legal Foundations of Female Emancipation*. Westport, CT: Greenwood Press.

Redding, Saunders. 1971. Sojourner Truth. In *Notable American Women, 1607–1950*, ed. Edward T. James, 3:479-81. Cambridge, MA: Belknap Press of Harvard University.

Richardson, Marilyn, ed. 1987. *Maria W. Stewart, America's First Black Woman Political Writer: Essays and Speeches*. Bloomington: Indiana University Press.

Robins-Mowry, Dorothy. 1983. *The Hidden Sun: Women of Modern Japan*. Boulder, CO: Westview Press.

Rorabaugh, W. J. 1980. *The Alcoholic Republic: An American Tradition*. New York: Oxford University Press.

Sanbonmatsu, Akira. 1971. Darrow and Rorke's Use of Burkeian Identification Strategies in *New York vs. Gitlow. Communication Monographs* 38:36-48.

Sartre, Jean-Paul. 1956. Existentialism is a Humanism. In *Existentialism from Dostoevsky to Sartre*, ed. Walter Kaufmann, 287-311. Cleveland: Meridian.

Sartre, Jean-Paul. 1962. Introduction to *Les Temps Modernes*. Trans. Françoise Ehrmann. In *Paths to the Present: Aspects of European Thought from Romanticism to Existentialism*, ed. Eugen Weber, 432-41. New York: Dodd, Mead.

Scott, Ann Firor. 1970. *The Southern Lady: From Pedestal to Politics, 1830–1930*. Chicago: University of Chicago Press.

Scott, Ann Firor. 1978. What, Then, is the American: This New Woman? *Journal of American History* 65:679-703.

Scott, Robert L. and Donald K. Smith. 1969. The Rhetoric of Confrontation. *Quarterly Journal of Speech* 55:1-8.

Shaw, Anna Howard. 1 July 1915. The Fundamental Principle of a Republic. The *Ogdenburg Advance and St. Lawrence Weekly Democrat*, pp. 2-3.

Shaw, Anna Howard. 1915. *Story of a Pioneer*. With Elizabeth Jordan. New York: Harper & Brothers.

Simons, Herbert W. 1970. Requirements, Problems, and Strategies: A Theory of Persuasion for Social Movements. *Quarterly Journal of Speech* 56:1-11.

Sklar, Kathryn Kish. 1986. Why Were Most Politically Active Women Opposed to the ERA in the 1920s? In *Rights of Passage: The Past and Future of the ERA*, ed. Joan Hoff-Wilson, 25-35. Bloomington: Indiana University Press.

Smith, Page. 1970. *Daughters of the Promised Land: Women in American History*. Boston: Little, Brown.

Smith-Rosenberg, Carroll. 1975. The Female World of Love and Ritual: Relations Between Women in Nineteenth-Century America. *Signs* 1:1-30.

Snow, Malinda. 1985. Martin Luther King's "Letter from Birmingham Jail" as Pauline Epistle. *Quarterly Journal of Speech* 71:318-34.

Sochen, June. 1973. *Movers and Shakers: American Women Thinkers and Activists, 1900–1970*. New York: Quadrangle/New York Times.

Solomon, Martha. 1988. Ideology as Rhetorical Constraint: The Anarchist Agitation of "Red Emma" Goldman. *Quarterly Journal of Speech* 74:184-200.

Stanton, Elizabeth Cady. 1854. *Address to the Legislature of New York, Adopted by the State Woman's Rights Convention, held at Albany, Tuesday and Wednesday, February 14 and 15, 1854*. Albany, NY: Weed, Parsons.

Stanton, Elizabeth Cady. 18 May 1860. Speech to the Anniversary of the American Anti-Slavery Society, May 1860. The *Liberator*, p. 78.

Stanton, Elizabeth Cady. 1861. *Address of Elizabeth Cady Stanton on the Divorce Bill, before the Judiciary Committee of the New York Senate, in the Assembly Chamber, Feb. 8, 1861*. Albany, NY: Weed, Parsons and Company.

Stanton, Elizabeth Cady. 1867. First speech in the Kansas State Referendum Campaign. Holograph. Topeka: Kansas State Historical Society.

Stanton, Elizabeth Cady. 19 May 1870. President's Address to the National Woman Suffrage Association Convention, 10 May 1870. *Revolution* 5:305-7.

Stanton, Elizabeth Cady. 1888. Statement. Hearing before the Committee on Woman Suffrage, United States Senate, April 2, 1888. 50th Cong. 2d sess. Report no. 2543, 9-17.

Stanton, Elizabeth Cady. 1892a. The Solitude of Self. The *Woman's Journal*, 23 January, pp. 1, 32.

Stanton, Elizabeth Cady. 1892b. Solitude of Self. *Hearings of the Woman Suffrage Association before the Committee on the Judiciary, 18 January 1892, House of Representatives*, 1-5. Washington, D.C.: U.S. Government Printing Office.

Stanton, Elizabeth Cady. 1983. Solitude of Self. In *We Shall Be Heard: Women Speakers in America*, eds. Patricia Scileppi Kennedy and Gloria Hartmann O'Shields, 66-74. Dubuque, IA: Kendall/Hunt.

Stanton, Elizabeth Cady. 1898; rpt. 1971. *Eighty Years and More: Reminiscences, 1815–1897*. New York: Schocken.

Stanton, Elizabeth Cady and the Revising Committee. 1892, 1895; rpt. 1974. *The Woman's Bible*. Seattle, WA: Seattle Coalition Task Force on Women and Religion.

Stanton, Theodore and Harriot Stanton Blatch, eds. 1922. *Elizabeth Cady Stanton: As Revealed in Her Letters, Diaries, and Reminiscences*. 2 vols. New York: Harper & Brothers.

Sterling, Dorothy. 1979. *Black Foremothers: Three Lives*. Old Westbury, New York: The Feminist Press.

Stewart, Maria W. Miller. 1835. *Productions of Mrs. Maria W. Stewart*. Boston: Friends of Freedom and Virtue.

Stewart, Maria W. Miller. 1879. *Meditations from the Pen of Mrs. Maria W. Stewart*. Washington, D.C.

Stewart, Maria W. Miller. 1971. Religion and the Pure Principles of Morality, Boston, October 1831. In *Early Negro Writing, 1760–1837*, ed. Dorothy Porter, 460-71. Boston: Beacon Press.

Stowe, Harriet Beecher. 1863. The Libyan Sibyl. *Atlantic Monthly* 11:473-81.

Stratton, Joanna L. 1981. *Pioneer Women: Voices from the Kansas Frontier*. Intro. Arthur M. Schlesinger, Jr. New York: Simon and Schuster.

Suhl, Yuri. 1959. *Ernestine L. Rose and the Battle for Human Rights*. New York: Reynal.

Terborg-Penn, Rosalyn. 1977. Afro-Americans in the Struggle for Woman Suffrage. Ph.D. diss., Howard University.

Terrell, Mary Church. 1893. Introduction of Ida B. Wells. In Mary Church Terrell Papers, Library of Congress Ms. 16976, Reel 20, container 28, 507-509.

Terrell, Mary Church. 1898. *The Progress of Colored Women* [Speech to NAWSA National Convention February 18, 1898]. Washington, D.C.: Smith Brothers.

Terrell, Mary Church. 1904. Speech at the 1904 International Congress of Women in Berlin. *Voice of the Negro* 1:454-461.

Terrell, Mary Church. 24 January 1907. What It Means to Be Colored in the Capital of the United States [1906]. The *Independent*, pp. 181-86.

Terrell, Mary Church. 1912; rpt. 1983. The Justice of Woman Suffrage. The *Crisis* 90:6.

Terrell, Mary Church. c.1913-1919. The Effects of Disfranchisement Upon the Colored Women of the South. 13 typed pp. Library of Congress, Ms. 16976, Reel 23, container 32, 385–397.

Terrell, Mary Church. 1940. *A Colored Woman in a White World*. Washington, D.C.: Ransdell.

Terrell, Mary Church. September 1943. If I Were Young Again. *Negro Digest*, pp. 57, 59.

Terrell, Mary Church. 1948. Something About Our Name. The *Delta* 18:57.

Tick, Judith. 1983. *American Women Composers before 1870*. Ann Arbor, MI: UMI Research Press.

Truth, Sojourner. 1 June 1867. Speeches delivered on May 9 and 10 at the First Annual Meeting of the American Equal Rights Association. *National Anti-Slavery Standard*, p. 3.

Truth, Sojourner. 1878; rpt. 1968. *Narrative of Sojourner Truth*. With Olive Gilbert. New York: Arno Press.

Van Voris, Jacqueline. 1987. *Carrie Chapman Catt: A Public Life*. New York: The Feminist Press at the City University of New York.

Vicinus, Martha. 1985. *Independent Women: Work and Community for Single Women, 1850–1920*. Chicago: University of Chicago Press.

Wagner, Sally Roesch. 1978. "That Word is Liberty": A Biography of Matilda Joslyn Gage. Ph.D. diss., University of California, Santa Cruz.

Wagner, Sally Roesch. 1987. *A Time of Protest: Suffragists Challenge the Republic, 1870–1887*. Sacramento, CA: Spectrum Publications.

Walker, Lola Carolyn. 1951. The Speeches and Speaking of Carrie Chapman Catt. Ph.D. diss., Northwestern University.

Wallace, John William. 1887. Silver v. Ladd. *Cases Argued and Adjudged in the Supreme Court of the United States, December term, 1868*, 7:219-28. New York: Banks and Brothers.

Washington, Booker T. 1901. Atlanta Exposition Address. In *Up from Slavery: An Autobiography*, 217-25. New York: Doubleday Page.

Wells, Ida B. 1892; rpt. 1969. Southern Horrors: Lynch Law in All Its Phases. In *On Lynchings: Southern Horrors, A Red Record, Mob Rule in New Orleans*, 4-24. New York: Arno Press.

Welter, Barbara. 1976. *Dimity Convictions: The American Woman in the Nineteenth*

Century. Athens: Ohio University Press.

Willard, Emma. 1819, rpt. 1893. A Plan for Improving Female Education. In *Woman and Higher Education*, ed. Anna Callender Brackett, 1-46. New York: Harper & Brothers.

Willard, Frances E. 1883. Temperance and Home Protection. Delivered at the Third Annual WCTU Convention in 1876. In Frances Willard, *Woman and Temperance*, 452-59. Hartford, CT: J. Betts.

Willard, Frances E. 6 August 1886. The White Cross and Social Purity. Delivered 4 August 1886. The *Chautauqua Assembly Herald*, p. 2.

Willard, Frances E. 1888. Presidential Address. *Minutes of the National Woman's Temperance Union, 14th Annual Meeting, 1887*. Chicago: Woman's Temperance Publication Association.

Willard, Frances E. 1889a. *Glimpses of Fifty Years, 1839–1889*. Chicago: Woman's Temperance Publication Association, H. J. Smith.

Willard, Frances E. 1889b. *Woman in the Pulpit*. Chicago: Woman's Temperance Publication Association.

Willard, Frances E. 1890. *A White Life for Two*. Chicago: Woman's Temperance Publishing Association.

Willard, Frances E. 2 August 1891. A White Life for Two, a lecture delivered in the Amphitheatre, August 1, 1891. *Chautuqua Assembly Herald*, p. 5.

Willard, Frances E. 7 December 1895. A White Life for Two. The *Lexington Church Record*. 1:2.1.

Wollstonecraft, Mary. 1792; rpt. 1976. *A Vindication of the Rights of Woman*. Ed. C.H. Poston. New York: Norton.

Woman's Rights Convention, held at Worcester, October 23 and 24, 1850. *Proceedings*. 1851. Boston: Prentiss and Sawyer.

Woman's Rights Conventions, held at Seneca Falls and Rochester, New York, July and August, 1848. *Proceedings*. 1870. New York: Robert J. Johnston.

Woman's Rights Convention, held at Syracuse, New York, September 8-10, 1852. *Proceedings*. 1852. Syracuse, NY: J. E. Masters.

Woman's Rights Convention, May 12, 1860. *Proceedings*. 1860. New York: Robert J. Johnston, Printer.

Woman's Rights Convention, May 10, 1866. *Proceedings*. 1866. New York: Robert J. Johnston.

Woodhull, Victoria Claflin. 1871. *A Lecture on Constitutional Equality delivered at Lincoln Hall, Washington, D.C., February 16, 1871*. New York: Journeymen Printers' Cooperative Association.

Yates, Gayle Graham. 1985. *Harriet Martineau on Women*. New Brunswick, NJ: Rutgers University Press.

Index

Abolitionism, 4, 22-35, 47-48, 49, 82-83, 105; Anti-Slavery Conventions of American Women, 18, 19, 26-28, 33, 69 n.1, 193

Adams, John Q., 61

Adams, Jane, 171, 182, 185

Afric-American Female Intelligence Society, 18

American Association of University Women, 155

American Civil Liberties Union, 185

American Equal Rights Association, 21, 49, 84, 85, 143, 193

American Medical Association, 182

American Woman Suffrage Association, 83, 84, 131, 159

Ames, Jessie Daniel, 149

Anderson, Judith, 17, 35, 185, 193

Antigone, 113

Anthony, Daniel, 115, 183

Anthony, Susan B., 5, 37, 51, 63, 74, 82, 83, 84, 86 n.6, 102, 118 n.1, 129, 131, 135, 143, 154, 157, 171, 177, 185, 189, 190, 193, 199; speech in defense of her vote, 105-18

Anti-suffrage, 3, 6, 157-58, 160-61

Aptheker, Bettina, 147, 193

Arguments: deductive, 109-13; from expediency (benefits), 14-15, 64, 87-88, 121-31; hermeneutical, 39, 40-41, 47; from natural rights (justice), 14-15, 22, 23, 44, 53, 55, 57, 60, 61, 64-65, 67, 73, 74, 87-88, 90, 92-93, 99, 100, 109, 114, 169-70

Aristotle, 1, 193

Armstrong, Richard, 193

Arnold, Carroll, 108, 118 n.2, 193

Association of Southern Women for the Prevention of Lynching (ASWPL), 149

Bacon, Margaret Hope, 25, 33, 35 n.1, 38, 40, 44, 45, 47, 193

Baker, Elizabeth, 184

Banner, Lois, 69 n.7, 193

Barnes, G. H., 25, 32, 193

Bartlett, Elizabeth, 193

Basch, Norma, 53, 194

Beard, Mary Ritter, 171

Becker, Susan, 86 n.5, 184, 194

Beecher, Catharine, 24, 42, 194

Beecher, Henry Ward, 71

Bennett, James Gordon, 68

Berg, Barbara, 10, 194

Berg, Christine, 31, 124, 194

Berry, Mary Frances, 191 n.1, 194

Berry, Philippa, 31, 124, 194

Birney, Catherine, 22, 25, 36, 194

Bitzer, Lloyd, 13, 194

Black, John, 108, 119 n.2, 194
Blackstone, William, 57
Blackwell, Antoinette Brown. *See* Antoinette Brown
Blackwell, Henry, 84, 85, 194
Blackwell, Samuel, 80
Blake, Nelson, 71, 73, 194
Bland, Sidney, 174, 175, 176, 194
Blatch, Harriot Stanton, 86 n.6, 144 n.1, 204
Blocker, Jack, 122, 132 n.2, 194
Bloomer, Amelia Jenks, 68, 103 n.1
Booth, Wayne, 69 n.3, 194-95
Bordin, Ruth, 5, 121, 122, 123, 127, 130, 131, 195
Branham, Lucy, 176
Brigance, William, 108, 195
Brown, Antoinette, 4, 37, 48 n.1, 59, 74, 82, 85, 140, 194; 1860 convention debate, 75-80
Bryant, Donald, 89, 195
Buhle, Mari Jo, 195
Burke, Kenneth, 139, 195
Burns, Lucy, 171
Butler, Benjamin, 107

Camhi, Jane, 15, 158, 164, 195
Campbell, Karlyn Kohrs, 9, 20, 143, 144 n.3, 189, 195
Cannon, Joe, 179 n.5
Catt, Carrie Chapman, 3, 6, 118, 131, 157, 158, 159, 164, 177, 178 n.2, 182, 185, 195. Speeches: 1902, 165-67; 1916, 167-68; 1917, 169-71
Cazden, Elizabeth, 48 n.1, 195
Chafe, William H., 181, 182, 183, 184, 185, 195
Channing, William Ellery, 43
Chapman, Maria Weston, 29
Charles F. Hovey Fund, 82-83
Chester, Ronald, 195
Child labor amendment, 6, 182
Choate, Rufus, 119 n.2
Christiansen, Adrienne, 88, 90, 93, 195-96
Civil War, 4, 48, 66, 80, 83, 84, 105, 118, 145, 167, 169
Clark, J. B. "Champ," 170, 179 n.5
Clark, Thomas D., 132 n.1, 196
Clarke, Edward, 12, 196

Clay, Laura, 8
Clevenger, Ima Fuchs, 165, 169, 196
Clinton, De Witt, 11
Colby, Clara Bewick, 8
Coleman, Willie Mae, 145, 196
Confrontation, 14, 41, 93, 94, 98, 99, 101, 102, 103 n.4, 129, 135, 156 n.3, 172, 174-77, 184, 190
Congressional Union. *See* National Woman's Party
Conrad, Charles, 86 n.7, 196
Consciousness-raising, 13-14, 53, 69 n.3
Convention of Anti-Slavery Women. *See* Abolitionism
Cook, Blanche Wiesen, 186, 187, 196
Cott, Nancy, 3, 10, 196
Cowper, William, 40, 46, 196
Credibility, 21, 34, 45-46, 115-16, 117, 130, 137
Cromwell, Otelia, 25, 47, 196
Cult of domesticity. *See* True womanhood
Curtis, Charles, 183

Daly, Mary, 196
Dana, Richard Henry, 38-39, 40, 42, 43, 46, 47, 117
Darrow, Clarence, 118 n.2
Darwin, Charles, 80, 125, 165
Davis, Angela, 145, 196
Davis, Marianna, 20, 196
Davis, Paulina Wright, 64, 68, 73-74, 196
Declaration of Independence, 16, 52-58, 64, 69, 109
Declaration of Sentiments: of American Anti-Slavery Society, 27-28, 52, 196; of Seneca Falls, 4, 16 n.5, 50, 52-58, 67, 68, 69 n.6, 144, 166
Divorce laws, 54, 71-85, 86 n.1
Dix, Dorothea, 43
Douglass, Frederick, 58, 69 n.2, 103 n.3, 135
Dow, Bonnie, 196
Drescher, Seymour, 196
Drish, Ruth Williamson, 196
DuBois, Ellen, 144, 196
DuBois, W.E.B., 146
Dumond, D. W., 25, 32, 193
Duniway, Abigail Scott, 8
Duster, Alfreda M., 196

Eastman, Crystal, 171, 183, 185, 186-88, 196
Emerson, Ralph Waldo, 45, 50
Engels, Friedrich, 65-66, 196
Equal Rights Amendment (ERA), 7, 87, 182, 183-85, 187, 188; Lucretia Mott Amendment, 183
Erskine, Lord Thomas, 118 n.2
Ethos. *See* Credibility

Farrell, Thomas, 13, 16 n.4, 197
Fauset, Arthur H., 35 n.3, 197
Fell, Margaret Askew, 36 n.7, 197
Fell, Sarah, 36 n.7, 197
Feminine style, 12-15, 16, 45-47, 63, 91-93, 129, 146-47, 150, 154, 190
Feminism, 3, 121-22, 133, 139, 185-87, 188
Fifteenth Amendment (U.S. Constitution), 106, 111-12, 114
Fitzgerald, Tracey, 145, 197
Flexner, Eleanor, 105, 158, 197
Foner, Philip, 69 n.2, 103 n.3, 197
Ford, Linda, 69 n.6, 197
Forster, Margaret, 135, 197
Foster, Abby Kelley. *See* Kelley, Abigail
Fourteenth Amendment (U.S. Constitution), 5, 21, 105-6, 107, 111, 114, 157
Fowler, Robert, 158, 197
Fox, George, 36 n.7
Freeman, Jo, 16 nn.3, 6, 197
French, William, 155 n.2
Friedman, Lawrence, 197
Fry, Amelia, 185, 197
Fry, Elizabeth, 43
Frye, Northrop, 33, 35 n.4, 139, 197
Fulkerson, Richard, 117, 197
Fuller, Margaret, 65

Gage, Matilda Joslyn, 38, 84, 106, 118, 118 n.1, 143, 197, 199
Gambone, Joseph, 90, 197
Gannett, Deborah Sampson, 17
Garrison, W. L., 22, 29, 69 n.3, 74, 81, 82, 85, 86 n.7
Giddings, Paula, 145, 150, 151, 197
Giele, Janet, 5, 35 n.1, 36 n.7, 197-98
Gifford, Carolyn, 124, 198
Gilman, Charlotte Perkins, 185-86, 191 n.2, 198

Goodman, James E., 86 n.4, 198
Goodrich, Chauncey, 119 n.2
Gornick, Vivian, 158, 198
Gougar, Helen Jackson, 8
Grady, Henry, 146, 198
Grant, Donald L., 147, 198
Greeley, Horace, 67, 68, 73, 82, 198
Greene, Dana, 9, 44, 48 n.3, 198
Griffith, Elisabeth, 69 n.7, 97, 103 n.6, 198
Grimké, Angelina, 3, 8, 17, 18, 19, 22-25, 34, 35, 36 n.8, 41, 49, 63, 65, 66, 80, 103 n.2, 135, 189, 198. Speech: 1838, 29-33
Grimké, Sarah, 3, 19, 22-25, 34, 35, 36, 37, 49, 65, 103 n.4, 193-94, 198
Grossberg, Michael, 198
Gurko, Miriam, 67, 68, 72, 74, 88, 198
Guy-Sheftall, Beverly, 145, 198

Hall, Jacqueline Dowd, 149, 198, 199
Hallowell, Anna Davis, 47, 199
Hamilton, Tullia Brown, 20, 199
Hardesty, Nancy, 125, 199
Harper, Ida Husted, 37, 108, 115, 116, 118, 135, 199
Harrison, Brian, 199
Hart, Joel, 126
Hayden, Dolores, 186, 199
Hersh, Blanche Glassman, 4, 10, 12, 137, 199
Herttell, Thomas, 54, 199
Higginson, Thomas Wentworth, 84, 199
Hodes, W. William, 157, 199
Hoff-Wilson, Joan, 157, 199
Homer, 1, 15-16 n.1, 199, 200
Hooks, Belle, 145, 200
Howe, Julia Ward, 84
Howell, Wilbur, 108, 119 n.2, 200
Hudson, Hoyt, 108, 119 n.2, 200
Hurlbut, Elisha, 46
Hurwitz, Edith, 178 n.2, 200

Ingram, Rosa, 155
International Council of Women, 118, 131, 146
International Woman Suffrage Alliance, 118, 178
Irwin, Inez Haynes, 158, 172, 174, 175, 176, 177, 200

James, Henry, 72, 200
Janeway, Elizabeth, 53, 200
Janis, Irving, 147, 200
Japp, Phyllis, 31, 200
Jefferson, Thomas, 16 n.5, 170
Jerry, E. Claire, 68, 200
Joan of Arc, 12, 62-63
Jones, Rufus, 48 n.2, 200

Katz, David, 164, 165-66, 200
Kelley, Abigail, 12, 29
Kelley, Florence, 182, 185
Kennedy, Patricia Scileppi, 144 n.3, 202
Kerber, Linda, 53, 200
Kettler, Ernestine, 175, 200
Kierkegaard, Søren, 140, 200
King, Martin Luther, Jr., 117
Kraditor, Aileen, 14, 37, 41, 121, 135, 200
Kropotkin, Peter, 141

Lane, Margaret, 17, 200
Langer, Susanne, 139, 200
Leach, William, 182, 200
League of Women Voters (LWV), 7, 178, 181, 183
Leff, Michael, 117, 200, 202
Lemons, J. Stanley, 181, 182, 183, 184, 185, 200
Lender, Mark, 5, 201
Lerner, Gerda, 22, 23, 24, 35, 36, 42, 44, 157, 201
Lewis, Dora, 171
Lincoln, Abraham, 117, 170
Linkugel, Wil, 3, 15, 159, 201
Lipking, Lawrence, 1, 9, 201
Lorant, Stefan, 201
Loughridge, William, 107
Lucas, Stephen, 52, 201
Lumpkin, Katherine DuPre, 22, 35, 36, 201
Lunardini, Christine, 201
Lutz, Alma, 11, 52, 67, 89, 115, 118, 135, 143, 201

Mäsel-Walters, Lynne, 134, 201
McClelland, David, 16 n.3, 201
McClintock, Mary Ann, 51
Mack, Phyllis, 31, 38, 179 n.4, 201
McMillan, Carol, 13, 201

Maloney, Martin, 108, 201
Mann, Horace, 43
Married women's disabilities, 5, 54, 64, 67, 71, 73-74, 87, 93-94, 145; property acts, 54-55, 64, 66, 72, 86 n.2, 103 n.5, 200
Martin, James, 5, 201
Martineau, Harriet, 46, 62, 65, 202, 206
Martyn, Henry, 202
Memorial, 106
Miller, Francis, 107, 108
Mills, Glen, 108, 119 n.2, 202
Minor v. Happersett et al., 5, 106, 117, 157
Minor, Francis, 106, 107
Minor, Virginia, 107, 117
Mitchell, S. Weir, 186
Mohrmann, G. P., 117, 200, 202
Mossell, Mrs. Nathan, 202
Motley, Constance Baker, 148, 202
Mott, James, 44, 52
Mott, Lucretia Coffin, 3, 4, 8, 9, 19, 20, 25, 29, 35 n.1, 38, 48 n.3, 50, 63, 65, 69 n.4, 80, 102, 103 n.2, 117, 129, 135, 183, 189, 190, 202; *Discourse on Woman*, 39-48
Muller v. Oregon, 183-84

National American Woman Suffrage Association (NAWSA), 6, 37, 105, 118, 122, 133, 134, 142, 143, 146, 159, 165, 167, 169, 171, 172, 178, 183
National Association for the Advancement of Colored People (NAACP), 146, 154
National Association of Colored Women (NACW), 151, 154
National Association Opposed to Woman Suffrage, 182
National Consumers League, 182
National Woman Suffrage Association, 66, 84, 105, 107, 118, 131, 143
National Woman's Party (NWP), 3, 6, 7, 69 n.6, 86 n.5, 105, 154, 158, 171-78
Natural rights philosophy, 14, 16 n.5, 23, 52-53, 55, 57, 64, 69, 85, 109, 129, 136, 158, 162, 167, 169, 170. *See also* Arguments, from natural rights
Nelson, Marjory, 184, 202
Nichols, Clarina Howard, 94, 96, 121,

129, 154, 189, 202. Speeches: 1851 and 1852, 88-93

O'Neill, William, 71, 121, 122, 181, 183, 188, 202
O'Shields, Gloria Hartmann, 144, 202
Owne, Robert Dale, 51, 198

Pankhurst, Christabel, 3, 188
Pankhurst, Emmeline, 3, 188
Paul, 1, 28, 31, 39, 41, 124
Paul, Alice, 6, 69 n.6, 158, 171-78, 178 n.2, 183, 187, 188
Peck, Mary Gray, 158, 165, 178 n.1, 203
Phillips, Brenda, 49, 50, 86 n.8, 90, 203
Phillips, Wendell, 50, 74, 84, 85, 86 nn.6, 7, 103 n.1; 1860 convention debate, 80-83
Pillsbury, Parker, 143
Plato, 95, 126
Pleck, Elizabeth, 72, 203
Preston, Amy, 59
Progressive movement, 6, 158
Prophecy. *See* Rhetorical strategies, persona
Protestantism, 39-40, 41, 55, 57, 122, 124, 135, 137, 138, 140
Purver, Andrew, 48 n.2

Quakers, 22, 23, 31, 35 n.1, 36 n.7, 38, 40, 41, 43, 45, 48 n.2, 171, 188

Rabkin, Peggy, 54-55, 203
Redding, Saunders, 33, 203
The *Revolution*, 105, 106, 107, 118, 143
Rhetoric, 1-3, 13, 16 n.6, 52-53, 89; forensic, 108, 113-15, 117, 118-19, 119 n.2; jeremiad, 33; sermon, 123-24, 132 n.1
Rhetorical barriers, 1, 9-12, 14, 23-27, 33, 45-46, 57-58, 88-89, 128-29, 134-35, 147, 149, 151-52, 189
Rhetorical strategies, 88, 89, 94, 96, 126, 128-29, 169, 170-71; analogy, 91, 95, 100; examples, 91, 102, 147-48, 149, 150, 151-52, 154; metaphors, 20, 97, 99, 136, 163; persona, 30, 31-32, 34, 45, 62, 91, 96-97; refutation, 20-21, 43, 60-62, 65, 78, 82, 101, 138-39, 146, 152, 159, 160-61; style, 18, 20, 22, 28, 29, 33,

35 n.4, 39, 45, 59, 66, 74-75, 78, 79, 94-95, 97, 149-50, 153, 159-60, 165, 167, 169, 189-90
Richardson, Marilyn, 9, 17, 19, 37, 203
Riddle, Albert, 107, 108
Robins-Mowry, Dorothy, 203
Root, Elihu, 170, 175
Rorabaugh, W. J., 5, 203
Rose, Ernestine Potowski, 49, 50, 59, 74, 78-80, 85, 86 n.3, 88, 177, 189. Speech: 1851, 63-66

Sanbonmatsu, Akira, 108, 118, 203
Sanger, Margaret Higgins, 185, 187
Sartre, Jean-Paul, 144 n.6, 203
Scott, Ann Firor, 10, 11, 35 n.2, 203
Scott, Robert, 172, 203
Scripture, 1, 18, 19, 25, 29, 40, 59, 91; arguments over, 86 n.9; Corinthians, 31, 39, 41, 48 n.1; Ezekiel, 40; Galatians, 32, 36 n.6, 124; Genesis, 36 n.6, 40; Hebrews, 30; Isaiah, 31; Joel, 62; John, 45; Luke, 31; Matthew, 29, 30, 31; Revelation, 36 n.6; Romans, 28; Samuel, 31; Thessalonians, 28; Timothy, 39, 48 n.1
Seneca Falls Convention, 4, 48, 50-63, 67-69, 131, 142, 143, 144, 183
Shafroth-Palmer Amendment, 178 n.3
Shakespeare, William, 38, 40, 95, 138, 144 n.5
Shaw, Anna Howard, 3, 6, 15, 35 n.4, 135, 165, 167, 173, 174, 177, 178, 189, 203. Speech: 1915, 158-64
Sheppard-Towner Act, 182
Shuler, Nettie, 131, 159, 195
Silver v. Ladd, 111, 205
Simons, Herbert, 83, 203
Sklar, Kathryn Kish, 184, 203
Smith, D. K., 172, 203
Smith, Gerrit, 23
Smith, Page, 74, 203
Smith, Sara T., 25, 26
Smith-Rosenberg, Carroll, 132 n.3, 203
Snow, Malinda, 117, 203
Sochen, June, 183, 204
Social movement, 4-7, 10, 34, 49-50, 72, 87, 133, 158, 168, 171-72; constituency, 86 n.8, 168; ideology, 56-59, 68-69; in-

ternal conflict, 5, 59, 71, 74, 80-85, 86 n.9, 89, 121, 183-85, 187; opposition, 67-68, 168, 175-77, 182-83; precipitating events, 34, 67; structural strain, 34, 53-54

Solomon, Martha, 140, 204

Spencer, Herbert, 80

Stanton, Elizabeth Cady, 3, 4, 8, 22, 37, 64, 69 n.7, 72-76, 84, 85, 86 nn.1, 6, 88, 103 nn.1, 4, 6, 105, 117, 118, 121, 123, 129, 133-44, 157, 165, 177, 189, 190, 199, 204. Speeches: 1848, 50-63, 142; 1854 and 1860, 93-102, 154; 1892, 133-44

Stanton, Henry, 48, 63

Stanton, Theodore, 86 n.6, 144 n.1, 204

Sterling, Dorothy, 150, 151, 155, 204

Stern, Madeleine, 186, 198

Stewart, Maria Miller, 9, 17-19, 33, 34, 37, 49, 145, 189, 204

Stone, Lucy, 3, 12, 51, 84, 103 n.1, 157

Stowe, Harriet Beecher, 33, 203

Stratton, Joanna, 204

Suffrage referenda, 102, 131, 157-58, 165, 178 nn.1, 3

Suhl, Yuri, 51, 204

Swisshelm, Jane Gray, 8

Terborg-Penn, Rosalyn, 20, 145, 204-5

Terrell, Mary Church, 8, 18, 19, 145-46, 155 nn.1, 2, 156 n.3, 205. Speech: 1906, 150-55

True womanhood, 6, 10, 15, 16, 19, 43, 50, 71, 75, 121, 122, 124, 127, 128, 129, 145, 176, 189, 190; biological rationale, 11-12, 37, 59, 87; sociological rationale, 37, 59, 61-62; theological rationale, 21, 37-38, 39-42, 47, 59, 99, 101

Truth, Sojourner, 17, 19-22, 33, 35 nn.3, 5, 59, 145, 160, 189, 205

U.S. Department of Labor, Women's Bureau, 184, 185, 285

Van Voris, Jacqueline, 158, 205

Vassar, Matthew, 72

Vicinus, Martha, 178-79 n.4, 205

Von Baer, Karl Ernst, 166

Wagner, Sally Roesch, 50, 90, 103 n.4, 205

Walker, Lola, 157, 164, 165, 169, 170, 205

Walker, Timothy, 46

Wallace, John, 205

Washington, Booker T., 146, 205

Webb, Samuel, 25, 199

Webster, Daniel, 61, 119 n.2

Weld, Theodore, 23, 25, 32, 36 n.8

Wells, Ida B., 3, 8, 19, 145-50, 151, 153, 189, 205

Welter, Barbara, 10, 205

Willard, Emma Hart, 11, 205

Willard, Frances E., 38, 86 n.5, 121-31, 132 nn.1, 3, 153, 154, 205-6. Speech: 1890, 123-28

Willis, Nathaniel, 46

Wilson, Woodrow, 170, 172, 173, 174, 175, 176

"Winning Plan," 6, 165, 167, 168

Wollstonecraft, Mary, 16 n.5, 65, 126, 206

Woman's Christian Temperance Union (WCTU), 5, 6, 15, 121, 122, 123, 132 n.2, 159, 183

Woman's Peace Party, 182

Woman's Rights Conventions, 35, 48 nn.1, 3, 51, 63, 66, 68, 73-74, 80, 89, 90, 117, 202, 206

Woman's Temperance Society (N.Y.), 63, 72, 143

Women's Bureau. *See* U.S. Department of Labor

Women's National Loyal League, 4, 35, 66, 118

Women's Social and Political Union, 3, 171, 188

Woodhull, Victoria Claflin, 106, 107-8, 206

Wordsworth, William, 126

World Anti-Slavery Convention, 4, 48

World War I, 6, 168, 170, 178, 182

Wright, Elizur, 22, 23

Wright, Frances, 17

Wright, Martha Coffin, 3, 51

Yates, Gayle Graham, 206

ABOUT THE AUTHOR

KARLYN KOHRS CAMPBELL is Professor of Speech-Communication
at the University of Minnesota at Minneapolis. Her publications include
Critiques of Contemporary Rhetoric, *Interplay of Influence*, and *The
Rhetorical Act*.